AN EVERYMAN ANTHOLOGY

Everyman, I will go with thee,
and be thy guide,
In thy most need to go by thy side

An Everyman Anthology

OF EXCERPTS GRAVE AND GAY FROM
EVERYMAN'S LIBRARY TO CELEBRATE
ITS DIAMOND JUBILEE MCMLXVI

INTRODUCED BY
J. B. PRIESTLEY

DENT: LONDON
EVERYMAN'S LIBRARY
DUTTON: NEW YORK

© *Introduction and editing, J. M. Dent & Sons Ltd, 1966*
All rights reserved
Printed in Great Britain by Western Printing Services Ltd, Bristol, for
J. M. Dent & Sons Ltd, Bedford Street, London
First published 1966
Reprinted 1966
Paperback Edition 1970

No. 1663

ISBN: 0 460 01663 6

INTRODUCTION

Far too many books are being published. I suspect that at least one out of every three new books never ought to have been sent to the printer, the binder, the bewildered and groaning booksellers. Such books come into existence to swell out the lists of publishers—and there are also too many of *them*—who are looking for good writers and are not finding them. Taking this view, then, clearly I must justify the appearance of this book I am introducing. It will not do simply to announce that Dent's, and Dutton's in the United States, are now celebrating the Diamond Jubilee of their famous *Everyman's Library*, and so have produced this anthology based on books and authors represented in that series. Do we want such a volume—or is it just another unnecessary book? My answers are Yes to the first question, No to the second.

This seems to me—and I had nothing whatever to do with the making of it—a book that can claim our attention by its own merits, quite apart from any Dent celebrations or the affectionate loyalty some of us feel for *Everyman's Library*. It isn't perfect. There are a few authors and passages I could have done without, and there are a few— a very few—rather surprising omissions. (But you must discover these for yourselves.) However, it is certainly an excellent anthology, a collection of tasting samples testifying to the richness and splendour of the cellars from which they have been fetched. The editor has looked for representative names, the authors we expect to find, but has been both industrious and clever in avoiding hackneyed passages, anthologized and quoted so often that their juice and flavour have vanished. So we have here, I feel, an admirable bedside book or travelling companion.

A lot of men about my age, weary of all this stuff about teenagers and their Pop nonsense, often declare that reading is going out, except on the 'There-was-a-dead-blonde-on-the-bed' level. Sometimes I feel this myself, especially after glancing at shelves of lurid paperbacks, where there are twenty bad writers to every good one. Yet I believe that we grumbling old codgers are wrong. The statistics are against us. (Except so far as they concern the sales of new and good hardcover fiction, which are far lower than they used to be.) In spite of television, running around in cars, listening to records, people of all ages still buy or borrow and read an astonishingly large number of good books. The figures exist to prove it. What has chiefly changed is the attitude towards books and reading.

I must now go back to the years just before the First War, let us say 1910–1914, when I was in my later teens. This was a time when the buying and reading of good books was rather a self-conscious business. There were innumerable references then to 'book-lovers' and 'book-men'. There were about half a dozen periodicals that were chiefly concerned with books and authors, old and new. My father, then the head of a large new elementary school, was very much a 'bookman' and regularly read several of these bookish periodicals. My friends and I, in our later teens or very early twenties, argued for hours about the latest novel by Wells, Conrad, Bennett. (Youngsters still argue, of course, but I suspect not so much about new novels as about ideas and the more serious non-fiction.) And all this, I think, was one aspect of a self-educating process, more often found in the industrial North than elsewhere in England, and very strong in cities like Manchester (see Neville Cardus's *Autobiography* for a wonderful account of it there) and my native city, Bradford. Along with this 'book-lover' thing went the 'Open Road' and 'Wind-on-the-heath, Brother' thing, which made us all acquire thick tweeds, pipes, brutal walking-sticks, and set us marching across the moors at week-ends. Here it must be remembered that before 1914, motoring was simply one of the hobbies of the rich, as far removed from us as champagne and caviare: I never sat in a car before the First War. And the country was the country then, before the roads and even the fields were noisy with internal-combustion engines; it began, green and quiet and smiling, a few miles outside any city. And in my part of the world you could rent a well-built stone cottage, on the edge of the moors, for ninepence a week. Too many of our streets might be grimy and monotonous—and are they much better now? But at least you could get away from them without half-killing yourself in the rat race.

We had no spare bookcases in the house, so when I furnished my attic bed-sitting-room I managed somehow—I have never been a handicraft man—to turn some crates into passable bookshelves. There came into existence then a collection of books that ultimately weighed eight tons, as we discovered to our horror when we moved from the Isle of Wight to Warwickshire. I call it, you notice, 'a collection of books' and not a Library, though it is certainly large enough to justify some proper cataloguing. I am not a Library man. I am not a genuine bibliophile. I have never been a real collector of books. The First

Edition thing has never enslaved me. I have never spent much money on special fancy editions. In one sense I am no 'book-lover'. There are two reasons why I have surrounded myself with more and more books. The first is this: I love reading anything that is worth reading, and very often I return, perhaps after months, perhaps after years, to books I have enjoyed. The second reason is a professional one. I have done most of my work in the country, far from libraries. Unless I am doing a huge job like *Literature and Western Man* or *Man and Time*, I may need only a few books for reference, but I like to feel that those books are somewhere in the house. And here I must add that all too often those books are not in the house—and God only knows what became of them. (A shattering question—do guests *steal* books?)

However, I must get back to 1910–1914, when I was filling those crates and orange boxes turned into bookshelves. There were of course plenty of cheap books around in those days. Several publishers were bringing out inexpensive reprints of the classics. My own favourite— and this explains my appearance here—was the *Everyman* series. It had not just arrived, for it began with 155 volumes, in 1906, when I was only twelve. By the time I began buying books, there were several hundred to choose from. I preferred the Everyman series because it seemed to me to offer more for your money—a shilling then—than any other series of reprints. A shilling was real money in those days, when I had a friend who provided himself with board and lodging, clothes, holidays, tobacco and beer, frequent visits to theatres and music halls, all on nineteen shillings a week. I had to practise all manner of economies, such as walking instead of taking trams and cutting down lunch from about ninepence to threepence, to find the shillings. But in the volumes I preferred to buy, *Everyman* offered me tremendous value for money, often several hundred pages, reasonably well printed and bound. These shilling books could take plenty of punishment and triumphantly survive. I know this for certain because I still have on my shelves those Everyman volumes I bought fifty-odd years ago, surviving so many moves that I begin to feel dizzy trying to remember them all.

The *Everyman's Library* figures leave me feeling rather dizzy too. On its fiftieth anniversary it issued its thousandth volume. The average stock of the Library the publishers have to keep in their warehouse is over two million volumes. The total sales have reached nearly fifty million and the annual sale is well over one million. My friend who lived on nineteen shillings a week would need about ten pounds a week now (and even then would probably have to economize on tobacco and beer), and publishing costs have risen more steeply than the general cost of living, so we need not feel surprised if *Everyman* prices have gone up and up. On the other hand, the books themselves seem to me altogether superior—in format, paper, printing, binding—to those of fifty years ago. They are still a notable bargain, and their sales suggest that a great many youngsters know this. I do not know what the pills called Purple Hearts do for one because I have never tried them, but I cannot imagine they are a better buy than a shelf or two of *Everyman* volumes, at once a solace and an enchantment. Like innumerable other readers, all over the world, I am deeply indebted to Dent's and their *Everyman's Library*, and this strong recommendation of their Diamond Jubilee anthology will not pay that debt. But it offers me a chance of doing something that is almost out of fashion these days—namely, showing some gratitude.

J. B. PRIESTLEY

ACKNOWLEDGEMENTS

For the use of the extracts reproduced J. M. Dent & Sons Ltd make grateful acknowledgements to the authors, editors, translators, and publishers, as detailed in the individual volumes of Everyman's Library, including:

Allen & Unwin Ltd, (Marx, *Capital*) trans. Eden and Cedar Paul; the Estate of Arnold Bennett *(The Old Wives' Tale)*; the Trustees of Joseph Conrad's estate *(Nostromo)*; Lord Dunsany trans. Horace 'Odes', in *The Collected Works of Horace*; John Grant (Rousseau *Confessions*); the Estates of George and Weedon Grossmith *(The Diary of a Nobody)*; E. R. Hughes *(Chinese Philosophy)*; S. Douglas Jackson (Sir Walter Raleigh 'An Account...' in Richard Hakluyt *Principal Navigations)*; the Executrix of Jerome K. Jerome *(Three Men in a Boat)*; Gwyn Jones *(The Mabinogion)*; A. D. Lindsay trans. Plato *The Republic*; the Executors of Karl Pearson *(The Grammar of Science)*; A. D. Peters & Co. (J. B. Priestley *Angel Pavement*) ; The Society of Authors (Heine 'English Fragments', trans. Havelock Ellis, in *Prose and Poetry)*; Reginald Spink (Hans Andersen *Fairy Tales and Stories)*; A. E. Taylor trans. Plato *The Laws*.

Book-loving Authors

I love an author the more for having been himself a lover of books. The idea of an ancient library perplexes our sympathy by its map-like volumes, rolled upon cylinders. Our imagination cannot take kindly to a yard of wit, or to thirty inches of moral observation, rolled out like linen in a draper's shop. But we conceive of Plato as of a lover of books; of Aristotle certainly; of Plutarch, Pliny, Horace, Julian, and Marcus Aurelius. Virgil, too, must have been one; and, after a fashion, Martial. May I confess, that the passage which I recollect with the greatest pleasure in Cicero, is where he says that books delight us at home, *and are no impediment abroad*; travel with us, ruralise with us. His period is rounded off to some purpose: '*Delectant domi, non impediunt foris; peregrinantur, rusticantur.*' I am so much of this opinion, that I do not care to be anywhere without having a book or books at hand, and like Dr Orkborne, in the novel of *Camilla*, stuff the coach or post-chaise with them whenever I travel. As books, however, become ancient, the love of them becomes more unequivocal and conspicuous. The ancients had little of what we call learning. They made it. They were also no very eminent buyers of books—they made books for posterity. It is true, that it is not at all necessary to love many books, in order to love them much. The scholar, in Chaucer, who would rather have

> At his beddes head
> A twenty bokes, clothed, in black and red,
> Of Aristotle and his philosophy,
> Than robès rich, or fiddle, or psaltry—

doubtless beat all our modern collectors in his passion for reading; but books must at least exist, and have acquired an eminence, before their lovers can make themselves known. There must be a possession, also, to perfect the communion; and the mere contact is much, even when our mistress speaks an unknown language. Dante puts Homer, the great ancient, in his Elysium, upon trust; but a few years afterwards, *Homer*, the book, made its appearance in Italy, and Petrarch, in a transport, put it upon his book-shelves, where he adored it, like 'the unknown God.' Petrarch ought to be the god of the bibliomaniacs, for he was a collector and a man of genius, which is an union that does not often happen. He copied out, with his own precious hand, the

9

manuscripts he rescued from time, and then produced others for time to reverence. With his head upon a book he died. Boccaccio, his friend, was another; nor can one look upon the longest and most tiresome works he wrote (for he did write some tiresome ones, in spite of the gaiety of his *Decameron*), without thinking, that in that resuscitation of the world of letters, it must have been natural to a man of genius to add to the existing stock of volumes, at whatsoever price. I always pitch my completest idea of a lover of books, either in these dark ages, as they are called,

(Cui cieco a torto il cieco volgo appella)—

or in the gay town days of Charles II, or a little afterwards. In both times the portrait comes out by the force of contrast. In the first, I imagine an age of iron warfare and energy, with solitary retreats, in which the monk or the hooded scholar walks forth to meditate, his precious volume under his arm. In the other, I have a triumphant example of the power of books and wit to contest the victory with sensual pleasure:—Rochester, staggering home to pen a satire in the style of Monsieur Boileau; Butler, cramming his jolly duodecimo with all the learning that he laughed at; and a new race of book poets come up, who, in spite of their periwigs and petit-maîtres, talk as romantically of 'the bays,' as if they were priests of Delphos. It was a victorious thing in books to beguile even the old French of their egotism, or at least to share it with them. Nature never pretended to do as much. And here is the difference between the two ages, or between any two ages in which genius and art predominate. In the one, books are loved because they are the records of Nature and her energies; in the other, because they are the records of those records, or evidences of the importance of the individuals, and proofs of our descent in the new and imperishable aristocracy. This is the reason why rank (with few exceptions) is so jealous of literature, and loves to appropriate or withhold the honours of it, as if they were so many toys and ribbons, like its own. It has an instinct that the two pretensions are incompatible. When Montaigne (a real lover of books) affected the order of St Michael, and pleased himself with possessing that fugitive little piece of importance, he did it because he would pretend to be above nothing that he really felt, or that was felt by men in general; but at the same time he vindicated his natural superiority over this weakness by praising and loving all higher and lasting things, and by placing his best glory in doing homage to the geniuses that had gone before him. He did not endeavour to think that an immortal renown was a fashion, like that of the cut of his scarf; or that by undervaluing the one, he should go shining down to posterity in the other, perpetual lord of Montaigne and of the ascendant.

I take our four great English poets to have all been fond of reading. Milton and Chaucer proclaim themselves for hard sitters at books. Spenser's reading is evident by his learning; and if there were nothing else to show for it in Shakespeare, his retiring to his native town, long before old age, would be a proof of it. It is impossible for a man to live in solitude without such assistance, unless he is a metaphysician or mathematician, or the dullest of mankind; and any country town would be solitude to Shakespeare, after the bustle of a metropolis and a theatre.

LEIGH HUNT (1784–1859)

Leonora's Library

Some Months ago, my Friend Sir ROGER, being in the Country, enclosed a Letter to me, directed to a certain Lady whom I shall here call by the Name of *Leonora*, and as it contained Matters of Consequence, desired me to deliver it to her with my own Hand. Accordingly I waited upon her Ladyship pretty early in the Morning, and was desired by her Woman to walk into her Lady's Library, till such time as she was in a Readiness to receive me. The very sound of a *Lady's Library* gave me a great Curiosity to see it; and, as it was some time before the Lady came to me, I had an Opportunity of turning over a great many of her Books, which were ranged together in a very beautiful Order. At the End of the *Folios* (which were finely bound and gilt) were great Jars of *China* placed one above another in a very noble piece of Architecture. The *Quartos* were separated from the *Octavos* by a pile of smaller Vessels, which rose in a delightful Pyramid. The *Octavos* were bounded by Tea Dishes of all Shapes Colours and Sizes, which were so disposed on a wooden Frame, that they looked like one continued Pillar indented with the finest Strokes of Sculpture, and stained with the greatest Variety of Dyes. That Part of the Library which was designed for the Reception of Plays and Pamphlets, and other loose Papers, was inclosed in a kind of Square, consisting of one of the prettiest Grotesque Works that ever I saw, and made up of Scaramouches, Lions, Monkies, Mandarines, Trees, Shells, and a thousand other odd Figures in *China* Ware. In the midst of the Room was a little Japan Table, with a Quire of gilt Paper upon it, and on the Paper a Silver Snuff-box made in the

Shape of a little Book. I found there were several other Counterfeit Books upon the upper Shelves, which were carved in Wood, and served only to fill up the Number, like Faggots in the Muster of a Regiment. I was wonderfully pleased with such a mixt kind of Furniture, as seemed very suitable both to the Lady and the Scholar, and did not know at first whether I should fancy my self in a Grotto, or in a Library.

Upon my looking into the Books, I found there were some few which the Lady had bought for her own use, but that most of them had been got together, either because she had heard them praised, or because she had seen the Authors of them. Among several that I examined, I very well remember these that follow...

All the Classick Authors in Wood. A Set of *Elzivers* by the same Hand. *Clelia*: Which opened of it self in the Place that describes two Lovers in a Bower. *Baker*'s Chronicle. Advice to a Daughter. The New *Atalantis*, with a Key to it. Mr *Steele*'s Christian Heroe. A Prayer Book: With a Bottle of *Hungary* Water by the side of it. Dr *Sacheverell*'s Speech. *Fielding*'s Tryal. *Seneca*'s Morals. *Taylor*'s Holy Living and Dying. *La Ferte*'s Instructions for Country Dances.

I was taking a Catalogue in my Pocket-Book of these, and several other Authors, when *Leonora* entred, and upon my presenting her with the Letter from the Knight, told me, with an unspeakable Grace, that she hoped Sir ROGER was in good Health: I answered *Yes*, for I hate long Speeches, and after a Bow or two retired.

Leonora was formerly a celebrated Beauty, and is still a very lovely Woman. She has been a Widow for two or three Years, and being unfortunate in her first Marriage, has taken a Resolution never to venture upon a second. She has no Children to take care of, and leaves the Management of her Estate to my good Friend Sir ROGER. But as the Mind naturally sinks into a kind of Lethargy, and falls asleep, that is not agitated by some Favourite Pleasures and Pursuits, *Leonora* has turned all the Passions of her Sex into a love of Books and Retirement. She converses chiefly with Men (as she has often said herself) but it is only in their Writings; and admits of very few Male-Visitants, except my Friend Sir ROGER, whom she hears with great Pleasure, and without Scandal. As her Reading has lain very much among Romances, it has given her a very particular Turn of Thinking, and discovers it self even in her House, her Gardens, and her Furniture. Sir ROGER has entertained me an Hour together with a Description of her Country-Seat, which is situated in a kind of Wilderness, about an hundred Miles distant from *London*, and looks like a little enchanted Palace. The Rocks about her are shaped into Artificial Grottoes, covered with Woodbines and Jessamines. The woods are cut into shady Walks, twisted into Bowers, and filled with Cages of Turtles. The Springs are made to run among Pebbles, and by that means taught to murmur very agreeably. They are likewise collected into a beautiful Lake, that is inhabited by a Couple of Swans, and empties it self by a little Rivulet which runs through a green Meadow, and is known in the Family by the Name of *The Purling Stream*. The Knight likewise tells me, that this Lady preserves her Game better than any of the Gentlemen in the Country; not (says Sir ROGER) that she sets so great a Value upon her Partridges and Pheasants, as upon her Larks and Nightingales. For she says that every Bird which is killed in her Ground, will spoil a Consort, and that she shall certainly miss him the next Year.

When I think how odly this Lady is improved by Learning, I look upon her with a mixture of Admiration and Pity. Amidst these innocent Entertainments which she has formed to her self, how much more Valuable does she appear than those of her Sex, who employ themselves in Diversions that are less Reasonable, though more in Fashion? What improvements would a Woman have made, who is so susceptible of Impressions from what she reads, had she been guided to such Books as have a tendency to enlighten the Understanding and rectifie the Passions, as well as to those which are of little more use than to divert the Imagination?

JOSEPH ADDISON (1676–1719)

The Isle of Albion

Britain, an island in the ocean, formerly called Albion, is situated between the north and west, facing, though at a considerable distance, the coasts of Germany, France, and Spain, which form the greatest part of Europe. It extends 800 miles in length towards the north, and is 200 miles in breadth, except where several promontories extend further in breadth, by which its compass is made to be 3,675 miles. To the south, as you pass along the nearest shore of the Belgic Gaul, the first place in Britain which opens to the eye is the city of Rutubi Portus, by the English corrupted into Reptacestir. The distance from hence across the sea to Gessoriacum, the nearest shore of the Morini, is fifty miles, or as some writers say, 450 furlongs. On the back of the island, where it opens upon the boundless ocean, it has the islands called Orcades.

Britain excels for grain and trees, and is well adapted for feeding cattle and beasts of burden. It also produces vines in some places, and has plenty of land and water-fowls of several sorts; it is remarkable also for rivers abounding in fish, and plentiful springs. It has the greatest plenty of salmon and eels; seals are also frequently taken, and dolphins, as also whales; besides many sorts of shell-fish, such as muscles, in which are often found excellent pearls of all colours, red, purple, violet, and green, but mostly white. There is also a great abundance of cockles, of which the scarlet dye is made; a most beautiful colour, which never fades with the heat of the sun or the washing of the rain; but the older it is, the more beautiful it becomes. . .

It has both salt and hot springs, and from them flow rivers which furnish hot baths, proper for all ages and sexes, and arranged according.

The island was formerly embellished with twenty-eight noble cities, besides innumerable castles, which were all strongly secured with walls, towers, gates, and locks. And, from its lying almost under the North Pole, the nights are light in summer, so that at midnight the beholders are often in doubt whether the evening twilight still continues, or that of the morning is coming on; for the sun, in the night, returns under the earth, through the northern regions at no great distance from them. For this reason the days are of a great length in summer, as, on the contrary, the nights are in winter, for the sun then withdraws into the southern parts, so that the nights are eighteen hours long. Thus the nights are extraordinarily short in summer, and the days in winter, that is, of only six equinoctial hours. Whereas, in Armenia, Macedonia, Italy, and other countries of the same latitude, the longest day or night extends but to fifteen hours, and the shortest to nine.

This island at present, following the number of the books in which the Divine law was written, contains five nations, the English, Britons, Scots, Picts, and Latins, each in its own peculiar dialect cultivating the sublime study of Divine truth. The Latin tongue is, by the study of the Scriptures, become common to all the rest.

BEDE (673-735)

The People of a Book

No greater moral change ever passed over a nation than passed over England during the years which parted the middle of the reign of Elizabeth from the meeting of the Long Parliament. England became the people of a book, and that book was the Bible. It was as yet the one English book which was familiar to every Englishman; it was read at churches and read at home, and everywhere its words, as they fell on ears which custom had not deadened to their force and beauty, kindled a startling enthusiasm. When Bishop Bonner set up the first six Bibles in St Paul's 'many well-disposed people used much to resort to the hearing thereof, especially when they could get any that had an audible voice to read to them. . . One John Porter used sometimes to be occupied in that goodly exercise, to the edifying of himself as well as others. This Porter was a fresh young man and of a big stature; and great multitudes would resort thither to hear him, because he could read well and had an audible voice.'

The popularity of the Bible was owing to other causes besides that of religion. The whole prose literature of England, save the forgotten tracts of Wyclif, has grown up since the translation of the Scriptures by Tyndall and Coverdale. No history, no romance, no poetry, save the little-known verse of Chaucer, existed for any practical purpose in the English tongue when the Bible was ordered to be set up in churches. Sunday after Sunday, day after day, the crowds that gathered round Bonner's Bibles in the nave of St Paul's, or the family group that hung on the words of the Geneva Bible in the devotional exercises at home, were leavened with a new literature. Legends and annals, war song and psalm, State-rolls and biographies, the mighty voices of prophets, the parables of Evangelists, stories of mission journeys of perils by the sea and among the heathen, philosophic arguments, apocalyptic visions, all were flung broadcast over minds unoccupied for the most part by any rival learning.

The disclosure of the stores of Greek literature had wrought the revolution of the Renaiscence. The disclosure of the older mass of Hebrew literature wrought the revolution of the Reformation. But the one revolution was far deeper and wider in its effects than the other. No version could transfer to another tongue the peculiar charm of language which gave their value to the authors of Greece and Rome. Classical letters, therefore, remained in the possession of the learned, that is of the few; and among these, with the exception of Colet and More, or of the pedants who revived a Pagan worship in the gardens of the Florentine Academy, their direct influence was purely intellectual. But the tongue of the Hebrew, the idiom of Hellenistic Greek, lent themselves with a curious felicity to the purposes of translation. As a mere literary monument, the English version of the Bible remains the noblest example of the English tongue. Its perpetual use made it from the instant of its appearance the standard of our language.

JOHN RICHARD GREEN (1837–1883)

London Gamesters

By and by I met with Mr Brisband; and having it in my mind this Christmas to do what I never can remember that I did, go to see the gaming at the groom-porter's, I having in my coming from the playhouse stepped into the two Temple halls, and there saw the dirty 'prentices and idle people playing; wherein I was mistaken, in thinking to have seen gentlemen of quality playing there, as I think it was when I was a little child, that one of my father's servants, John Bassum, I think, carried me in his arms thither. I did tell Brisband of it, and he did lead me thither, where, after staying an hour, they begun to play at about eight at night, where to see how differently one man took his losing from another, one cursing and swearing, and another only muttering and grumbling to himself, a third without any apparent discontent at all.

To see how the dice will run good luck in one hand for half an hour together, and another have no good luck at all. To see how easily here, where they play nothing but guineas, a £100 is won or lost. To see two or three gentlemen come in there drunk, and putting their stock of gold together, one 22 pieces, the second 4, and the third 5 pieces; and these two play one with another, and forget how much each of them brought, but he that brought the 22 thinks that he brought no more than the rest. To see the different humours of gamesters to change their luck when it is bad, how ceremonious they are to call for new dice, to shift their places, to alter their manner of throwing, and that with great industry, as if there was anything in it. To see how some old gamesters, that have no money now to spend as formerly, do come and sit and look on, and among others Sir Lewis Dives, who was here, and hath been a great gamester in his time. To hear their cursing and damning to no purpose, as one man being to throw a seven if he could, and failing to do it after a great many throws, cried he would be damned if ever he flung seven more while he lived, his despair of throwing it being so great, while others did it as their luck served almost every throw. To see how persons of the best quality do here sit down and play with people of any, though meaner. And to see how people in ordinary clothes shall come hither, and play away 100 or 200 or 300 guineas without any kind of difficulty.

And lastly, to see the formality of the groom-porter, who is their judge of all disputes in play and all quarrels that may arise therein, and how his under-officers are there to observe true play at each table and to give new dice, is a consideration I never could have thought had been in the world, had I not now seen it. And mighty glad I am that I did see it, and it may be will find another evening before Christmas be over to see it again, when I may stay later, for their heat of play begins not till about eleven or twelve o'clock; which did give me another pretty observation of a man, that did win mighty fast when I was there. I think he won £100 at single pieces in a little time. While all the rest envied him his good fortune he cursed it, saying, 'It comes so early upon me, for this fortune two hours hence would be worth something to me, but then I shall have no such luck.' This kind of profane, mad entertainment they give themselves. And so I, having enough for once, refusing to venture, though Brisband pressed me hard and tempted me with saying that no man was ever known to lose the first time, the devil being too cunning to discourage a gamester; and he offered me also to lend me ten pieces to venture, but I did refuse and so went away.

SAMUEL PEPYS (1633–1703)

Gossip of the Town

I thank you heartily for the sow, if you have no occasion for her, I have; and if his l$^{dp.}$ will be so kind as to drive her up to town, will gladly give him forty shillings and the chitterlings into the bargain. I could repay you with the story of my Lady F$^{r.}$ but (I doubt) you know my sow already, especially as you dwell near Raby. However I'll venture; it may be you have not heard it. About two months ago Mr Creswick (the D. of Cleveland's managing man) received an anonymous letter as from a lady, offering him (if he would bring about a match between her and his lord) £3,000 to be paid after marriage out of the estate. If he came into the proposal, a place was named where he might speak with the party. He carried the letter directly to the old Lady Darlington, and they agreed he should go to the place. He did so, and found there a man, agent for the lady; but, refusing to treat with any but principals, after a little difficulty was conducted to her in person, and found it was my Lady F. (S$^{r.}$ Ev. F.'s fine young widow). What passed between them I know not; but that very night she was at Lady Darl$^{n.}$'s assembly (as she had used to be) and no notice taken. The next morning she received a card to say Lady D. had not expected to see her after *what had passed*; otherwise she would have ordered her porter not to let her in. The whole affair was immediately told to everybody. Yet she had continued going about all public places *tête levée*, and solemnly denying the whole to her acquaintance. Since that I hear she owns it, and says her children were unprovided for, and desires to know which of her friends would not have done the same? But as neither of these expedients succeed very well, she has hired a small house, and is going into the country for the summer.

Here has just been a duel between the Duke of Bolton and Mr Stewart (a candidate for the county of Hampshire at the late election), what the quarrel was I do not know; but they met near Mary-le-bone, and the D. in making a pass over-reached himself, fell down and hurt his knee, the other bid him get up, but he could not; then he bid him ask his life, but he would not; so he let him alone, and that's all. Mr Stewart was slightly wounded.

The old Pundles that sat on L^d. G. Sackville (for they were all such, but two, Gen. Cholmondeley and L^d. Albermarle) have at last hammered out their sentence. He is declared disobedient and unfit for all military command. It is said that nine (out of the fifteen) were for death, but as two-thirds must be unanimous, some of them came over to the merciful side. I do not affirm the truth of this. What he will do with himself, nobody guesses. The poor old duke went into the country some time ago, and (they say) can hardly bear the sight of anybody. The unembarrassed countenance, the looks of sovereign contempt and superiority, that his l^dp. bestowed on his accusers during the trial, were the admiration of all: but his usual talents and art did not appear, in short his cause would not support him. Be that as it will, everybody blames *somebody*, who has been out of all temper and intractable during the whole time. Smith (the aid-de-camp, and principal witness for L^d. G.) had no sooner finished his evidence, but he was forbid to mount guard, and ordered to sell out. The court and the criminal went halves in the expence of the shorthand writer, so L^d. G. has already published the trial, before the authentic copy appears; and in it are all the foolish questions that were asked, and the absurdities of his judges, you may think perhaps that he intends to go abroad and hide his head: *au contraire*, all the world visits him on his condemnation. He says himself his situation is better than ever it was; the Scotch have all along affected to take him under their protection; his wife has been daily walking with Lady Augusta (during the trial) in Leicester Gardens, and Lord B.'s chariot stands at his door by the hour.

L^d. Ferrers has entertained the town for three days; I was not there, but Mason and Stonehewer were in the D. of Ancaster's gallery, and in the greatest danger (which I believe they do not yet know themselves), for the cell underneath them (to which the prisoner retires) was on fire during the trial, and the D. of Anc^r· with the workmen, by sawing away some timbers, and other assistance, contrived to put it out without any alarm given to the court: several now recollect they smelt burning, and heard a noise of sawing, but none guessed as to the cause. Miss Johnson, daughter to the murthered man, appeared so cool, and gave so gentle an evidence, that at first sight every one concluded she was bought off; but this could do him little good. The surgeon and his own servants laid open such a scene of barbarity and long-meditated malice, as left no room for his plea of lunacy, nor any thought of pity in the hearers. The oddest thing was this plea of temporary lunacy, and his producing two brothers of his to prove it, one a clergyman (suspended for Methodism by the B^p· of London); the other a sort of squire, that goes in the country by the name of *Ragged and Dangerous*. He managed the cause himself with more cleverness than any of his counsel, and (when found guilty) asked pardon for his plea, and laid it upon the persuasions of his family. Mrs Shirley (his mother), Lady Huntingdon, and others of the relations were at court yesterday with a petition for mercy; but on the 5th of May he is to be hanged at Tyburn.

The town are reading the K. of Prussia's poetry ('Le Philosophe sans souci'), and I have done like the town; they do not seem so sick of it as I am. It is all the scum of Voltaire and Bolingbroke, the *crambe recocta* of our worst Freethinkers, tossed up in German-French rhyme. *Tristram Shandy* is still a greater object of admiration, the man as well as the book. One is invited to dinner, where he dines, a fortnight beforehand. His portrait is done by Reynolds, and now engraving. Dodsley gives £700 for a second edition, and two new volumes not yet written; and to-morrow will come out two volumes of sermons by him. Your friend, Mr Hall, has printed two lyric epistles, one to my Cousin Shandy on his coming to town, the other to the grown gentlewomen, the misses of York: they seem to me to be absolute madness.

THOMAS GRAY (1716–1771)

East End, West End

I had made up my mind not to be astonished at that immensity of London of which I had heard so much. But it happened to me as to the poor schoolboy, who had made up his mind not to feel the whipping he was to receive. The facts of the case were, that he expected to get the usual blows with the usual stick in the usual way on the back, whereas he received a most unusually severe thrashing on an unusual place with a slender switch. I anticipated great palaces, and saw nothing but mere small houses. But their very uniformity and their limitless extent are wonderfully impressive.

These houses of brick, owing to the damp atmosphere and coal smoke, become uniform in colour, that is to say, of a brown olive green; they are all of the same style of building, generally two or three windows wide, three stories high, and adorned above with small red tiles, which remind one of newly-extracted bleeding teeth; so that the broad and accurately-squared streets seem to be bordered by endlessly long barracks. This has its reason in the fact that every English family, though it consist of only two persons, must still have a house to itself for its own castle, and rich speculators, to meet the demand' build wholesale entire streets of these dwellings, which they retail singly. In the principal streets of the city, where the business of London is most at home, where old-fashioned buildings are mingled with the new, and where the fronts of the houses are covered with names and signs, yards in length, generally gilt, and in relief, this characteristic uniformity is less striking—the less so, indeed, because the eye of the stranger is incessantly caught by the new and brilliant articles exposed for sale in the windows. And these articles do not merely produce an effect because the Englishman completes so perfectly everything which he manufactures, and because every article of luxury, every astral lamp and every boot, every tea-kettle and every woman's dress, shines out so invitingly and so 'finished'; there is a peculiar charm in the art of arrangement, in the contrast of colours, and in the variety of the English shops; even the most commonplace necessaries of life appear in a startling magic light through this artistic power of setting forth everything to advantage. Ordinary articles of food attract us by the new light in which they are placed, even uncooked fish lie so delightfully dressed that the rainbow gleam of their scales attracts us; raw meat lies, as if painted, on neat and many-coloured porcelain plates, garlanded about with parsley—yes, everything seems painted, reminding us of the brilliant, yet modest, pictures of Franz Mieris. Only the people are not so cheerful as in the Dutch paintings; they sell the most delightful playthings with the most serious faces, and the cut and colour of their clothes is as uniform as that of their houses.

At the opposite side of the town, which they call the West End, where the more aristocratic add less-occupied world lives, this uniformity is still more dominant; yet here there are very long and broad streets, where all the houses are large as palaces, though outwardly anything but distinguished, unless we except the fact that in these, as in all the better class of houses in London, the windows of the first story are adorned with iron-barred balconies, and also on the ground floor there is a black railing protecting the entrance to certain cellar apartments buried in the earth. In this part of the city there are also great squares, where rows of houses, like those already described, form a quadrangle, in whose centre there is a garden enclosed by a black iron railing, and containing some statue or other. In all of these squares and streets the eye is never shocked by the dilapidated huts of misery. Everywhere we are stared down on by wealth and respectability, while crammed away in retired lanes and dark, damp alleys poverty dwells with her rags and her tears.

The stranger who wanders through the great streets of London and does not chance right into the regular quarters of the people, sees little or nothing of the misery there. Only here and there, at the mouth of some dark alley, stands a ragged woman with a suckling babe at her wasted breast, and begs with her eyes. Perhaps if those eyes are still beautiful, one glances into them and shrinks back at the world of wretchedness within them. The common beggars are old people, generally blacks, who stand at the corners of the streets cleaning pathways—a very necessary thing in muddy London—and ask for 'coppers' in reward. It is in the dusky twilight that Poverty with her mates, Vice and Crime, glide forth from their lairs. They shun daylight the more anxiously, the more cruelly their wretchedness contrasts with the pride of wealth which glitters everywhere; only hunger sometimes drives them at noonday from their dens, and then they stand with silent, speaking eyes, staring beseechingly at the rich merchant who hurries along, busy and jingling gold, or at the lazy lord who, like a surfeited god, rides by on his high horse, casting now and then an aristocratically indifferent glance at the mob below, as though they were swarming ants, or, at all events, a mass of baser beings, whose joys and sorrows have nothing in common with his feelings. Yes, over the vulgar multitude which sticks fast to the soil, soar, like beings of a higher nature, England's nobility, who regard their little island as only a temporary resting-place, Italy as their summer garden, Paris as their social saloon, and the whole world as their inheritance.

HEINRICH HEINE (c. 1797–1856)

London

I wander thro' each charter'd street
Near where the charter'd Thames does flow,
And mark in every face I meet
Marks of weakness, marks of woe.

In every cry of every Man,
In every Infant's cry of fear,
In every voice, in every ban,
The mind-forg'd manacles I hear.

How the Chimney-sweeper's cry
Every black'ning Church appalls,
And the hapless Soldier's sigh
Runs in blood down Palace walls.

But most thro' midnight streets I hear
How the youthful Harlot's curse
Blasts the new born Infant's tear,
And blights with plagues the Marriage hearse.

WILLIAM BLAKE (1757–1827)

Angel Pavement

Many people who think they know the City well have been compelled to admit that they do not know Angel Pavement. You could go wandering half a dozen times between Bunhill Fields and London Wall, or across from Barbican to Broad Street Station, and yet miss Angel Pavement. Some of the street maps of the district omit it altogether; taxi-drivers often do not even pretend to know it; policemen are frequently not sure; and only the postmen who are caught within half a dozen streets of it are triumphantly positive. This all suggests that Angel Pavement is of no great importance. Everybody knows Finsbury Pavement, which is not very far away, because Finsbury Pavement is a street of considerable length and breadth, full of shops, warehouses, and offices, to say nothing of buses and trams, for it is a real thoroughfare. Angel Pavement is not a real thoroughfare, and its length and breadth are inconsiderable. You might bombard the postal districts of

E.C.1 and E.C.2 with letters for years, and yet never have to address anything to Angel Pavement. The little street is old, and has its fair share of sooty stone and greasy walls, crumbling brick and rotting woodwork, but somehow it has never found itself on the stage of history. Kings, princes, great bishops, have never troubled it; murders it may have seen, but they have all belonged to private life; and no literary masterpiece has ever been written under one of its roofs. The guide-books, the volumes on London's byways, have not a word to say about it, and those motor coaches, complete with guide, that roam about the city in the early evening never go near it. The guide himself, who knows all about Henry the Eighth and Wren and Dickens and is so highly educated that he can still talk with an Oxford accent and at the very top of his voice, could probably tell you nothing about Angel Pavement.

It is a typical City side-street, except that it is shorter, narrower, and dingier than most. At one time it was probably a real thoroughfare, but now only pedestrians can escape at the western end, and they do this by descending the six steps at the corner. For anything larger and less nimble than a pedestrian, Angel Pavement is a *cul-de-sac*, for all that end, apart from the steps, is blocked up by *Chase & Cohen : Carnival Novelties*, and not even by the front of Chase & Cohen but by their sooty, mouldering, dusty-windowed back. Chase & Cohen do not believe it is worth while offering Angel Pavement any of their carnival novelties—many of which are given away, with a thirty-shilling dinner and dance, in the West End every gala night—and so they turn the other way, not letting Angel Pavement have so much as a glimpse of a pierrot hat or a false nose. Perhaps this is as well, for if the pavementeers could see pierrot hats and false noses every day, there is no telling what might happen.

What you do see there, however, is something quite different. Turning into Angel Pavement from that crazy jumble and jangle of buses, lorries, drays, private cars, and desperate bicycles, the main road, you see on the right, first a nondescript blackened building that is really the side of a shop and a number of offices; then *The Pavement Dining Rooms : R. Ditton, Propr.*, with R. Ditton's usual window display of three coco-nut buns, two oranges, four bottles of cherry cider picturesquely grouped, and if not the boiled ham, the meat and potato pie; then a squashed little house or bundle of single offices that is hopelessly to let; and then the bar of the *White Horse*, where you have the choice of any number of mellowed whiskies or fine sparkling ales, to be consumed on or off the premises, and if on, then either publicly or privately. You are now half way down the street, and could easily throw a stone through one of Chase & Cohen's windows, which is precisely what somebody, maddened perhaps by the thought of the Carnival Novelties, has already done. On the other side, the southern side, the left-hand side when you turn in from the outer world, you begin, rather splendidly, with *Dunbury & Co.: Incandescent Gas Fittings*, and two windows almost bright with sample fittings. Then you arrive at *T. Benenden: Tobacconist*, whose window is filled with dummy packets of cigarettes and tobacco that have long ceased even to pretend they have anything better than air in them; though there are also, as witnesses to T. Benenden's enterprise, one or two little bowls of dry and dusty stuff that mutter, in faded letters, 'Our Own Mixture, Cool Sweet Smoking, Why not try it?' To reach T. Benenden's little counter, you go through the street doorway and then turn through another door on the left. The stairs in front of you—and very dark and dirty they are, too—belong to *C. Warstein: Tailors' Trimmings*. Next to T. Benenden and C. Warstein is a door, a large, stout, old door from which most of the paint has flaked and shredded away. This door has no name on it, and nobody, not even T. Benenden, has seen it open or knows what there is behind it. There it is, a door, and it does nothing but gather dust and cobwebs and occasionally drop another flake of dried paint on the worn step below. Perhaps it leads into another world. Perhaps it will open, one morning, to admit an angel, who, after looking up and down the little street for a moment, will suddenly blow the last trumpet. Perhaps that is the real reason why the street is called Angel Pavement. What is certain, however, is that this door has no concern with the building next to it and above it, the real neighbour of T. Benenden and C. Warstein and known to the postal authorities as No. 8, Angel Pavement.

J. B. PRIESTLEY (b. 1894)

The Industrial North

It was dark before we reached Sheffield; so that we saw the iron furnaces in all the horrible splendour of their everlasting blaze. Nothing can be conceived more grand or more terrific than the yellow waves of fire that incessantly issue from the top of these furnaces, some of which are close by the way-side. Nature has placed the beds of iron and the beds of coal alongside of each other, and art has taught man to make one to operate upon the other, as to turn the iron-stone into liquid matter, which is drained off from the bottom of the furnace, and afterwards moulded into blocks and bars, and all sorts of things. The combustibles are put into the top of the furnace, which stands thirty, forty, or fifty feet up in the air, and the ever-blazing mouth of which is kept supplied with coal and coke and iron-stone from little iron waggons forced up by steam, and brought down again to be refilled. It is a surprising thing to behold; and it is impossible to behold it without being convinced that, whatever other nations may do with cotton and with wool, they will never equal England with regard to things made of iron and steel. This Sheffield, and the land all about it, is one bed of iron and coal. They call it black Sheffield, and black enough it is; but from this one town and its environs go nine-tenths of the knives that are used in the whole world; there being, I understand, no knives made at Birmingham; the manufacture of which place consists of the larger sort of implements, of locks of all sorts, and guns and swords, and of all the endless articles of hardware which go to the furnishing of a house...

The trade of Sheffield has fallen off less in proportion than that of the other manufacturing districts. North America, and particularly the United States, where the people have so much victuals to cut, form a great branch of the custom of this town. If the people of Sheffield could only receive a tenth part of what their knives sell for by retail in America, Sheffield might pave its streets with silver. A *gross* of knives and forks is sold to the Americans for less than three knives and forks can be bought at retail in a country store in America. No fear of rivalship in this trade. The Americans may lay on their tariff, and double it, and triple it; but as long as they continue to *cut* their victuals from Sheffield they must have the things to cut it with.

The ragged hills all round about this town are bespangled with groups of houses inhabited by the working cutlers. They have not suffered like the working weavers; for to make knives there must be the hand of man. Therefore, machinery cannot come to destroy the wages of the labourer. The home demand has been very much diminished; but still the depression has here not been what it has been, and what it is where the machinery can be brought into play. We are here just upon the borders of Derbyshire, a nook of which runs up and separates Yorkshire from Nottinghamshire. I went to a village, the day before yesterday, called *Mosborough*, the whole of the people of which are employed in the making of *sickles* and *scythes*; and where, as I was told, they are very well off even in these times. A prodigious quantity of these things go to the United States of America.

In short, there are about twelve millions of people there continually consuming these things; and the hardware merchants here have their agents and their stores in the great towns of America; which country, as far as relates to this branch of business, is still a part of old England.

WILLIAM COBBETT (1762–1835)

Edinburgh

The main street . . . is the most spacious, the longest, and best inhabited street in Europe; its length I have describ'd; the buildings are surprizing both for strength, for beauty, and for height; all, or the greatest part of free-stone, and so firm is every thing made, that tho' in so high a situation, and in a country where storms and violent winds are so frequent, 'tis very rare that any damage is done here. No blowing of tiles about the streets, to knock people on the head as they pass; no stacks of chimneys and gable-ends of houses falling in to bury the inhabitants in their ruins, as we often find it in London, and other of our paper built cities in England; but all is fix'd, and strong to the top, tho' you have, in that part of the city call'd the Parliament-close, houses, which, on the south side, appear to be eleven or twelve story high, and inhabited to the very top.

From the palace gate, westward, this street is call'd the Cannon-Gate, vulgarly the Canni-gate, which part, tho' a suburb, is a kind of corporation by itself, as Westminster to London; and has a toll-booth, a prison, and a town-guard by itself, tho' under the government of the provost and bailiffs of Edinburgh as Leith itself also is. In this part of the street, tho' otherwise not so well inhabited as the city itself, are several very magnificent houses of the nobility, built for their residence when the court was in town, and on their other occasions, just as was the case in the Strand between London and Whitehall, before the encrease of the city prompted the building those fine houses into streets.

Of those the Duke of Queensberry's, the Earl of Wintoun's, the Duke of Roxburgh's, and the Earl of Murray's are the chief; the first and last are very magnificent, large and princely buildings, all of free-stone, large in front, and with good gardens behind them, and the other are very fine buildings, too many to be describ'd.

At the upper, or west end of this street, and where it joins to the city, is a gate which, just as Ludgate, or Temple-Bar, stands parting the city itself from the suburb, but not at all discontinuing the street, which rather widens, and is more spacious when you are thro' the gate than before. This gate, or Bow, is call'd the Nether-Bow, or, by some, the Nether-Bow port.

Just at this port, on the outside, turn away two streets, one goes south to a gate or port which leads out of the city into the great road for England, by the way of Kelso, and is call'd St Mary Wynde; and, on the right hand of it, another port turns away west, into the low street, mention'd before, where was a lough formerly fill'd up, and is call'd the Cowgate, because, by this street, the cattle are driven to and from the great market-place, call'd the Grass-market, where such cattle are bought and sold, as also where is a horse-market weekly, as in Smithfield. This street, call'd the Cowgate, runs parallel with the high street, but down in a bottom, as has been said. But to go back to the Nether-Bow Port, as this turning is on the left hand going into the city, so on the right hand goes another street, which they call Leith Wynd, and leads down to a gate which is not in the city wall immediately, but adjoining to a church call'd the College-Kirk, and thro' which gate, a suburb runs out north, opening into the plain, leads to Leith; and all along by the road side, the road itself pav'd with stones like a street, is a broad causeway, or, as we call it, a foot way, very firm, and made by hand at least 20 foot broad, and continued to the town of Leith. This causeway is very well kept at the publick expence, and no horses suffer'd to come upon it.

DANIEL DEFOE (c. 1661–1731)

John Bull

John Bull, to all appearance, is a plain, downright, matter-of-fact fellow, with much less of poetry about him than rich prose. There is little of romance in his nature, but a vast deal of strong natural feeling. He excels in humour more than in wit; is jolly rather than gay; melancholy rather than morose; can easily be moved to a sudden tear, or surprised into a broad laugh; but he loathes sentiment, and has no turn for light pleasantry. He is a boon companion, if you allow him to have his humour, and to talk about himself; and he will stand by a friend in a quarrel, with life and purse, however soundly he may be cudgelled. . .

He is a little fond of playing the magnifico abroad; of pulling out a long purse; flinging his money bravely about at boxing-matches, horse-races, cock-fights, and carrying a high head among 'gentlemen of

27

the fancy': but immediately after one of these fits of extravagance, he will be taken with violent qualms of economy; stop short at the most trivial expenditure; talk desperately of being ruined and brought upon the parish; and in such moods will not pay the smallest tradesman's bill without violent altercation. He is, in fact, the most punctual and discontented paymaster in the world; drawing his coin out of his breeches pocket with infinite reluctance; paying to the uttermost farthing, but accompaning every guinea with a growl.

With all his talk of economy, however, he is a bountiful provider, and a hospitable housekeeper. His economy is of a whimsical kind, its chief object being to devise how he may afford to be extravagant; for he will begrudge himself a beefsteak and pint of port one day, that he may roast an ox whole, broach a hogshead of ale, and treat all his neighbours on the next.

His domestic establishment is enormously expensive: not so much from any great outward parade, as from the great consumption of solid beef and pudding; the vast number of followers he feeds and clothes; and his singular disposition to pay hugely for small services. He is a most kind and indulgent master, and, provided his servants humour his peculiarities, flatter his vanity a little now and then, and do not peculate grossly on him before his face, they may manage him to perfection. Everything that lives on him seems to thrive and grow fat. His house-servants are well paid and pampered, and have little to do. His horses are sleek and lazy, and prance slowly before his state carriage; and his house-dogs sleep quietly about the door, and will hardly bark at a house-breaker.

His family mansion is an old castellated manor-house, gray with age, and of a most venerable, though weather-beaten appearance. It has been built upon no regular plan, but is a vast accumulation of parts, erected in various tastes and ages. The centre bears evident traces of Saxon architecture, and is as solid as ponderous stone and old English oak can make it. Like all the relics of that style, it is full of obscure passages, intricate mazes, and dusky chambers; and though these have been partially lighted up in modern days, yet there are many places where you must still grope in the dark. Additions have been made to the original edifice from time to time, and great alterations have taken place; towers and battlements have been erected during wars and tumults; wings built in time of peace; and outhouses, lodges, and offices, run up according to the whim or convenience of different generations, until it has become one of the most spacious, rambling tenements imaginable. . .

A great part of his park, also, is turned into paddocks, where his broken-down chargers are turned loose to graze undisturbed for the remainder of their existence—a worthy example of grateful recollection, which, if some of his neighbours were to imitate, would not be to their discredit. Indeed, it is one of his great pleasures to point out these old steeds to his visitors, to dwell on their good qualities, extol their past services, and boast, with some little vainglory, of the perilous adventures and hardy exploits through which they have carried him.

He is given, however, to indulge his veneration for family usages, and family incumbrances, to a whimsical extent. His manor is infested by gangs of gipsies; yet he will not suffer them to be driven off, because they have infested the place time out of mind, and been regular poachers upon every generation of the family. He will scarcely permit a dry branch to be lopped from the great trees that surround the house, lest it should molest the rooks, that have bred there for centuries. Owls have taken possession of the dovecot; but they are hereditary owls, and must not be disturbed. Swallows have nearly choked up every chimney with their nests; martins build in every frieze and cornice; crows flutter about the towers, and perch on every weathercock; and old gray-headed rats may be seen in every quarter of the house, running in and out of their holes undauntedly in broad daylight. In short, John has such a reverence for everything that has been long in the family, that he will not hear even of abuses being reformed, because they are good old family abuses.

WASHINGTON IRVING (1783–1859)

At the Wordsworths'

That night, after hearing conversation superior by much, in its tone and subject, to any which I had ever heard before—one exception only being made, in favour of Coleridge, whose style differed from Wordsworth's in this, that being far more agile and more comprehensive, consequently more showy and surprising, it was less impressive and weighty; for Wordsworth's was slow in its movement, solemn, majestic. After a luxury so rare as this, I found myself, about eleven at night, in a pretty bedroom, about fourteen feet by twelve. Much I feared that this might turn out the best room in the house; and it illustrates the hospitality of my new friends, to mention that it was. Early in the morning, I was awoke by a little voice, issuing from a little cottage bed in an opposite corner, soliloquizing in a low tone. I soon recognized the words—'Suffered under Pontius Pilate; was crucified, dead, and buried'; and the voice I easily conjectured to be that of the eldest amongst Wordsworth's children, a son, and at that time about three years old. He was a remarkably fine boy in strength and size, promising (which has in fact been realized) a much more powerful person, physically, than that of his father. Miss Wordsworth I found making breakfast in the little sitting-room. No urn was there; no glittering breakfast service; a kettle boiled upon the fire, and everything was in harmony with these unpretending arrangements. I, the son of a merchant, and naturally, therefore, in the midst of luxurious (though not ostentatious) display from my childhood, had never seen so humble a *ménage*: and contrasting the dignity of the man with this honourable poverty, and this courageous avowal of it, his utter absence of all effort to disguise the simple truth of the case, I felt my admiration increase to the uttermost by all I saw. This, thought I to myself, is, indeed, in his own words—

'Plain living, and high thinking.'

This is indeed to reserve the humility and the parsimonies of life for its bodily enjoyments, and to apply its lavishness and its luxury to its enjoyments of the intellect. So might Milton have lived; so Marvel.

THOMAS DE QUINCEY (1785–1859)

Village Cricket

I doubt if there be any scene in the world more animating or delightful than a cricket match—I do not mean a set match at Lord's ground for money, hard money, between a certain number of gentlemen and players, as they are called—people who make a trade of that noble sport, and degrade it into an affair of bettings, and hedgings, and cheatings, it may be, like boxing or horse-racing; nor do I mean a pretty fête in a gentleman's park, where one club of cricketing dandies encounters another such club, and where they show off in graceful costume to a gay marquee of admiring belles, who condescend so to purchase admiration, and while away a long summer morning in partaking cold collations, conversing occasionally, and seeming to understand the game—the whole being conducted according to ball-room etiquette, so as to be exceedingly elegant and exceedingly dull.

No! the cricket that I mean is a real solid old-fashioned match between neighbouring parishes, where each attacks the other for honour and a supper, glory and half a crown a man. If there be any gentlemen amongst them, it is well—if not, it is so much the better. Your gentleman cricketer is in general rather an anomalous character. Elderly gentlemen are obviously good for nothing; and young beaux are, for the most part, hampered and trammelled by dress and habit: the stiff cravat, the pinched-in waist, the dandy-walk—oh, they will never do for cricket! Now, our country lads, accustomed to the flail or the hammer (your blacksmiths are capital hitters), have the free use of their arms; they know how to move their shoulders; and they can move their feet too—they can run; then they are so much better made, so much more athletic, and yet so much lissomer—to use a Hampshire phrase, which deserves at least to be good English. Here and there, indeed, one meets with an old Etonian, who retains his boyish love for that game which formed so considerable a branch of his education: some even preserve their boyish proficiency, but in general it wears away like the Greek, quite as certainly, and almost as fast; a few years of Oxford, or Cambridge, or the Continent, are sufficient to annihilate both the power and the inclination. No! a village match is the thing—where our highest officer, our conductor (to borrow a musical term), is but a little farmer's second son; where a day-labourer is our bowler, and a blacksmith our long-stop; where the spectators consist of the retired cricketers, the veterans of the green, the careful mothers, the girls, and all the boys of two parishes, together with a few amateurs, little above them in rank, and not at all in pretension; where laughing and shouting, and the very ecstasy of merriment and good humour, prevail.

MARY R. MITFORD (1787–1855)

The Raw Material of Politics

Hereby it is manifest, that during the time men live without a common Power to keep them all in awe, they are in that condition which is called Warre; and such a warre, as is of every man, against every man. For Warre, consisteth not in Battell onely, or the act of fighting; but in a tract of time, wherein the Will to contend by Battell is sufficiently known: and therefore the notion of *Time*, is to be considered in the nature of Warre; as it is in the nature of Weather. For as the nature of Foule weather, lyeth not in a showre or two of rain; but in an inclination thereto of many dayes together; So the nature of War, consisteth not in actuall fighting; but in the known disposition thereto, during all the time there is no assurance to the contrary. All other time is Peace.

Whatsoever therefore is consequent to a time of Warre, where every man is Enemy to every man; the same is consequent to the time, wherein men live without other security, than what their own strength, and their own invention shall furnish them withall. In such condition, there is no place for Industry; because the fruit thereof is uncertain: and consequently no Culture of the Earth, no Navigation, nor use of the commodities that may be imported by Sea; no commodious Building; no Instruments of moving, and removing such things as require much force; no Knowledge of the face of the Earth; no account of Time; no Arts; no Letters; no Society; and which is worst of all, continuall feare, and danger of violent death; And the life of man, solitary, poore, nasty, brutish, and short. . .

To this warre of every man against every man, this also is consequent; that nothing can be Unjust. The notions of Right and Wrong, Justice and Injustice have there no place. Where there is no common Power, there is no Law: where no Law, no Injustice. Force, and Fraud, are in warre the two Cardinall vertues. Justice, and Injustice are none of the Faculties neither of the Body, nor Mind. If they were, they might be in a man that were alone in the world, as well as his Senses, and Passions. They are Qualities, that relate to men in Society, not in Solitude. It is consequent also to the same condition, that there be no Propriety, no Dominion, no *Mine* and *Thine* distinct; but onely that to be every mans, that he can get; and for so long, as he can keep it. And thus much for the ill condition, which man by meer Nature is actually placed in; though with a possibility to come out of it, consisting partly in the Passions, partly in his Reason.

The Passions that encline men to Peace, are Feare of Death; Desire of such things as are necessary to commodious living; and a Hope by their Industry to obtain them. And Reason suggesteth convenient Articles of Peace, upon which men may be drawn to agreement. These Articles, are they, which otherwise are called the Lawes of Nature.

THOMAS HOBBES (1588–1679)

The Allegiance of an M.P.

I am sorry I cannot conclude without saying a word on a topic touched upon by my worthy colleague. I wish that topic had been passed by at a time when I have so little leisure to discuss it. But since he has thought proper to throw it out I owe you a clear explanation of my poor sentiments on this subject.

He tells you that 'the topic of instructions has occasioned much alteration and uneasiness in this city;' and he expresses himself (if I understand him rightly) in favour of the coercive authority of such instructions.

Certainly, gentlemen, it ought to be the happiness and glory of a representative to live in the strictest union, the closest correspondence, and the most unreserved communication with his constituents. Their wishes ought to have great weight with him; their opinion, high respect; their business, unremitted attention. It is his duty to sacrifice his repose, his pleasures, his satisfactions, to theirs; and above all, ever, and in all cases, to prefer their interest to his own. But his unbiassed opinion, his mature judgment, his enlightened conscience, he ought not to sacrifice to you, to any man, or to any set of men living. These he does not derive from your pleasure; no, nor from the law and the constitution. They are a trust from Providence, for the abuse of which he is deeply answerable. Your representative owes you, not his industry only, but his judgment; and he betrays, instead of serving you, if he sacrifices it to your opinion.

My worthy colleague says, his will ought to be subservient to yours. If that be all, the thing is innocent. If government were a matter of will upon any side, yours, without question, ought to be superior. But government and legislation are matters of reason and judgment, and not of inclination; and what sort of reason is that, in which the determination precedes the discussion; in which one set of men deliberate, and another decide; and where those who form the conclusion are perhaps three hundred miles distant from those who hear the arguments?

To deliver an opinion, is the right of all men; that of constituents is a weighty and respectable opinion, which a representative ought always to rejoice to hear; and which he ought always most seriously to consider. But *authoritative* instructions; *mandates* issued, which the member is bound blindly and implicitly to obey, to vote, and to argue for, though contrary to the clearest conviction of his judgment and conscience,—these are things utterly unknown to the laws of this land, and which arise from a fundamental mistake of the whole order and tenor of our constitution.

Parliament is not a *congress* of ambassadors from different and hostile interests; which interests each must maintain, as an agent and advocate, against other agents and advocates; but parliament is a *deliberative* assembly of *one* nation, with *one* interest, that of the whole; where, not local purposes, not local prejudices, ought to guide, but the general good, resulting from the general reason of the whole. You choose a member indeed; but when you have chosen him, he is not member for Bristol, but he is a member of *parliament*. If the local constituent should have an interest, or should form an hasty opinion, evidently opposite to the real good of the rest of the community, the member for that place ought to be as far, as any other, from any endeavour to give it effect. I beg pardon for saying so much on this subject. I have been unwillingly drawn into it; but I shall ever use a respectful frankness of communication with you. Your faithful friend, your devoted servant, I shall be to the end of my life: a flatterer you do not wish for. On this point of instructions, however, I think it scarcely possible we ever can have any sort of difference. Perhaps I may give you too much, rather than too little, trouble.

From the first hour I was encouraged to court your favour, to this happy day of obtaining it, I have never promised you anything but humble and persevering endeavours to do my duty. The weight of that duty, I confess, makes me tremble; and whoever well considers what it is, of all things in the world, will fly from what has the least likeness to a positive and precipitate engagement. To be a good member of parliament is, let me tell you, no easy task; especially at this time, when there is so strong a disposition to run into the perilous extremes of servile compliance or wild popularity. To unite circumspection with vigour, is absolutely necessary; but it is extremely difficult. We are now members for a rich commercial *city*; this city, however, is but a part of a rich commercial *nation*, the interests of which are various, multiform, and intricate. We are members for that great nation, which however is itself but part of a great *empire*, extended by our virtue and our fortune to the farthest limits of the east and of the west. All these wide-spread interests must be considered; must be compared; must be reconciled, if possible. We are members for a *free* country; and surely we all know, that the machine of a free constitution is no simple thing; but as intricate and as delicate as it is valuable. We are members in a great and ancient *monarchy*; and we must preserve religiously the true legal rights of the sovereign, which form the key-stone that binds together the noble and well-constructed arch of our empire and our constitution. A constitution made up of balanced powers must ever be a critical thing. As such I mean to touch that part of it which comes within my reach. I know my inability, and I wish for support from every quarter. In particular I shall aim at the friendship, and shall cultivate the best correspondence, of the worthy colleague you have given me.

EDMUND BURKE (1729-1797)

No Representation, No Taxation

When it shall be said in any country in the world my poor are happy; neither ignorance nor distress is to be found among them; my jails are empty of prisoners, my streets of beggars; the aged are not in want; the taxes are not oppressive; the rational world is my friend, because I am the friend of its happiness: When these things can be said, then may that country boast its Constitution and its Government.

Within the space of a few years we have seen two Revolutions, those of America and France. In the former the contest was long, and the conflict severe; in the latter the Nation acted with such a consolidated impulse, that, having no foreign enemy to contend with, the Revolution was complete in power the moment it appeared. From both those instances it is evident that the greatest forces that can be brought into the field of Revolutions are reason and common interest. Where these can have the opportunity of acting opposition dies with fear, or crumbles away by conviction. It is a great standing which they have now universally obtained; and we may hereafter hope to see Revolutions, or changes in Governments, produced with the same quiet operation, by which any measure, determinable by reason and discussion, is accomplished.

When a Nation changes its opinion and habits of thinking it is no longer to be governed as before; but it would not only be wrong, but bad policy, to attempt by force what ought to be accomplished by reason. Rebellion consists in forcibly opposing the general will of a Nation, whether by a party or by a Government. There ought, therefore, to be in every Nation a method of occasionally ascertaining the state of public opinion with respect to Government. On this point the old Government of France was superior to the present Government of England, because, on extraordinary occasions, recourse could be had to what was then called the States-General. But in England there are no such occasional bodies; and as to those who are now called representatives, a great part of them are mere machines of the Court, placemen, and dependents.

I presume that though all the people of England pay taxes, not an hundredth part of them are electors, and the members of one of the

Houses of Parliament represent nobody but themselves. There is, therefore, no power but the voluntary will of the people that has a right to act in any matter respecting a general reform; and by the same right that two persons can confer on such a subject, a thousand may. The object in all such preliminary proceedings, is to find out what the general sense of a Nation is and to be governed by it. If it prefer a bad or defective Government to a reform, or chuse to pay ten times more taxes than there is occasion for, it has a right so to do: and so long as the majority do not impose conditions on the minority, different from what they impose on themselves, though there may be much error, there is no injustice. Neither will the error continue long. Reason and discussion will soon bring things right, however wrong they may begin. By such a process no tumult is to be apprehended. The poor in all countries are naturally both peaceable and grateful in all reforms in which their interest and happiness is included. It is only by neglecting and rejecting them that they become tumultuous.

TOM PAINE (1737–1809)

A Patchwork Administration

I have done with the third period of your policy, that of your repeal, and the return of your ancient system, and your ancient tranquillity and concord. Sir, this period was not as long as it was happy. Another scene was opened, and other actors appeared on the stage. The state, in the condition I have described it, was delivered into the hands of Lord Chatham—a great and celebrated name—a name that keeps the name of this country respectable in every other on the globe. It may be truly called—

Clarum et venerabile nomen
Gentibus, et multum nostræ quod proderat urbi.

Sir, the venerable age of this great man, his merited rank, his superior eloquence, his splendid qualities, his eminent services, the vast space he fills in the eye of mankind, and, more than all the rest, his fall from power, which, like death, canonises and sanctifies a great character, will not suffer me to censure any part of his conduct. I am afraid to flatter him; I am sure I am not disposed to blame him. Let those who have betrayed him by their adulation insult him with their malevolence. But what I do not presume to censure I may have leave to lament. For a wise man, he seemed to me at that time to be governed too much by general maxims. I speak with the freedom of history, and

I hope without offence. One or two of these maxims, flowing from an opinion not the most indulgent to our unhappy species, and surely a little too general, led him into measures that were greatly mischievous to himself, and for that reason among others fatal to his country; measures, the effects of which, I am afraid, are for ever incurable. He made an administration, so chequered and speckled; he put together a piece of joinery, so crossly indented and whimsically dovetailed; a cabinet so variously inlaid; such a piece of diversified mosaic; such a tessellated pavement without cement; here a bit of black stone, and there a bit of white; patriots and courtiers, king's friends and republicans; whigs and tories; treacherous friends and open enemies—that it was indeed a very curious show, but utterly unsafe to touch, and unsure to stand on. The colleagues whom he had assorted at the same boards stared at each other, and were obliged to ask, 'Sir, your name?—Sir, you have the advantage of me—Mr Such-a-one—I beg a thousand pardons—' I venture to say, it did so happen that persons had a single office divided between them, who had never spoke to each other in their lives until they found themselves, they knew not how, pigging together, heads and points, in the same truckle-bed.

EDMUND BURKE (1729–1797)

Political Exile

 . . . so comes before mine eye
 The time prepared for thee. Such as driven out
 From Athens, by his cruel stepdame's wiles,
 Hippolytus departed; such must thou
 Depart from Florence. This they wish, and this
 Contrive, and will ere long effectuate, there,
 Where gainful merchandize is made of Christ
 Throughout the live-long day. The common cry,
 Will, as 'tis ever wont, affix the blame
 Unto the party injured: but the truth
 Shall, in the vengeance it dispenseth, find
 A faithful witness. Thou shalt leave each thing
 Beloved most dearly: this is the first shaft
 Shot from the bow of exile. Thou shalt prove
 How salt the savour is of other's bread;
 How hard the passage, to descend and climb
 By other's stairs. But that shall gall thee most,

Will be the worthless and vile company,
With whom thou must be thrown into these straits.
For all ungrateful, impious all, and mad,
Shall turn 'gainst thee: but in a little while,
Theirs, and not thine, shall be the crimson'd brow.
Their course shall so evince their brutishness,
To have ta'en thy stand apart shall well become thee.

DANTE ALIGHIERI (1265–1321)

To Control Faction

Complaints are everywhere heard from our most considerate and virtuous citizens, equally the friends of public and private faith, and of
public and personal liberty, that our governments are too unstable,
that the public good is disregarded in the conflicts of rival parties, and
that measures are too often decided, not according to the rules of justice
and the rights of the minor party, but by the superior force of an
interested and overbearing majority. However anxiously we may wish
that these complaints had no foundation, the evidence of known facts
will not permit us to deny that they are in some degree true. It will
be found, indeed, on a candid review of our situation, that some of the
distresses under which we labour have been erroneously charged on
the operation of our governments; but it will be found, at the same
time, that other causes will not alone account for many of our heaviest
misfortunes; and, particularly, for that prevailing and increasing distrust of public engagements, and alarm for private rights, which are
echoed from one end of the continent to the other. These must be
chiefly, if not wholly, effects of the unsteadiness and injustice with
which a factious spirit has tainted our public administrations.

By a faction, I understand a number of citizens, whether amounting
to a majority or minority of the whole, who are united and actuated by
some common impulse of passion, or of interest, adverse to the rights
of other citizens, or to the permanent and aggregate interests of the
community.

There are two methods of curing the mischiefs of faction: the one,
by removing its causes; the other, by controlling its effects.

There are again two methods of removing the causes of faction: the
one, by destroying the liberty which is essential to its existence; the
other, by giving to every citizen the same opinions, the same passions,
and the same interests.

It could never be more truly said than of the first remedy, that it was worse than the disease. Liberty is to faction what air is to fire, an aliment without which it instantly expires. But it could not be less folly to abolish liberty, which is essential to political life, because it nourishes faction, than it would be to wish the annihilation of air, which is essential to animal life, because it imparts to fire its destructive agency.

The second expedient is as impracticable as the first would be unwise. As long as the reason of man continues fallible, and he is at liberty to exercise it, different opinions will be formed. As long as the connection subsists between his reason and his self-love his opinions and his passions will have a reciprocal influence on each other; and the former will be objects to which the latter will attach themselves. The diversity in the faculties of men, from which the rights of property originate, is not less an insuperable obstacle to a uniformity of interests. The protection of these faculties is the first object of government. From the protection of different and unequal faculties of acquiring property, the possession of different degrees and kinds of property immediately results; and from the influence of these on the sentiments and views of the respective proprietors, ensues a division of the society into different interests and parties.

The latent causes of faction are thus sown in the nature of man; and we see them everywhere brought into different degrees of activity, according to the different circumstances of civil society. A zeal for different opinions concerning religion, concerning government, and many other points, as well of speculation as of practice; an attachment of different leaders ambitiously contending for pre-eminence and power; or to persons of other descriptions whose fortunes have been interesting to the human passions, have, in turn, divided mankind into parties, inflamed them with mutual animosity, and rendered them much more disposed to vex and oppress each other than to co-operate for their common good. So strong is this propensity of mankind to fall into mutual animosities, that where no substantial occasion presents itself, the most frivolous and fanciful distinctions have been sufficient to kindle their unfriendly passions and excite their most violent conflicts. But the most common and durable source of factions has been the various and unequal distribution of property. Those who hold and those who are without property have ever formed distinct interests in society. Those who are creditors, and those who are debtors, fall under a like discrimination. A landed interest, a manufacturing interest, a mercantile interest, a moneyed interest, with many lesser interests, grow up of necessity in civilised nations, and divide them into different classes, actuated by different sentiments and views. The regulation of these various and interfering interests forms the principal task of modern legislation, and involves the spirit of party and faction in the necessary and ordinary operations of the government.

ALEXANDER HAMILTON (1757–1804)

The Moralities of Princes

When civil government has been established over the greatest part of mankind, and different societies have been formed contiguous to each other, there arises a new set of duties among the neighbouring states, suitable to the nature of that commerce which they carry on with each other. Political writers tell us, that in every kind of intercourse, a body politic is to be considered as one person; and, indeed, this assertion is so far just, that different nations, as well as private persons, require mutual assistance; at the same time that their selfishness and ambition are perpetual sources of war and discord. But though nations in this particular resemble individuals, yet as they are very different in other respects, no wonder they regulate themselves by different maxims, and give rise to a new set of rules, which we call *the laws of nations*. Under this head we may comprise the sacredness of the persons of ambassadors, the declaration of war, the abstaining from poisoned arms, with other duties of that kind, which are evidently calculated for the commerce that is peculiar to different societies.

But though these rules be superadded to the laws of nature, the former do not entirely abolish the latter; and one may safely affirm, that the three fundamental rules of justice, the stability of possession, its transference by consent, and the performance of promises, are duties of princes as well as of subjects. The same interest produces the same effect in both cases. Where possession has no stability, there must be perpetual war. Where property is not transferred by consent, there can be no commerce. Where promises are not observed, there can be no leagues nor alliances. The advantages, therefore, of peace, commerce, and mutual succour, make us extend to different kingdoms the same notions of justice which take place among individuals.

There is a maxim very current in the world, which few politicians are willing to avow, but which has been authorised by the practice of all ages, *that there is a system of morals calculated for princes, much more free than that which ought to govern private persons*. It is evident this is not to be understood of the lesser *extent* of public duties and obligations; nor will any one be so extravagant as to assert, that the most solemn treaties ought to have no force among princes. For as princes do actually form treaties among themselves, they must propose some advantage from the execution of them; and the prospect of such advantage for the future must engage them to perform their part, and must establish that law of nature. The meaning, therefore, of this political maxim is, that though the morality of princes has the same *extent*, yet it has not the same *force* as that of private persons, and may lawfully be transgressed from a more trivial motive. However shocking such a proposition may appear to certain philosophers, it will be easy to defend it upon those principles, by which we have accounted for the origin of justice and equity.

When men have found by experience that it is impossible to subsist without society, and that it is impossible to maintain society, while they give free course to their appetites; so urgent an interest quickly restrains their actions, and imposes an obligation to observe those rules which we call *the laws of justice*. This obligation of interests rests not here; but, by the necessary course of the passions and sentiments, gives rise to the moral obligation of duty; while we approve of such actions as tend to the peace of society, and disapprove of such as tend to its disturbance. The same *natural* obligation of interest takes place among independent kingdoms, and gives rise to the same *morality*; so that no one of ever so corrupt morals will approve of a prince who voluntarily, and of his own accord, breaks his word, or violates any treaty. But here we may observe, that though the intercourse of different states be advantageous, and even sometimes necessary, yet it is not so necessary nor advantageous as that among individuals, without which it is utterly impossible for human nature ever to subsist. Since, therefore, the *natural* obligation to justice, among different states, is not so strong as among individuals, the *moral* obligation which arises from it must partake of its weakness; and we must necessarily give a greater indulgence to a prince or minister who deceives another, than to a private gentleman who breaks his word of honour.

DAVID HUME (1711–1776)

Have States a Legal Code?

The grandest function of the Law of Nature was discharged in giving birth to modern International Law and to the modern Law of War, but this part of its effects must here be dismissed with consideration very unequal to its importance.

Among the postulates which form the foundation of International Law, or of so much of it as retains the figure which it received from its original architects, there are two or three of pre-eminent importance. The first of all is expressed in the position that there is a determinable Law of Nature. Grotius and his successors took the assumption directly from the Romans, but they differed widely from the Roman jurisconsults and from each other in their ideas as to the mode of determination. The ambition of almost every Publicist who has flourished since the revival of letters has been to provide new and more manageable definitions of Nature and of her law, and it is indisputable that the conception in passing through the long series of writers on Public Law has gathered round it a large accretion, consisting of fragments of ideas derived from nearly every theory of ethics which has in its turn taken possession of the schools. Yet it is a remarkable proof of the essentially historical character of the conception that, after all the efforts which have been made to evolve the code of nature from the necessary characteristics of the natural state, so much of the result is just what it would have been if men had been satisfied to adopt the dicta of the Roman lawyers without questioning or reviewing them. Setting aside the Conventional or Treaty Law of Nations, it is surprising how large a part of the system is made up of pure Roman law. Wherever there is a doctrine of the jurisconsults affirmed by them to be in harmony with the Jus Gentium, the publicists have found a reason for borrowing it, however plainly it may bear the marks of a distinctively Roman origin. . .

The assumption that Natural Law is binding on states *inter se* is the next in rank of those which underlie International Law. A series of assertions or admissions of this principle may be traced up to the very infancy of modern juridical science, and at first sight it seems a direct inference from the teaching of the Romans. The civil condition of society being distinguished from the natural by the fact that in the first there is a distinct author of law, while in the last there is none, it appears as if the moment a number of *units* were acknowledged to obey no common sovereign or political superior they were thrown back on the ulterior behests of the Law Natural. States are such units; the hypothesis of their independence excludes the notion of a common lawgiver, and draws with it, therefore, according to a certain range of ideas, the notion of subjection to the primeval order of nature. The alternative is to consider independent communities as not related to each other by any law, but this condition of lawlessness is exactly the vacuum which the Nature of the jurisconsults abhorred. There is certainly apparent reason for thinking that if the mind of a Roman lawyer rested on any sphere from which civil law was banished, it would instantly fill the void with the ordinances of Nature. It is never safe, however, to assume that conclusions, however certain and immediate in our own eyes, were actually drawn at any period of history. No passage has ever been adduced from the remains of Roman law which, in my judgment, proves the jurisconsults to have believed natural law to have obligatory force between independent commonwealths; and we cannot but see that to citizens of the Roman empire who regarded their sovereign's dominions as conterminous with civilisation, the equal subjection of states to the Law of Nature, if contemplated at all, must have seemed at most an extreme result of curious speculation. The truth appears to be that modern International Law, undoubted as is its descent from Roman law, is only connected with it by an irregular filiation. The early modern interpreters of the jurisprudence of Rome, misconceiving the meaning of Jus Gentium, assumed without hesitation that the Romans had bequeathed to them a system of rules for the adjustment of international transactions. This 'Law of Nations' was at first an authority which had formidable competitors to strive with, and the condition of Europe was long such as to preclude its universal reception. Gradually, however, the western world arranged itself in a form more favourable to the theory of the civilians; circumstances destroyed the credit of rival doctrines; and at last, at a peculiarly felicitous conjuncture, Ayala and Grotius were able to obtain for it the enthusiastic assent of Europe, an assent which has been over and over again renewed in every variety of solemn engagement. The great men to whom its triumph is chiefly owing attempted, it need scarcely be said, to place it on an entirely new basis, and it is unquestionable that in the course of this displacement they altered much of its structure, though far less of it than is commonly supposed. Having adopted from the Antonine jurisconsults the position that the Jus Gentium and the Jus Naturæ were identical, Grotius, with his immediate predecessors and his immediate successors, attributed to the Law of Nature an authority which would never perhaps have been claimed for it, if 'Law of Nations' had not in that age been an ambiguous expression. They laid down unreservedly that Natural Law is the code of states, and thus put in operation a process which has continued almost down to our own day, the process of engrafting on the international system rules which are supposed to have been evolved from the unassisted contemplation of the conception of Nature. There is too one consequence of immense practical importance to mankind which, though not unknown during the early modern history of Europe, was never clearly or universally acknowledged till the doctrines of the Grotian school had prevailed. If the society of nations is governed by Natural Law, the atoms which compose it must be absolutely equal. Men under the sceptre of Nature are all equal, and accordingly commonwealths are equal if the international state be one of nature. The proposition that independent communities, however different in size and power, are all equal in the view of the law of nations, has largely contributed to the happiness of mankind, though it is constantly threatened by the political tendencies of each successive age.

SIR HENRY MAINE (1822–1888)

A Confidential Talk

In the meantime, after dinner, Tadpole and Taper, who were among the guests of Mr Ormsby, withdrew to a distant sofa, out of earshot, and indulged in confidential talk.

'Such a strength in debate was never before found on a Treasury bench,' said Mr Tadpole; 'the other side will be dumfounded.'

'And what do you put our members at now?' inquired Mr Taper.

'Would you take fifty-five for our majority?' rejoined Mr Tadpole.

'It is not so much the tail they have, as the excuse their junction will be for the moderate, sensible men to come over,' said Taper. 'Our friend, Sir Everard for example, it would settle him.'

'He is a solemn impostor,' rejoined Mr Tadpole; 'but he is a baronet and a county member, and very much looked up to by the Wesleyans. The other men, I know, have refused him a peerage.'

'And we might hold out judicious hopes,' said Taper.

'No one can do that better than you,' said Tadpole. 'I am apt to say too much about those things.'

'I make it a rule never to open my mouth on such subjects,' said Taper. 'A nod or a wink will speak volumes. An affectionate pressure of the hand will sometimes do a great deal; and I have promised many a peerage without committing myself by an ingenuous habit of deference which cannot be mistaken by the future noble.'

'I wonder what they will do with Rigby,' said Tadpole.

'He wants a good deal,' said Taper.

'I tell you what, Mr Taper; the time is gone by when a Marquess of Monmouth was Letter A. No. 1.'

'Very true, Mr Tadpole. A wise man would do well now to look to the great middle class, as I said the other day to the electors of Shabbyton.'

'I had sooner be supported by the Wesleyans,' said Mr Tadpole, 'than by all the marquesses in the peerage.'

'At the same time,' said Mr Taper, 'Rigby is a considerable man. If we want a slashing article—'

'Pooh!' said Mr Tadpole. 'He is quite gone by. He takes three months for his slashing articles. Give me a man who can write a leader. Rigby can't write a leader.'

'Very few can,' said Mr Taper. 'However, I don't think much of the press. Its power is gone by. They overdid it.'

'There is Tom Chudleigh,' said Tadpole. 'What is he to have?'

'Nothing, I hope,' said Taper. 'I hate him. A coxcomb! cracking his jokes and laughing at us.'

'He has done a good deal for the party, though,' said Tadpole. 'That, to be sure, is only an additional reason for throwing him over, as he is too far committed to venture to oppose us. But I am afraid from something that dropped to-day, that Sir Robert thinks he has claims.'

'We must stop them,' said Taper, growing pale. 'Fellows like Chudleigh when they once get in, are always in one's way. I have no objection to young noblemen being put forward, for they are preferred so rapidly, and then their fathers die, that in the long run they do not practically interfere with us.'

'Well, his name was mentioned,' said Tadpole. 'There is no concealing that.'

'I will speak to Earwig,' said Taper. 'He shall just drop into Sir Robert's ear by chance, that Chudleigh used to quiz him in the smoking-room. Those little bits of information do a great deal of good.'

'Well, I leave him to you,' said Tadpole. 'I am heartily with you in keeping out all fellows like Chudleigh. They are very well for opposition; but in office we don't want wits.'

'And when shall we have the answer from Knowsley?' inquired Taper. 'You anticipate no possible difficulty?'

'I tell you it is "carte blanche",' replied Tadpole. 'Four places in the cabinet. Two secretaryships at the least. Do you happen to know any gentlemen of your acquaintance, Mr Taper, who refuse secretaryships of state so easily, that you can for an instant doubt of the present arrangement?'

'I know none, indeed,' said Mr Taper, with a grim smile.

'The thing is done,' said Mr Tadpole.

'And now for our cry,' said Mr Taper.

'It is not a cabinet for a good cry,' said Tadpole; 'but then on the other hand, it is a cabinet that will sow dissension in the opposite ranks, and prevent them having a good cry.'

'Ancient institutions and modern improvements, I suppose, Mr Tadpole?'

'Ameliorations is the better word; ameliorations. Nobody knows exactly what it means.'

'We go strong on the Church?' said Mr Taper.

'And no repeal of the malt tax; you were right, Taper. It can't be listened to for a moment.'

'Something might be done with prerogative,' said Mr Taper; 'the king's constitutional choice.'

'Not too much,' replied Mr Tadpole. 'It is a raw time yet for prerogative.'

'Ah! Tadpole,' said Mr. Taper, getting a little maudlin; 'I often think, if the time should ever come, when you and I should be joint secretaries of the treasury!'

'We shall see, we shall see. All we have to do is to get into parliament, work well together, and keep other men down.'

'We will do our best,' said Taper. 'A dissolution you hold inevitable?'

'How are you and I to get into parliament, if there be not one? We must make it inevitable. I tell you what, Taper, the lists must prove a dissolution inevitable. You understand me? If the present parliament goes on, where shall we be? We shall have new men cropping up every session.'

'True, terribly true,' said Mr Taper. 'That we should ever live to see a Tory government again! We have reason to be very thankful.'

'Hush!' said Mr Tadpole. 'The time has gone by for Tory governments; what the country requires is a sound Conservative government.'

'A sound Conservative government,' said Taper musingly. 'I understand: Tory men and Whig measures.'

LORD BEACONSFIELD (1804–1881)

The Inns of Court

But besides all this, there is in and about this city a whole university, as it were, of students, practicers or pleaders, and judges of the laws of this realm, not living of common stipends, as in other universities it is for the most part done, but of their own private maintenance, as being altogether fed either by their places or practice, or otherwise by their proper revenue, or exhibition of parents and friends; for that the younger sort are either gentlemen or the sons of gentlemen, or of other most wealthy persons. Of these houses there be at this day fourteen in all; whereof nine do stand within the liberties of this city, and five in the suburbs thereof; to wit:

Serjeants' inn in Fleet Street, Serjeants' inn in Chancery lane; for judges and sergeants only.

The Inner temple, the Middle temple, in Fleet street; houses of court.

Clifford's inn in Fleet street, Thavies inn in Oldborne, Furnival's inn in Oldborne, Barnard's inn in Oldborne, Staple inn in Oldborne; houses of Chancery. . .

The houses of court be replenished partly with young students, and partly with graduates and practisers of the law; but the inns of Chancery being, as it were, provinces, severally subjected to the inns of court, be chiefly furnished with officers, attorneys, solicitors, and clerks, that follow the courts of the King's Bench or Common Pleas; and yet there want not some other being young students, that come thither sometimes from one of the Universities, and sometimes immediately from grammar schools; and these having spent some time in studying upon the first elements and grounds of the law, and having performed the exercise of their own houses (called Boltas Mootes, and putting of cases), they proceed to be admitted, and become students in some of these four houses or inns of court, where continuing by the space of seven years or thereabouts, they frequent readings, meetings, boltings, and other learned exercises, whereby growing ripe in the knowledge of the laws, and approved withal to be of honest conversation, they are either, by the general consent of the benchers or readers, being of the most ancient, grave, and judicial men of every inn of the court, or by the special privilege of the present reader there, selected and called to the degree of utter barristers, and so enabled to be common counsellors, and to practice the law, both in their chambers and at the bars.

Of these, after that they be called to a further step of preferment, called the Bench, there are twain every year chosen among the benchers of every inn of court to be readers there, who do make their readings at two times in the year also; that is, one in Lent, and the other at the beginning of August.

And for the help of young students in every of the inns of Chancery, they do likewise choose out of every one inn of court a reader, being no bencher, but an utter barrister there, of ten or twelve years' continuance, and of good profit in study. Now, from these of the said degree of counsellors, or utter barristers, having continued therein the space of fourteen or fifteen years at the least, the chiefest and best learned are by the benchers elected to increase the number, as I said, of the bench amongst them; and so in their time do become first single, and then double, readers to the students of those houses of court; after which last reading they be named apprentices at the law, and, in default, of a sufficient number of sergeants at law, these are, at the pleasure of the prince, to be advanced to the places of sergeants; out of which number of sergeants also the void places of judges are likewise ordinarily filled; albeit, now and then some be advanced, by the special favour of the prince, to the estate, dignity, and place, both of sergeant and judge, as it were in one instant. But from thenceforth they hold not any room in those inns of court, being translated to one of the said two inns, called Sergeante's inns, where none but the sergeants and judges do converse.

JOHN STOW (c. 1525–1605)

Let the Seller Beware

In the matter of buying and selling estates, it is provided amongst us by the civil constitutions, that he who is the seller should tell all the faults that he knows of to the purchaser: for the twelve tables ordering no more than this, that the seller should be bound to make good those faults which were expressly mentioned by word of mouth in the bargain, and which whoever denied was to pay double damages, the lawyers have appointed a punishment for those who themselves do not discover the defects of what they sell: for they have so decreed, that if the seller of an estate, when he made the bargain, did not tell all the faults in particular that he knew of it, he should afterwards be bound to make them good to the purchaser. Titus Claudius Centumalus, to give an example, had a house that stood on the Coelian hill, and hindered the augurs as they made their observations from the Capitoline mount; who therefore gave him orders to pull that down which was such a hindrance to their business. Instead of this, Claudius put a bill over the door, that the house was to be sold; and quickly put it off, P. Calpurnius Lanarius being the man that bought it. The augurs in a short time sent him the same orders, and he accordingly took care to perform them: but afterwards, coming to understand that Claudius had not set the house to sale till after he had been ordered by the augurs to demolish it, he brought in against him an action at law, to receive such satisfaction as in conscience and equity he was bound to make him. Marcus Cato, the father of him that is lately dead (for as others are distinguished by the names of their fathers, so he that begot this incomparable person should be named from his son), sat as judge in the case, and gave this sentence on the whole matter; that since Claudius knew this inconvenience beforehand, and did not discover it when he sold the estate, he was obliged in equity to make it good to the purchaser: he judged it therefore to be a part of honesty that the seller should fairly declare to the buyer all the faults which he knows in the thing to be sold. If, then, this judgement were just and equitable, neither the merchant that brought the corn, nor the supposed seller of the infectious house, did well in concealing what either of them knew: but all the particular sorts of concealing could never be taken notice of by the laws of the city: however, such as could were very carefully provided against.

CICERO (106–43 B.C.)

The Just and the Expedient

Is, then, the difference between the Just and the Expedient a merely imaginary distinction? Have mankind been under a delusion in thinking that justice is a more sacred thing than policy, and that the latter ought only to be listened to after the former has been satisfied? By no means. The exposition we have given of the nature and origin of the sentiment, recognises a real distinction; and no one of those who profess the most sublime contempt for the consequences of actions as an element in their morality, attaches more importance to the distinction than I do. While I dispute the pretensions of any theory which sets up an imaginary standard of justice not grounded on utility, I account the justice which is grounded on utility to be the chief part, and incomparably the most sacred and binding part, of all morality. Justice is a name for certain classes of moral rules, which concern the essentials of human well-being more nearly, and are therefore of more absolute obligation, than any other rules for the guidance of life; and the notion which we have found to be of the essence of the idea of justice, that of a right residing in an individual, implies and testifies to this more binding obligation.

The moral rules which forbid mankind to hurt one another (in which we must never forget to include wrongful interference with each other's freedom) are more vital to human well-being than any maxims, however important, which only point out the best mode of managing some department of human affairs. They have also the peculiarity, that they are the main element in determining the whole of the social feelings of mankind. It is their observance which alone preserves peace among human beings: if obedience to them were not the rule, and disobedience the exception, every one would see in every one else an enemy, against whom he must be perpetually guarding himself. What is hardly less important, these are the precepts which mankind have the strongest and the most direct inducements for impressing upon one another. By merely giving to each other prudential instruction or exhortation, they may gain, or think they gain, nothing: in inculcating on each other the duty of positive beneficence they have an unmistakable interest, but far less in degree: a person may possibly not need the benefits of others; but he always needs that they should not do him hurt. Thus the moralities which protect every individual from being harmed by others, either directly or by being hindered in his freedom of pursuing his own good, are at once those which he himself has most at heart, and those which he has the strongest interest in publishing and enforcing by word and deed. It is by a person's observance of these that his fitness to exist as one of the fellowship of human beings is tested and decided; for on that depends his being a nuisance or not to those with whom he is in contact. Now it is these moralities primarily which compose the obligations of justice. The most marked cases of injustice, and those which give the tone to the feeling of repugnance which characterises the sentiment, are acts of wrongful aggression, or wrongful exercise of power over some one; the next are those which consist in wrongfully withholding from him something which is his due; in both cases, inflicting on him a positive hurt, either in the form of direct suffering, or of the privation of some good which he had reasonable ground, either of a physical or of a social kind, for counting upon.

The same powerful motives which command the observance of these primary moralities, enjoin the punishment of those who violate them; and as the impulses of self-defence, of defence of others, and of vengeance, are all called forth against such persons, retribution, or evil for evil, becomes closely connected with the sentiment of justice, and is universally included in the idea. Good for good is also one of the dictates of justice; and this, though its social utility is evident, and though it carries with it a natural human feeling, has not at first sight that obvious connection with hurt or injury, which, existing in the most elementary cases of just and unjust, is the source of the characteristic intensity of the sentiment. But the connection, though less obvious, is not less real. He who accepts benefits, and denies a return of them when needed, inflicts a real hurt, by disappointing one of the most natural and reasonable of expectations, and one which he must at least tacitly have encouraged, otherwise the benefits would seldom have been conferred. The important rank, among human evils and wrongs, of the disappointment of expectation, is shown in the fact that it constitutes the principal criminality of two such highly immoral acts as a breach of friendship and a breach of promise. Few hurts which human beings can sustain are greater, and none wound more, than when that on which they habitually and with full assurance relied, fails them in the hour of need; and few wrongs are greater than this mere withholding of good; none excite more resentment, either in the person suffering, or in a sympathising spectator. The principle, therefore, of giving to each what they deserve, that is, good for good as well as evil for evil, is not only included within the idea of Justice as we have defined it, but is a proper object of that intensity of sentiment, which places the Just, in human estimation, above the simply Expedient.

JOHN STUART MILL (1806–1873)

Science catches up with the Arts

From 1660 to the present day the English have made greater progress in all the arts than in all preceding ages. I will not here repeat what I have said elsewhere of Milton. . . Criticism indeed exhausts itself, but never praise. Milton remains at once the glory and wonder of England; he is compared to Homer, whose defects are as great, and he is preferred to Dante, whose conceptions are yet more fantastic.

Among the large number of pleasing poets who graced the reign of Charles II, such as Waller, the Earl of Dorset and the Earl of Rochester, the Duke of Buckingham and many others, we must single out Dryden, who distinguished himself in every branch of poetry; his works are full of details both brilliant and true to nature, lively, vigorous, bold and passionate, merits in which none of his own nation equals him nor any of the ancients surpass him. If Pope, who succeeded him, had not written late in life his *Essay on Man*, he could not be compared to Dryden.

No other nation has treated moral subjects in poetry with greater depth and vigour than the English; there lies, it seems to me, the greatest merit of her poets.

There is another kind of elegant writing which requires at once a mind more cultured and more universal; such was Addison's; he achieved immortal fame with his *Cato*, the only English tragedy written from beginning to end in an elegant and lofty style, and his other moral and critical works breathe a perfect taste; in all he wrote, sound sense appears adorned by a lively fancy, and his manner of writing is an excellent model for any country. Dean Swift left several passages whose like is not to be found among the writers of antiquity—a Rabelais made perfect. . .

It is, moreover, remarkable that this insular people, separated from the rest of the world and so lately cultured, should have acquired at least as much knowledge of antiquity as the Italians have been able to gather in Rome, which was for so long the meeting-place of the nations. Marsham penetrated the mysteries of ancient Egypt. No Persian had such a knowledge of the Zoroastrian religion as the scholar Hyde. The Turks were unacquainted with the history of Mahomet and the preceding centuries, and its interpretation was left to the Englishman Sale, who turned his travels in Arabia to such good profit. . .

It is above all in philosophy that the English have become the teachers of other nations. It is no mere question of ingenious systems. The false myths of the Greeks should have disappeared long ago and modern myths should never have appeared at all. Roger Bacon broke fresh ground by declaring that Nature must be studied in a new way, that experiments must be made; Boyle devoted his life to making them. This is no place for a dissertation on physics; it is enough to say that after three thousand years of fruitless research, Newton was the first to find and demonstrate the great natural law by which all elements of matter are mutually attracted, the law by which all the stars are held in their courses. He was indeed the first to see the light; before him it was unknown.

His principles of mathematics, which include a system of physics at once new and true, are based on the discovery of the calculus, incorrectly called *infinitesimal*, a supreme effort of geometry, and one which he made at the age of twenty-four. It was a great philosopher, the learned Halley, who said of him 'that it is not permitted to any mortal to approach nearer to divinity.'

A host of expert geometricians and physicists were enlightened by his discoveries and inspired by his genius. Bradley discovered the aberration of the light of fixed stars, distant at least twelve billion leagues from our small globe.

Halley, whom I have quoted above, though but an astronomer, received the command of one of the king's ships in 1698. It was on this ship that he determined the position of the stars of the Antarctic Pole, and noted the variations of the compass in all parts of the known globe. The voyage of the Argonauts was in comparison but the crossing of a bark from one side of a river to the other. Yet Halley's voyage has been hardly spoken of in Europe.

The indifference we display towards great events become too familiar, and our admiration of the ancient Greeks for trivial ones, is yet another proof of the wonderful superiority of our age over that of the ancients. Boileau in France and Sir William Temple in England obstinately refused to acknowledge such a superiority; they were eager to disparage their own age, in order to place themselves above it: but the dispute between the ancients and the moderns has been at last decided, at any rate in the field of philosophy. There is not a single ancient philosopher whose works are taught to-day to the youth of any enlightened nation.

Locke alone should serve as a good example of the advantage of our age over the most illustrious ages of Greece. From Plato to Locke there is indeed nothing; no one in that interval developed the operations of the human mind, and a man who knew the whole of Plato and only Plato, would know little and that not well. . .

Locke alone has developed the *human understanding* in a book where there is naught but truths, a book made perfect by the fact that these truths are stated clearly.

To complete our review of the superiority of the past century over all others, we may cast our eyes towards Germany and the North. Hevelius of Danzig was the first astronomer to study deeply the planet of the moon; no man before him surveyed the heavens with greater care: and of all the great men that the age produced, none showed more plainly why it should be justly called the age of Louis XIV. A magnificent library that he possessed was destroyed by fire; upon which the King of France bestowed on the astronomer of Danzig a present which more than compensated him for the loss

Mercator of Holstein was the forerunner of Newton in geometry; and the Bernouillis in Switzerland were worthy pupils of that great man. Leibnitz was for some time regarded as his rival.

The celebrated Leibnitz was born at Leipzig; and died, full of learning, in the town of Hanover; like Newton, worshipping a god, and seeking counsel of no man. He was perhaps the most universal genius in Europe: a historian assiduous in research; a sagacious lawyer, enlightening the study of law with science, foreign to that subject though it seem; a metaphysician sufficiently open-minded to endeavour to reconcile theology with metaphysics; even a Latin poet, and finally a mathematician of sufficient calibre to dispute with the great Newton the invention of the infinitesimal calculus, so that for some time the issue remained uncertain.

It was the golden age of geometry; mathematicians frequently challenged one another, that is to say, they sent each other problems to be solved, almost as the ancient kings of Asia and Egypt are reported to have sent each other riddles to divine. The problems propounded by the geometricians were more difficult than the ancient riddles; and in Germany, England, Italy and France, not one of them was left unsolved. Never was intercourse between philosophers more universal; Leibnitz did much to encourage it. A republic of letters was being gradually established in Europe, in spite of different religions. Every science, every art, was mutually assisted in this way, and it was the academies which formed this republic. Italy and Russia were allied by literature. The Englishman, the German and the Frenchman went to Leyden to study. The celebrated physician Boerhaave was consulted both by the Pope and by the Czar. His greatest pupils attracted the notice of foreigners and thus became to some extent the physicians of the nation; true scholars in every branch drew closer the bonds of this great fellowship of intellect, spread everywhere and everywhere independent. This intercourse still obtains, and is indeed one of the consolations for those ills which political ambition scatters throughout the earth.

VOLTAIRE (1694–1778)

The Grayling

The Umber and Grayling are thought by some to differ as the Herring and Pilchard do. But though they may do so in other nations, I think those in England differ nothing but in their names. Aldrovandus says, they be of a Trout kind; and Gesner says, that in his country, which is Switzerland, he is accounted the choicest of all fish. And in Italy, he is, in the month of May, so highly valued, that he is sold there at a much higher rate than any other fish. The French, which call the Chub Un Villain, call the Umber of the lake Leman Un Umble Chevalier; and they value the Umber or Grayling so highly, that they say he feeds on gold; and say, that many have been caught out of their famous river of Loire, out of whose bellies grains of gold have been often taken. And some think that he feeds on water thyme, and smells of it at his first taking out of the water; and they may think so with as good reason as we do that our Smelts smell like violets at their being first caught, which I think is a truth. Aldrovandus says, the Salmon, the Grayling, and Trout, and all fish that live in clear and sharp streams, are made by their mother Nature of such exact shape and pleasant colours purposely to invite us to a joy and contentedness in feasting with her. Whether this is a truth or not, is not my purpose to dispute: but 'tis certain, all that write of the Umber declare him to be very medicinable. And Gesner says, that the fat of an Umber or Grayling, being set, with a little honey, a day or two in the sun, in a little glass, is very excellent against redness or swarthiness, or anything that breeds in the eyes. Salvian takes him to be called Umber from his swift swimming, or gliding out of sight more like a shadow or a ghost than a fish. Much more might be said both of his smell and taste: but I shall only tell you that St Ambrose, the glorious bishop of Milan, who lived when the church kept fasting-days, calls him the flower-fish, or flower of fishes; and that he was so far in love with him, that he would not let him pass without the honour of a long discourse; but I must; and pass on to tell you how to take this dainty fish.

First note, that he grows not to the bigness of a Trout; for the biggest of them do not usually exceed eighteen inches. He lives in such rivers as the Trout does; and is usually taken with the same baits as the Trout is, and after the same manner; for he will bite both at the minnow, or worm, or fly, though he bites not often at the minnow, and is very gamesome at the fly; and much simpler, and therefore bolder than a Trout; for he will rise twenty times at a fly, if you miss him, and yet rise again. He has been taken with a fly made of the red feathers of a paroquet, a strange outlandish bird; and he will rise at a fly not unlike a gnat, or a small moth, or, indeed, at most flies that are not too big.

ISAAK WALTON (1593–1683)

Gold Fish

Not long since I spent a fortnight at the house of a friend where there was such a vivary, to which I paid no small attention, taking every occasion to remark what passed within its narrow limits. It was here that I first observed the manner in which fishes die. As soon as the creature sickens, the head sinks lower and lower, and it stands as it were on its head; till, getting weaker, and losing all poise, the tail turns over, and at last it floats on the surface of the water with its belly uppermost. The reason why fishes, when dead, swim in that manner is very obvious; because, when the body is no longer balanced by the fins of the belly, the broad muscular back preponderates by its own gravity, and turns the belly uppermost, as lighter from its being a cavity, and because it contains the swimming-bladders, which contribute to render it buoyant. Some that delight in gold and silver fishes have adopted a notion that they need no aliment. True it is that they will subsist for a long time without any apparent food but what they can collect from pure water frequently changed; yet they must draw some support from animalcula, and other nourishment supplied by the water; because, though they seem to eat nothing, yet the consequences of eating often drop from them. That they are best pleased with such jejune diet may easily be confuted, since if you toss them crumbs, they will seize them with great readiness, not to say greediness: however, bread should be given sparingly, lest, turning sour, it corrupt the water. They will also feed on the water-plant called *lemna* (duck's meat), and also on small fry.

When they want to move a little they gently protrude themselves with their *pinnæ pectorales*; but it is with their strong muscular tails only that they and all fishes shoot along with such inconceivable rapidity. It has been said that the eyes of fishes are immoveable: but these apparently turn them forward or backward in their sockets as their occasions require. They take little notice of a lighted candle, though applied close to their heads, but flounce and seem much frightened by a sudden stroke of the hand against the support whereon the bowl is hung; especially when they have been motionless, and are perhaps asleep. As fishes have no eyelids, it is not easy to discern when they are sleeping or not, because their eyes are always open.

Nothing can be more amusing than a glass bowl containing such fishes: the double refractions of the glass and water represent them, when moving, in a shifting and changeable variety of dimensions, shades, and colours; while the two mediums, assisted by the concavo-convex shape of the vessel, magnify and distort them vastly; not to mention that the introduction of another element and its inhabitants into our parlours engages the fancy in a very agreeable manner.

Gold and silver fishes, though originally natives of China and Japan, yet are become so well reconciled to our climate as to thrive and multiply very fast in our ponds and stews. Linnæus ranks this species of fish under the genus of *cyprinus*, or carp, and calls it *cyprinus auratus*.

Some people exhibit this sort of fish in a very fanciful way; for they cause a glass bowl to be blown with a large hollow space within, that does not communicate with it. In this cavity they put a bird occasionally; so that you may see a goldfinch or a linnet hopping as it were in the midst of the water, and the fishes swimming in a circle round it. The simple exhibition of the fishes is agreeable and pleasant; but in so complicated a way becomes whimsical and unnatural.

GILBERT WHITE (1720–1793)

Anomalies of an Archipelago

I have not as yet noticed by far the most remarkable feature in the natural history of this archipelago; it is, that the different islands to a considerable extent are inhabited by a different set of beings. My attention was first called to this fact by the Vice-Governor, Mr Lawson, declaring that the tortoises differed from the different islands, and that he could with certainty tell from which island any one was brought. I did not for some time pay sufficient attention to this statement, and I had already partially mingled together the collections from two of the islands. I never dreamed that islands, about fifty or sixty miles apart, and most of them in sight of each other, formed of precisely the same rocks, placed under a quite similar climate, rising to a nearly equal height, would have been differently tenanted; but we shall soon see that this is the case. It is the fate of most voyagers, no sooner to discover what is most interesting in any locality, than they are hurried from it; but I ought, perhaps, to be thankful that I obtained sufficient material to establish this most remarkable fact in the distribution of organic beings.

The inhabitants, as I have said, state that they can distinguish the tortoises from the different islands; and that they differ not only in size, but in other characters. Captain Porter has described those from Charles and from the nearest island to it, namely, Hood Island, as having their shells in front thick and turned up like a Spanish saddle, whilst the tortoises from James Island are rounder, blacker, and have a better taste when cooked. M. Bibron, moreover, informs me that he has seen what he considers two distinct species of tortoise from the Galapagos, but he does not know from which islands. The specimens that I brought from three islands were young ones; and probably owing to this cause, neither Mr Gray nor myself could find in them any specific differences. I have remarked that the marine Amblyrhynchus was larger at Albemarle Island than elsewhere; and M. Bibron informs me that he has seen two distinct aquatic species of this genus; so that the different islands probably have their representative species or races of the Amblyrhynchus, as well as of the tortoise. My attention was first thoroughly aroused, by comparing together the numerous specimens, shot by myself and several other parties on board, of the mocking-thrushes, when, to my astonishment, I discovered that all those from Charles Island belonged to one species (Mimus trifasciatus); all from Albemarle Island to M. parvulus; and all from James and Chatham Islands (between which two other islands are situated, as connecting links) belonged to M. melanotis. These two latter species are closely allied, and would by some ornithologists be considered as only well-marked races or varieties; but the Mimus trifasciatus is very distinct. Unfortunately most of the specimens of the finch tribe were mingled together; but I have strong reasons to suspect that some of the species of the sub-group Geospiza are confined to separate islands. If the different islands have their representatives of Geospiza, it may help to explain the singularly large number of the species of this sub-group in this one small archipelago, and as a probable consequence of their numbers, the perfectly graduated series in the size of their beaks. Two species of the sub-group Cactornis, and two of Camarhynchus, were procured in the archipelago; and of the numerous specimens of these two sub-groups shot by four collectors at James Island, all were found to belong to one species of each; whereas the numerous specimens shot either on Chatham or Charles Island (for the two sets were mingled together) all belonged to the two other species: hence we may feel almost sure that these islands possess their representative species of these two sub-groups. In land-shells this law of distribution does not appear to hold good. In my very small collection of insects, Mr Waterhouse remarks, that of those which were ticketed with their locality, not one was common to any two of the islands.

CHARLES DARWIN (1809–1882)

The Life-Blood of Science

There is another aspect from which it is right that we should regard pure science—one that makes no appeal to its utility in practical life, but touches a side of our nature which the reader may have thought that I have entirely neglected. There is an element in our being which is not satisfied by the formal processess of reasoning; it is the imaginative or aesthetic side, the side to which the poets and philosophers appeal, and one which science cannot, to be scientific, disregard. We have seen that the imagination must not replace the reason in the deduction of relation and law from classified facts. But, none the less, disciplined imagination has been at the bottom of all great scientific discoveries. All great scientists have, in a certain sense, been great artists; the man with no imagination may collect facts, but he cannot make great discoveries. If I were compelled to name the Englishmen who during our generation have had the widest imaginations and exercised them most beneficially, I think I should put the novelists and poets on one side and say Michael Faraday and Charles Darwin. Now it is very needful to understand the exact part imagination plays in pure science. We can, perhaps, best achieve this result by considering the following proposition: Pure science has a further strong claim upon us on account of the exercise it gives to the imaginative faculties and the gratification it provides for the aesthetic judgment. The exact meaning of the terms 'scientific fact' and 'scientific law' will be considered in later chapters, but for the present let us suppose an elaborate classification of such facts has been made, and their relationships and sequences carefully traced. What is the next stage in the process of scientific investigation? Undoubtedly it is the use of the imagination. The discovery of some single statement, some brief *formula* from which the whole group of facts is seen to flow, is the work, not of the mere cataloguer, but of the man endowed with creative imagination. The single statement, the brief formula, the few words of which replace in our minds a wide range of relationships between isolated phenomena, is what we term a scientific *law*. Such a law, relieving our memory from the burden of individual sequences, enables us, with the minimum of intellectual fatigue, to grasp a vast complexity of natural or social phenomena. The discovery of law is therefore the peculiar function of the creative imagination. But this imagination has to be a *disciplined* one. It has in the first place to appreciate the whole range of facts, which require to be resumed in a single statement; and then when the law is reached— often by what seems solely the inspired imagination of genius—it must be tested and criticized by its discoverer in every conceivable way, till he is certain that the imagination has not played him false, and that his law is in real agreement with the whole group of phenomena which it resumes. Herein lies the key-note to the scientific use of the imagination. Hundreds of men have allowed their imagination to solve the universe, but the men who have contributed to our real understanding of natural phenomena have been those who were unstinting in their application of criticism to the product of their imaginations. It is such criticism which is the essence of the scientific use of the imagination, which is, indeed, the very life-blood of science.

KARL PEARSON (1857–1936)

The Bean-field

Meanwhile my beans, the length of whose rows, added together, was seven miles already planted, were impatient to be hoed, for the earliest had grown considerably before the latest were in the ground; indeed, they were not easily to be put off. What was the meaning of this so steady and self-respecting, this small Herculean labour, I knew not. I came to love my rows, my beans, though so many more than I wanted. They attached me to the earth, and so I got strength like Antæus. But why should I raise them? Only Heaven knows. This was my curious labour all summer,—to make this portion of the earth's surface, which had yielded only cinquefoil, blackberries, johnswort, and the like, before, sweet wild fruits and pleasant flowers, produce instead this pulse. What shall I learn of beans or beans of me? I cherish them, I hoe them, early and late I have an eye to them; and this is my day's work. It is a fine broad leaf to look on. My auxiliaries are the dews and rains which water this dry soil, and what fertility is in the soil itself, which for the most part is lean and effete. My enemies are worms, cool days, and most of all woodchucks. The last have nibbled for me a quarter of an acre clean. But what right had I to oust johnswort and the rest, and break up their ancient herb garden? Soon, however, the remaining beans will be too tough for them, and go forward to meet new foes.

When I was four years old, as I well remember, I was brought from Boston to this my native town, through these very woods and this field, to the pond. It is one of the oldest scenes stamped on my memory. And now to-night my flute has waked the echoes over that very water. The pines still stand here, older than I; or, if some have fallen, I have cooked my supper with their stumps, and a new growth is rising all around, preparing another aspect for new infant eyes. Almost the same johnswort springs from the same perennial root in this pasture, and even I have at length helped to clothe that fabulous landscape of my infant dreams, and one of the results of my presence and influence is seen in these bean leaves, corn blades, and potato vines.

I planted about two acres and a-half of upland; and as it was only about fifteen years since the land was cleared, and I myself had got out two or three cords of stumps, I did not give it any manure; but in the course of the summer it appeared by the arrow-heads which I turned up in hoeing, that an extinct nation had anciently dwelt here and planted corn and beans ere white men came to clear the land, and so, to some extent, had exhausted the soil for this very crop.

Before yet any woodchuck or squirrel had run across the road, or the sun had got above the shrub oaks, while all the dew was on, though the farmers warned me against it,—I would advise you to do all your work if possible while the dew is on,—I began to level the ranks of haughty weeds in my bean-field and throw dust upon their heads. Early in the morning I worked barefooted, dabbling like a plastic artist in the dewy and crumbling sand, but later in the day the sun blistered my feet. There the sun lighted me to hoe beans, pacing slowly backward and forward over that yellow gravelly upland, between the long green rows, fifteen rods, the one end terminating in a shrub oak copse where I could rest in the shade, the other in a blackberry field where the green berries deepened their tints by the time I had made another bout. Removing the weeds, putting fresh soil about the bean stems, and encouraging this weed which I had sown, making the yellow soil express its summer thought in bean leaves and blossoms rather than in wormwood and piper and millet grass, making the earth say beans instead of grass,—this was my daily work. As I had little aid from horses or cattle, or hired men or boys, or improved implements of husbandry, I was much slower, and became much more intimate with my beans than usual. But labour of the hands, even when pursued to the verge of drudgery, is perhaps never the worst form of idleness. It has a constant and imperishable moral, and to the scholar it yields a classic result. A very *agricola laboriosus* was I to travellers bound westward through Lincoln and Wayland to nobody knows where; they sitting at their ease in gigs, with elbows on knees, and reins loosely hanging in festoons; I the home-staying, laborious native of the soil. But soon my homestead was out of their sight and thought. It was the only open and cultivated field for a great distance on either side of the road, so they made the most of it; and sometimes the man in the field heard more of travellers' gossip and comment than was meant for his ear: 'Beans so late! peas so late!'—for I continued to plant when others had began to hoe,—the ministerial husbandman had not suspected it. 'Corn, my boy, for fodder; corn for fodder.' 'Does he *live* there?' asks the black bonnet of the grey coat; and the hard-featured farmer reins up his grateful dobbin to inquire what you are doing when he sees no manure in the furrow, and recommends a little chip dirt, or any little waste stuff, or it may be ashes or plaster. But here were two acres and a-half of furrows, and only a hoe for cart and two hands to draw it,—there being an aversion to other carts and horses,—and chip dirt far away. Fellow-travellers as they rattled by compared it aloud with the fields which they had passed, so that I came to know how I stood in the agricultural world. This was one field not in Mr Coleman's report. And, by the way, who estimates the value of the crop which Nature yields in the still wilder fields unimproved by man? The crop of *English* hay is carefully weighed, the moisture calculated, the silicates and the potash; but in all dells and pond holes in the woods and pastures and swamps grows a rich and various crop only unreaped by man. Mine was, as it were, the connecting link between wild and cultivated fields; as some states are civilised, and others half-civilised, and others savage or barbarous, so my field was, though not in a bad sense, a half-cultivated field.

HENRY DAVID THOREAU (1817–1862)

The Guardian of the Granary

Cat! who hast pass'd thy grand climacteric,
  How many mice and rats hast in thy days
  Destroy'd?—How many tit bits stolen? Gaze
With those bright languid segments green, and prick
Those velvet ears—but pr'ythee do not stick
  Thy latent talons in me—and upraise
  Thy gentle mew—and tell me all thy frays
Of fish and mice, and rats and tender chick.
Nay, look not down, nor lick thy dainty wrists—
  For all the wheezy asthma,—and for all
Thy tail's tip is nick'd off—and though the fists
  Of many a maid have given thee many a maul,
Still is that fur as soft as when the lists
  In youth thou enter'dst on glass-bottled wall.

JOHN KEATS (1795–1821)

The Professions

It has been considered as of so much importance that a proper number of young people should be educated for certain professions, that sometimes the public and sometimes the piety of private founders have established many pensions, scholarships, exhibitions, bursaries, etc., for this purpose, which draw many more people into those trades than could otherwise pretend to follow them. In all Christian countries, I believe, the education of the greater part of churchmen is paid for in this manner. Very few of them are educated altogether at their own expense. The long, tedious, and expensive education, therefore, of those who are, will not always procure them a suitable reward, the church being crowded with people who, in order to get employment, are willing to accept of a much smaller recompense than what such an education would otherwise have entitled them to; and in this manner the competition of the poor takes away the reward of the rich. It would be indecent, no doubt, to compare either a curate or a chaplain with a journeyman in any common trade. The pay of a curate or chaplain, however, may very properly be considered as of the same nature with the wages of a journeyman. They are, all three, paid for their work according to the contract which they may happen to make with their respective superiors. Till after the middle of the fourteenth century, five merks, containing about as much silver as ten pounds of our present money, was in England the usual pay of a curate or a stipendiary parish priest, as we find it regulated by the decrees of several different national councils. At the same period fourpence a day, containing the same quantity of silver as a shilling of our present money, was declared to be the pay of a master mason, and threepence a day, equal to ninepence of our present money, that of a journeyman mason. The wages of both these labourers, therefore, supposing them to have been constantly employed, were much superior to those of the curate. The wages of the master mason, supposing him to have been without employment one third of the year, would have fully equalled them. By the 12th of Queen Anne, c. 12, it is declared, 'That whereas for want of sufficient maintenance and encouragement to curates, the cures have in several places been meanly supplied, the bishop is, therefore, empowered to appoint by writing under his hand and seal a sufficient certain stipend or allowance, not exceeding fifty and not less than twenty pounds a year.' Forty pounds a year is reckoned at present very good pay for a curate, and notwithstanding this act of parliament there are many curacies under twenty pounds a year. There are journeymen shoemakers in London who earn forty pounds a year, and there is scarce an industrious workman of any kind in that metropolis who does not earn more than twenty. This last sum indeed does not exceed what is frequently earned by common labourers in many country parishes. Whenever the law has attempted to regulate the wages of workmen, it has always been rather to lower them than to raise them. But the law has upon many occasions attempted to raise the wages of curates, and for the dignity of the church, to oblige the rectors of parishes to give them more than the wretched maintenance which they themselves might be willing to accept of. And in both cases the law seems to have been equally ineffectual, and has never either been able to raise the wages of curates, or to sink those of labourers to the degree that was intended; because it has never been able to hinder either the one from being willing to accept of less than the legal allowance, on account of the indigence of their situation and the multitude of their competitors; or the other from receiving more, on account of the contrary competition of those who expected to derive either profit or pleasure from employing them.

The great benefices and other ecclesiastical dignities support the honour of the church, notwithstanding the mean circumstances of some of its inferior members. The respect paid to the profession, too, makes some compensation even to them for the meanness of their pecuniary recompense. In England, and in all Roman Catholic countries, the lottery of the church is in reality much more advantageous than is necessary. The example of the churches of Scotland, of Geneva, and of several other protestant churches, may satisfy us that in so creditable a profession, in which education is so easily procured, the hopes of much more moderate benefices will draw a sufficient number of learned, decent, and respectable men into holy orders.

In professions in which there are no benefices, such as law and physic, if an equal proportion of people were educated at the public expense, the competition would soon be so great as to sink very much their pecuniary reward. It might then not be worth any man's while to educate his son to either of those professions at his own expense. They would be entirely abandoned to such as had been educated by those public charities, whose numbers and necessities would oblige them in general to content themselves with a very miserable recompense, to the entire degradation of the now respectable professions of law and physic.

That unprosperous race of men commonly called men of letters are pretty much in the situation which lawyers and physicians probably would be in upon the foregoing supposition. In every part of Europe the greater part of them have been educated for the church, but have been hindered by different reasons from entering into holy orders. They have generally, therefore, been educated at the public expense, and their numbers are everywhere so great as commonly to reduce the price of their labour to a very paltry recompense.

Before the invention of the art of printing, the only employment by which a man of letters could make anything by his talents was that of a public or private teacher, or by communicating to other people the curious and useful knowledge which he had acquired himself: and this is still surely a more honourable, a more useful, and in general even a more profitable employment than that other of writing for a bookseller, to which the art of printing has given occasion. The time and study, the genius, knowledge, and application requisite to qualify an eminent teacher of the sciences, are at least equal to what is necessary for the greatest practitioners in law and physic. But the usual reward of the eminent teacher bears no proportion to that of the lawyer or physician; because the trade of the one is crowded with indigent people who have been brought up to it at the public expense; whereas those of the other two are encumbered with very few who have not been educated at their own. The usual recompense, however, of public and private teachers, small as it may appear, would undoubtedly be less than it is, if the competition of those yet more indigent men of letters who write for bread was not taken out of the market. Before the invention of the art of printing, a scholar and a beggar seem to have been terms very nearly synonymous. The different governors of the universities before that time appear to have often granted licences to their scholars to beg.

ADAM SMITH (1723–1790)

The Self-Help State

I have reflected much on the subject of the poor-laws, and hope therefore that I shall be excused in venturing to suggest a mode of their gradual abolition to which I confess that at present I can see no material objection. Of this indeed I feel nearly convinced that, should we ever become so fully sensible of the widespreading tyranny, dependence, indolence, and unhappiness which they create as seriously to make an effort to abolish them, we shall be compelled by a sense of justice to adopt the principle, if not the plan, which I shall mention. It seems impossible to get rid of so extensive a system of support, consistently with humanity, without applying ourselves directly to its vital principle, and endeavouring to counteract that deeply-seated cause which occasions the rapid growth of all such establishments and invariably renders them inadequate to their object.

As a previous step even to any considerable alteration in the present system, which would contract or stop the increase of the relief to be given, it appears to me that we are bound in justice and honour formally to disclaim the *right* of the poor to support.

To this end, I should propose a regulation to be made, declaring that no child born from any marriage, taking place after the expiration of a year from the date of the law, and no illegitimate child born two years from the same date, should ever be entitled to parish assistance. And to give a more general knowledge of this law, and to enforce it more strongly on the minds of the lower classes of people, the clergyman of each parish should, after the publication of banns, read a short address stating the strong obligation on every man to support his own children; the impropriety, and even immorality, of marrying without a prospect of being able to do this; the evils which had resulted to the poor themselves from the attempt which had been made to assist by public institutions in a duty which ought to be exclusively appropriated to parents; and the absolute necessity which had at length appeared of abandoning all such institutions, on account of their producing effects totally opposite to those which were intended.

This would operate as a fair, distinct, and precise notice, which no man could well mistake; and, without pressing hard on any particular individuals, would at once throw off the rising generation from that miserable and helpless dependence upon the government and the rich, the moral as well as physical consequences of which are almost incalculable.

After the public notice which I have proposed had been given, and the system of poor-laws had ceased with regard to the rising generation, if any man chose to marry, without a prospect of being able to support a family, he should have the most perfect liberty so to do. Though to marry, in this case, is, in my opinion, clearly an immoral act, yet it is not one which society can justly take upon itself to prevent or punish; because the punishment provided for it by the laws of nature falls directly and most severely upon the individual who commits the act, and through him, only more remotely and feebly, on the society. When nature will govern and punish for us, it is a very miserable ambition to wish to snatch the rod from her hand and draw upon ourselves the odium of executioner. To the punishment therefore of nature he should be left, the punishment of want. He has erred in the face of a most clear and precise warning, and can have no just reason to complain of any person but himself when he feels the consequences of his error. All parish assistance should be denied him; and he should be left to the uncertain support of private charity. He should be taught to know that the laws of nature, which are the laws of God, had doomed him and his family to suffer for disobeying their repeated admonitions; that he had no claim of *right* on society for the smallest portion of food, beyond that which his labour would fairly purchase; and that if he and his family were saved from feeling the natural consequences of his imprudence he would owe it to the pity of some kind benefactor, to whom, therefore, he ought to be bound by the strongest ties of gratitude.

If this system were pursued, we need be under no apprehensions that the number of persons in extreme want would be beyond the power and the will of the benevolent to supply. The sphere for the exercise of private charity would, probably, not be greater than it is at present; and the principal difficulty would be to restrain the hand of benevolence from assisting those in distress in so indiscriminate a manner as to encourage indolence and want of foresight in others.

THOMAS RICHARD MALTHUS (1766–1834)

The Marshalsea

To this prison of the Court of the Marshalsea, and of the King's Palace Court of Westminster, are brought debtors arrested for the lowest sums, anywhere within twelve miles of the palace, except in the City of London: and also persons committed for piracy.

The deputy marshal, under whose particular custody this prison is, has his appointment from the knight marshal of the king's household for the time being. The great abuses practised by this officer were reported to Parliament by the gaol committee in 1729.

This prison is held under several leases by the widow of the late deputy marshal at the yearly rent of £101. It is an old irregular building (rather several buildings) in a spacious court. There are, in the whole, near sixty rooms; and yet only six of them left for common-side debtors. Of the other rooms—five were let to a man who was not a prisoner: in one of them he kept a chandler's shop; in two he lived with his family: the other two he let to prisoners. Four rooms, the Oaks, were for women. They were too few for the number; and the more modest women complained of the bad company, in which they were confined. There were about forty rooms for men on the master's-side, in which were about sixty beds; yet at my first visits, many prisoners had no beds nor any place to sleep in, but the chapel, and the tap-room. The chamber-rent wants regulation; for in several rooms where four lie in two beds, and in some dark rooms where two lie in one bed, each pays 3s. 6d. a week for his lodging.

The prison is greatly out of repair. No infirmary. The court is well supplied with water. In it the prisoners play at rackets, etc., and in a little back court, the Park, at skittles.

The tap was let to a prisoner in the rules of the King's Bench Prison; this prison being just within those rules. I was credibly informed, that one Sunday in the summer 1775, about six hundred pots of beer were brought in from a public house in the neighbourhood (Ashmore's), the prisoners not then liking the tapster's beer.

In March 1775, when the number of prisoners was a hundred and seventy-five, there were with them in this incommodious prison wives and children forty-six.

Since the Act of the nineteenth of George III, chap. lxx, there are not so many debtors in this prison as formerly; yet they are increasing, for I find here, and in other prisons, many debtors whose original debts are much under £10, but for the purpose of imprisoning such debtors, they are prosecuted either in the Court of Exchequer, or in other inferior courts, until the expenses of such prosecutions which added to the original debt amount to £10. A fresh action is then taken out in the superior courts, for the small original debt, and the accumulated costs of prosecution. Thus the salutary purposes of the said Act are defeated.

Mr Henry Allnott, who was many years since a prisoner here, had, during his confinement, a large estate bequeathed to him. He learned sympathy by his sufferings; and left £100 a year for discharging poor debtors from hence, whose debts do not exceed £4. As he bound his manor of Goring in Oxfordshire for charitable uses, this is called the Oxford charity. Many are cleared by it every year.

JOHN HOWARD (C. 1726–1790)

Interest at Five per cent

To serve both intentions, the way would be briefly thus. That there be two rates of usury; the one free and general for all; the other under licence only, to certain persons and in certain places of merchandizing. First, therefore, let usury in general be reduced to five in the hundred; and let that rate be proclaimed to be free and current; and the state let shut itself out to take any penalty for the same. This will preserve borrowing from any general stop or dryness. This will ease infinite borrowers in the country. This will, in good part, raise the price of land, because land purchased at sixteen years' purchase will yield six in the hundred and somewhat more, whereas this rate of interest yields but five. This, by like reason, will encourage and edge industrious and profitable improvements; because many will rather venture in that kind than take five in the hundred, especially having been used to greater profit. Secondly, let there be certain persons licensed to lend to known merchants upon usury at a higher rate; and let it be with the cautions following. Let the rate be, even with the merchant himself, somewhat more easy than that he used formerly to pay; for by that means all borrowers shall have some ease by this reformation, be he merchant or whosoever. Let it be no bank or common stock, but every man be master of his own money: not that I altogether mislike banks, but they will hardly be brooked, in regard of certain suspicions. Let the state be answered some small matter for the licence, and the rest left to the lender; for if the abatement be but small, it will no whit discourage the lender. For he, for example, that took before ten or nine in the hundred, will sooner descend to eight in the hundred, than give over his trade of usury, and go from certain gains to gains of hazard. Let these licensed lenders be in number indefinite, but restrained to certain principal cities and towns of merchandizing; for then they will be hardly able to colour other men's moneys in the country: so as the licence of nine will not suck away the current rate of five; for no man will lend his moneys far off, nor put them into unknown hands.

If it be objected that this doth, in a sort, authorize usury, which before was in some places but permissive; the answer is, that it is better to mitigate usury by declaration, than to suffer it to rage by connivance.

FRANCIS BACON (1561–1626)

Paper Money

A currency is in its most perfect state when it consists wholly of paper money, but of paper money of an equal value with the gold which it professes to represent. The use of paper instead of gold substitutes the cheapest in place of the most expensive medium, and enables the country, without loss to any individual, to exchange all the gold which it before used for this purpose for raw materials, utensils, and food; by the use of which both its wealth and its enjoyments are increased.

In a national point of view, it is of no importance whether the issuers of this well regulated paper money be the government or a bank, it will, on the whole, be equally productive of riches whether it be issued by one or by the other; but it is not so with respect to the interest of individuals. In a country where the market rate of interest is 7 per cent., and where the state requires for a particular expense £70,000 per annum, it is a question of importance to the individuals of that country whether they must be taxed to pay this £70,000 per annum, or whether they could raise it without taxes. Suppose that a million of money should be required to fit out an expedition. If the state issued a million of paper and displaced a million of coin, the expedition would be fitted out without any charge to the people; but if a bank issued a million of paper, and lent it to government at 7 per cent., thereby displacing a million of coin, the country would be charged with a continual tax of £70,000 per annum: the people would pay the tax, the bank would receive it, and the society would in either case be as wealthy as before; the expedition would have been really fitted out by the improvement of our system, by rendering capital of the value of a million productive in the form of commodities instead of letting it remain unproductive in the form of coin; but the advantage would always be in favour of the issuers of paper; and as the state represents the people, the people would have saved the tax if they, and not the bank, had issued this million.

I have already observed that if there were perfect security that the power of issuing paper money would not be abused, it would be of no importance with respect to the riches of the country collectively by whom it was issued; and I have now shown that the public would have a direct interest that the issuers should be the state, and not a company of merchants or bankers. The danger, however, is that this power would be more likely to be abused if in the hands of government than if in the hands of a banking company. A company would, it is said, be more under the control of law, and although it might be their interest to extend their issues beyond the bounds of discretion, they would be limited and checked by the power which individuals would have of calling for bullion or specie. It is argued that the same check would not be long respected if government had the privilege of issuing money; that they would be too apt to consider present convenience rather than future security, and might, therefore, on the alleged grounds of expediency, be too much inclined to remove the checks by which the amount of their issues was controlled.

Under an arbitrary government this objection would have great force; but in a free country, with an enlightened legislature, the power of issuing paper money, under the requisite checks of convertibility at the will of the holder, might be safely lodged in the hands of commissioners appointed for that special purpose, and they might be made totally independent of the control of ministers.

The sinking fund is managed by commissioners responsible only to Parliament, and the investment of the money entrusted to their charge proceeds with the utmost regularity; what reason can there be to doubt that the issues of paper money might be regulated with equal fidelity, if placed under similar management?

DAVID RICARDO (1772–1823)

Lines Written on a Banknote

Wae worth thy power, thou cursed leaf,
Fell source o' a' my woe and grief;
For lack o' thee I've lost my lass,
For lack o' thee I scrimp my glass:
I see the children of affliction
Unaided, through thy curst restriction:

I've seen the oppressor's cruel smile
Amid his hapless victim's spoil;
And for thy potence vainly wished,
To crush the villain in the dust:
For lack o' thee, I leave this much-lov'd shore,
Never, perhaps, to greet old Scotland more.

ROBERT BURNS (1759–1796)

No Admittance Except on Business

In countries where the capitalist method of production has become established, labour power is not paid for until it has functioned throughout the period specified in the contract; not, for instance, until the end of the week. Everywhere, therefore, the worker advances to the capitalist the use-value of his labour power; the seller of labour power allows the buyer to consume its use-value before the seller gets the price; everywhere the worker gives credit to the capitalist. That this credit is not a mere fiction we may learn, not only from the occasional loss of wages when a capitalist goes bankrupt, but also from the study of more lasting consequences. Nevertheless, whether money is used as means of purchase or as means of payment, this makes no difference to the nature of the exchange of commodities. The price of labour power is fixed by the bargain, although the labour power is not realised until after the bargain is struck. (The same thing happens when a house is rented, for the tenant only realises the advantage of his bargain by degrees.) The labour power has been sold, though it is not paid for until later. We shall, therefore, be helped to a clear understanding of the nature of the relation by assuming, for the nonce, that the owner of the labour power receives the stipulated price at the moment when he sells it.

We now know how the value paid by the owner of money to the owner of this peculiar commodity, labour power, is determined. The use-value which the owner of money gets in exchange for his money is only manifested in the actual usufruct, in the process whereby the labour power is consumed. All the articles requisite for the labour process, such as raw material, etc., are bought by the owner of money in the commodity market, and paid for by him at their full price. The process whereby labour power is consumed is, at the same time, the process whereby commodities and surplus value are produced. The consumption of labour power, like the consumption of every other commodity, takes place outside the market, outside the sphere of circulation. Let us, therefore, leave this noisy region of the market, where all that goes on is done in full view of every one's eyes, where everything seems open and above board. We will follow the owner of money and the owner of labour power into the hidden foci of production, crossing the threshold of the portal above which is written: 'No admittance except on business.' Here we shall discover, not only how capital produces, but also how it is itself produced. We shall at last discover the secret of the making of surplus value.

The sphere we are leaving, that of circulation or of the exchange of commodities, the sphere within whose confines the purchase and the sale of labour power are effected, is, in fact, a paradise of the rights of man. Here, liberty, equality, property, and Jeremy Bentham, are supreme. Liberty, because the buyer and seller of a commodity, such as labour power, buy and sell at their own sweet will. They enter into bargains as free individuals, equals before the law. The contract between them is the final outcome of the expression of their joint wills. Equality, because they enter into relations only as owners of commodities, and exchange equivalent for equivalent. Property, because each of them disposes exclusively of his own. Jeremy Bentham, because each of the pair is only concerned with his own interest. The power which brings them together, which makes them enter into relation one with another, is self-interest, and nothing more. Every one for himself alone, no one with any concern for another. Thanks to this, owing to the preestablished harmony of things, or under the auspices of an all-wise providence, they work together for their mutual advantage, for the commonweal, on behalf of the common interest of them all.

As we quit this sphere of simple circulation or of the exchange of commodities, which provides the common or garden free trader with his views and ideas, and with the standard by which he judges a society based upon capital and wage labour, we seem to note a change in the physiognomy of our persons of the drama. The one who came to the market as the owner of money, leaves it striding forward as a capitalist; the one who came to the market as the owner of labour power, brings up the rear as a worker. One of them, self-important, self-satisfied, with a keen eye to business; the other, timid, reluctant, like a man who is bringing his own skin to market, and has nothing to expect but a tanning.

KARL MARX (1818–1883)

Machinists versus Antimachinists

It was during my stay in the City of the Colleges of Unreason—a city whose Erewhonian name is so cacophonous that I refrain from giving it—that I learned the particulars of the revolution which had ended in the destruction of so many of the mechanical inventions which were formerly in common use.

Mr Thims took me to the rooms of a gentleman who had a great reputation for learning, but who was also, so Mr Thims told me, rather a dangerous person, inasmuch as he had attempted to introduce an adverb into the hypothetical language. He had heard of my watch and been exceedingly anxious to see me, for he was accounted the most learned antiquary in Erewhon on the subject of mechanical lore. We fell to talking upon the subject, and when I left he gave me a reprinted copy of the work which brought the revolution about.

It had taken place some five hundred years before my arrival; people had long become thoroughly used to the change, although at the time that it was made the country was plunged into the deepest misery, and a reaction which followed had very nearly proved successful. Civil war raged for many years, and is said to have reduced the number of the inhabitants by one-half. The parties were styled the machinists and the anti-machinists, and in the end, as I have said already, the latter got the victory, treating their opponents with such unparalleled severity that they extirpated every trace of opposition.

The wonder was that they allowed any mechanical appliances to remain in the kingdom, neither do I believe that they would have done so had not the Professors of Inconsistency and Evasion made a stand against the carrying of the new principles to their legitimate conclusions. These Professors, moreover, insisted that during the struggle the anti-machinists should use every known improvement in the art of war, and several new weapons, offensive and defensive, were invented while it was in progress. I was surprised at their remaining so many mechanical specimens as are seen in the museums, and at students having rediscovered their past uses so completely; for at the time of the revolution the victors wrecked all the more complicated machines, and burned all treatises on mechanics, and all engineers' workshops—thus, so they thought, cutting the mischief out root and branch, at an incalculable cost of blood and treasure.

Certainly they had not spared their labour, but work of this description can never be perfectly achieved; and when, some two hundred years before my arrival, all passion upon the subject had cooled down, and no one save a lunatic would have dreamed of reintroducing forbidden inventions, the subject came to be regarded as a curious antiquarian study, like that of some long-forgotten religious practices among ourselves. Then came the careful search for whatever fragments could be found, and for any machines that might have been hidden away, and also numberless treatises were written showing what the functions of each rediscovered machine had been; all being done with no idea of using such machinery again, but with the feelings of an English antiquarian concerning Druidical monuments or flint arrowheads.

SAMUEL BUTLER (1835–1902)

Man's Ally—Machinery

Up to the present, man has been, to a certain extent, the slave of machinery, and there is something tragic in the fact that as soon as man had invented a machine to do his work he began to starve. This, however, is, of course, the result of our property system and our system of competition. One man owns a machine which does the work of five hundred men. Five hundred men are, in consequence, thrown out of employment, and, having no work to do, become hungry and take to thieving. The one man secures the produce of the machine and keeps it, and has five hundred times as much as he should have, and probably, which is of much more importance, a great deal more than he really wants. Were that machine the property of all, everybody would benefit by it. It would be an immense advantage to the community. All unintellectual labour, all monotonous, dull albour, all labour that deals with dreadful things, and involves unpleasant conditions, must be done by machinery. Machinery must work for us in coal mines, and do all sanitary services, and be the stoker of steamers, and clean the streets, and run messages on wet days, and do anything that is tedious or distressing. At present machinery competes against man. Under proper conditions machinery will serve man. There is no doubt at all that this is the future of machinery; and just as trees grow while the country gentleman is asleep, so while Humanity will be amusing itself, or enjoying cultivated leisure—which, and not labour, is the aim of man—or making beautiful things, or reading beautiful things, or simply contemplating the world with admiration and delight, machinery will be doing all the necessary and unpleasant work. The fact is, that civilization requires slaves. The Greeks were quite right there. Unless there are slaves to do the ugly, horrible, uninteresting work, culture and contemplation become almost impossible. Human slavery is wrong, insecure, and demoralizing. On mechanical slavery, on the slavery of the machine, the future of the world depends. And when scientific men are no longer called upon to go down to a depressing East End and distribute bad cocoa and worse blankets to starving people, they will have delightful leisure in which to devise wonderful and marvellous things for their own joy and the joy of every one else. There will be great storages of force for every city, and for every house if required, and this force man will convert into heat, light, or motion, according to his needs. Is this Utopian? A map of the world that does not include Utopia is not worth even glancing at, for it leaves out the one country at which Humanity is always landing. And when Humanity lands there, it looks out, and, seeing a better country, sets sail. Progress is the realization of Utopias.   OSCAR WILDE (1854–1900)

When do we need Friends most?

Do we need friends more in prosperity than in adversity? They are sought after in both; for while men in adversity need help, in prosperity they need people with whom to live, and upon whom they may confer their benefits in order to satisfy their urge to do good. Friendship then is more necessary when fortune is against us, and in these circumstances we have need of useful friends; but it is more noble in prosperity, and so we also seek virtuous men as our friends, since it is more desirable to do well by and to live with these. The very presence of friends is pleasant in bad fortune as well as in good, for grief is lightened when friends sorrow with us. Hence one might ask whether they share as it were our burden, or—if that is not so—their delightful presence, and the thought of their grieving with us lessens our pain. We need not concern ourselves with the question whether it is for these reasons or for some other that our grief is lightened; the fact remains that what we have described does in fact occur.

The presence of a friend, however, seems to be compounded of several elements. The very sight of him is pleasant, especially if one is in adversity, and becomes a safeguard against grief; but to see him pained at one's misfortunes is painful, for no man is willing to be the cause of pain to his friends. For this reason people of a manly nature take care not to let their friends grieve with them; such a man, unless he is exceptionally insensible to pain, cannot endure the pain that results for his friends, and in general does not admit fellow mourners because he himself is not prone to mourning. Women and effeminate men, however, enjoy the sympathy of others in their grief, and love them as friends and companions in sorrow. One ought, of course, to imitate the better type of persons in all things.

In prosperity, on the other hand, the presence of friends means that we pass our time pleasantly, and also that we enjoy the thought of their pleasure at our own good fortune. So it would seem that while we ought gladly to invite our friends to share our prosperity (for beneficence is a noble quality), we should hesitate before calling upon them in misfortune; for it is our duty to give them as small a share as possible of evil, whence the saying, 'My own misfortune is enough.' In particular we should call upon our friends when it is probable that by suffering a little inconvenience they will render us a great service.

Conversely it is right and proper to go unasked and gladly to the help of those in adversity, for it is characteristic of a friend to render services, especially to those who are in need and have not asked for them; such conduct is nobler and more pleasant for both parties. But when our friends are prosperous we should join readily in their activities (for they need friends for these also), but be slow to put ourselves forward as prospective beneficiaries; for it is not honourable, to be keen for one's own advantage. At the same time we must, of course, take care not to earn the reputation of being killjoys by repulsing them, as occasionally happens.

The presence of friends then seems desirable in all circumstances.

ARISTOTLE (384–322 B.C.)

How to Get On!

Have friends. A friend is a second self. Every friend is virtuous and wise in the eyes of his friend. Between friends, everything turns out well. Each man has the value which others may choose to put upon him; and to gain their regard he must win their lips through their hearts. There is no charm so efficacious as a good turn; and the best way to win friendship is to make friends. The greatest and best that we have depends upon others. We must live, among either friends or enemies: try to find a friend every day, if not as a boon companion, then as a well-wisher; for some of these will later become intimates when once you have contrived to win their regard.

The friends of one's choice. Such friends must pass the test of discretion and the examination of fortune; their degrees must be granted not only by the will but also by the understanding. And although the ability to choose friends is the most important accomplishment in life, it is the one which is fostered with least care. For some, diversion is the motive, for the majority, chance; a man is known by the friends he has, for a wise man never associates with the ignorant; but to enjoy a man's company does not imply intimacy, for the satisfaction may proceed from the good times his wit may provide rather than from confidence in his abilities. Some friendships are legitimate, and others illicit; the latter are for pleasure, the former conducive to success in abundance. A man has few friends who love him for himself, and many who love him for his money. The cordial understanding of one friend is worth more than masses of goodwill from others: so make your friends by choice and not by chance.

Let no one be entirely in your confidence, nor you in his: blood relationship, friendship, the most pressing obligation, are not sufficient [to justify such intimacy], for there is a big difference between giving your affection and surrendering your will. The closest intimacy allows for exceptions; and the laws of good breeding are not thereby offended. A friend always keeps some secret to himself, and even a son hides something from his father; certain things which you conceal from one you reveal to another, and vice versa; hence you eventually disclose everything and withhold everything by making a distinction between individual members of your circle.

BALTASAR GRACIÁN (1601–1658)

The Graces

Of all the men that ever I knew in my life (and I knew him extremely well), the late Duke of Marlborough possessed the Graces in the highest degree, not to say engrossed them; and, indeed, he got the most by them, for I will venture (contrary to the custom of profound historians, who always assign deep causes for great events) to ascribe the better half of the Duke of Marlborough's greatness and riches to those Graces. He was eminently illiterate; wrote bad English, and spelled it still worse. He had no share of what is commonly called *parts*; that is, he had no brightness, nothing shining in his genius. He had, most undoubtedly, an excellent good plain understanding, with sound judgment. But these alone would probably have raised him but something higher than they found him, which was page to King James the Second's Queen. There the Graces protected and promoted him; for, while he was an Ensign of the Guards, the Duchess of Cleveland, then favourite mistress to King Charles the Second, struck by those very Graces, gave him five thousand pounds, with which he immediately bought an annuity for his life, of five hundred pounds a-year, of my grandfather, Halifax, which was the foundation of his subsequent fortune. His figure was beautiful, but his manner was irresistible, by either man or woman. It was by this engaging, graceful manner, that he was enabled, during all his war, to connect the various and jarring powers of the Grand Alliance, and to carry them on to the main object of the war, notwithstanding their private and separate views, jealousies, and wrongheadednesses. Whatever Court he went to (and he was often obliged to go himself to some resty and refractory ones), he as constantly prevailed, and brought them into his measures. The Pensionary Heinsius, a venerable old minister, grown grey in business, and who had governed the republic of the United Provinces for more than forty years, was absolutely governed by the Duke of Marlborough, as that republic feels to this day. He was always cool, and nobody ever observed the least variation in his countenance; he could refuse more gracefully than other people could grant; and those who went away from him the most dissatisfied as to the substance of their business, were yet personally charmed with him, and, in some degree, comforted by his manner. With all his gentleness and gracefulness, no man living was more conscious of his situation, nor maintained his dignity better.

LORD CHESTERFIELD (1694–1773)

Proverbs of Hell

As I was walking among the fires of hell, delighted with the enjoyments of Genius, which to Angels look like torment and insanity, I collected some of their Proverbs, thinking that as the sayings used in a nation mark its character, so the Proverbs of Hell shew the nature of Infernal wisdom better than any description of buildings or garments.

When I came home, on the abyss of the five senses, where a flat sided steep frowns over the present world, I saw a mighty Devil folded in black clouds hovering on the sides of the rock: with corroding fires he wrote the following sentence now percieved by the minds of men, & read by them on earth.

> How do you know but ev'ry Bird that cuts the airy way,
> Is an immense world of delight, clos'd by your senses five?

In seed time learn, in harvest teach, in winter enjoy.
Drive your cart and your plow over the bones of the dead.
The road of excess leads to the palace of wisdom.
Prudence is a rich ugly old maid courted by Incapacity.
He who desires but acts not, breeds pestilence.
The cut worm forgives the plow.
Dip him in the river who loves water.
A fool sees not the same tree that a wise man sees.
He whose face gives no light, shall never become a star.
Eternity is in love with the productions of time.
The busy bee has no time for sorrow.
The hours of folly are measur'd by the clock, but of wisdom no clock can measure.
All wholsom food is caught without a net or a trap.
Bring out number weight & measure in a year of dearth.
No bird soars too high if he soars with his own wings.
A dead body revenges not injuries.
The most sublime act is to set another before you.
If the fool would persist in his folly he would become wise.
Folly is the cloke of knavery.

Shame is Pride's cloke.

Prisons are built with stones of Law, Brothels with bricks of Religion.

The pride of the peacock is the glory of God.

The lust of the goat is the bounty of God.

The wrath of the lion is the wisdom of God.

The nakedness of woman is the work of God.

Excess of sorrow laughs. Excess of joy weeps.

The roaring of lions, the howling of wolves, the raging of the stormy sea, and the destructive sword, are portions of eternity too great for the eye of man.

The fox condemns the trap, not himself.

Joys impregnate. Sorrows bring forth.

Let man wear the fell of the lion, woman the fleece of the sheep.

The bird a nest, the spider a web, man friendship.

WILLIAM BLAKE (1757–1827)

The Shame of Incorruptibility

Virtue may choose the high or low degree,
'Tis just alike to virtue, and to me;
Dwell in a monk, or light upon a king,
She's still the same beloved, contented thing.
Vice is undone, if she forgets her birth,
And stoops from angels to the dregs of earth:
But 'tis the fall degrades her to a whore;
Let greatness own her, and she's mean no more,
Her birth, her beauty, crowds and courts confess,
Chaste matrons praise her, and grave bishops bless;
In golden chains the willing world she draws,
And hers the gospel is, and hers the laws,
Mounts the tribunal, lifts her scarlet head,
And sees pale Virtue carted in her stead.
Lo! at the wheels of her triumphal car,
Old England's genius, rough with many a scar,
Dragg'd in the dust! his arms hang idly round,
His flag inverted trails along the ground!
Our youth, all liveried o'er with foreign gold,
Before her dance: behind her, crawl the old!
See thronging millions to the pagod run,
And offer country, parent, wife, or son!

Hear her black trumpet through the land proclaim,
That NOT TO BE CORRUPTED IS THE SHAME!
In soldier, churchman, patriot, man in power,
'Tis avarice all, ambition is no more!
See, all our nobles begging to be slaves!
See, all our fools aspiring to be knaves!
The wit of cheats, the courage of a whore,
Are what ten thousand envy and adore:
All, all look up, with reverential awe,
At crimes that 'scape, or triumph o'er the law:
While truth, worth, wisdom, daily they decry—
'Nothing is sacred now but villainy.'

ALEXANDER POPE (1688–1744)

The First Sin

Thus *Eve* with Countnance blithe her storie told;
But in her Cheek distemper flushing glowd.
On th' other side, *Adam*, soon as he heard
The fatal Trespass don by *Eve*, amaz'd,
Astonied stood and Blank, while horror chill
Ran through his veins, and all his joints relaxd;
From his slack hand the Garland wreath'd for *Eve*
Down dropd, and all the faded Roses shed:
Speechless he stood and pale, till thus at length
First to himself he inward silence broke.

O fairest of Creation, last and best
Of all Gods works, Creature in whom excelld
Whatever can to sight or thought be formd,
Holy, divine, good, amiable, or sweet!
How art thou lost, how on a sudden lost,
Defac't, deflowrd, and now to Death devote?
Rather how hast thou yielded to trangress
The strict forbiddance, how to violate
The sacred Fruit forbidden! som cursed fraud
Of Enemie hath beguil'd thee, yet unknown,
And mee with thee hath ruind, for with thee
Certain my resolution is to Die;
How can I live without thee, how forgoe
Thy sweet Converse and Love so dearly joind,

To live again in these wilde Woods forlorn?
Should God create another *Eve*, and I
Another Rib afford, yet loss of thee
Would never from my heart; no no, I feel
The Link of Nature draw me: Flesh of Flesh,
Bone of my Bone thou art, and from thy State
Mine never shall be parted, bliss or woe.

JOHN MILTON (1608-1674)

The Woman's Point of View

This relation may serve, therefore, to let the ladies see, that the advantage is not so much on the other side as the men think it is; and that though it may be true, the men have but too much choice among us, and that some women may be found who will dishonour themselves, be cheap, and too easy to come at, yet if they will have women worth having, they may find them as uncomeatable as ever, and that those that are otherwise have often such deficiencies, when had, as rather recommend the ladies that are difficult, than encourage the men to go on with their easy courtship, and expect wives equally valuable that will come at first call.

Nothing is more certain than that the ladies always gain of the men by keeping their ground, and letting their pretended lovers see they can resent being slighted, and that they are not afraid of saying no. They insult us mightily, with telling us of the number of women; that the wars, and the sea, and trade, and other incidents have carried the men so much away, that there is no proportion between the numbers of the sexes; but I am far from granting that the number of the women is so great, or the number of the men so small; but if they will have me tell the truth, the disadvantage of the women is a terrible scandal upon the men, and it lies here only; namely, that the age is so wicked, and the sex so debauched, that, in short, the number of such men as an honest woman ought to meddle with is small indeed, and it is but here and there that a man is to be found who is fit for an honest woman to venture upon.

But the consequence even of that too amounts to no more than this, that women ought to be the more nice; for how do we know the just character of the man that makes the offer? To say that the woman should be the more easy on this occasion, is to say we should be the forwarder to venture because of the greatness of the danger, which is very absurd.

On the contrary, the women have ten thousand times the more reason to be wary and backward, by how much the hazard of being betrayed is the greater; and would the ladies act the wary part, they would discover every cheat that offered; for, in short, the lives of very few men nowadays will bear a character; and if the ladies do but make a little inquiry, they would soon be able to distinguish the men and deliver themselves. As for women that do not think their own safety worth their own thought, that, impatient of their present state, run into matrimony as a horse rushes into the battle, I can say nothing to them but this, that they are a sort of ladies that are to be prayed for among the rest of distempered people, and they look like people that venture their estates in a lottery where there is a hundred thousand blanks to one prize.

No man of common sense will value a woman the less for not giving up herself at the first attack, or for not accepting his proposal without inquiring into his person or character; on the contrary, he must think her the weakest of all creatures, as the rate of men now goes; in short, he must have a very contemptible opinion of her capacities, that having but one cast for her life, shall cast that life away at once, and make matrimony, like death, be a leap in the dark.

I would fain have the conduct of my sex a little regulated in this particular, which is the same thing in which, of all the parts of life, I think at this time we suffer most in; 'tis nothing but lack of courage, the fear of not being married at all, and of that frightful state of life called an old maid. This, I say, is the woman's snare; but would the ladies once but get above that fear, and manage rightly, they would more certainly avoid it by standing their ground, in a case so absolutely necessary to their felicity, than by exposing themselves as they do; and if they did not marry so soon, they would make themselves amends by marrying safer. She is always married too soon who gets a bad husband, and she is never married too late who gets a good one; in a word, there is no woman, deformity or lost reputation excepted, but if she manages well may be married safely one time or other; but if she precipitates herself, it is ten thousand to one but she is undone.

DANIEL DEFOE (c. 1661–1731)

Destroying Fiend or Guardian Angel

In the commerce of lovers, the man makes the address, assails, and betrays; and yet stands in the same degree of acceptance as he was in before he committed that treachery. The woman, for no other crime but believing one who she thought loved her, is treated with shyness and indifference at the best, and commonly with reproach and scorn. He that is past the power of beauty may talk of this matter with the same unconcern as of any other subject; therefore I shall take upon me to consider the sex, as they live within rules, and as they transgress them. The ordinary class of the good or the ill have very little influence upon the actions of others; but the eminent, in either kind, are those who lead the world below. The ill are employed in communicating scandal, infamy, and disease, like furies; the good distribute benevolence, friendship, and health, like angels. The ill are damped with pain and anguish at the sight of all that is laudable, lovely, or happy. The virtuous are touched with commiseration towards the guilty, the disagreeable, and the wretched. There are those who betray the innocent of their own sex, and solicit the lewd of ours. There are those who have abandoned the very memory, not only of innocence, but shame. There are those who never forgave, nor could ever bear being forgiven. There are those also who visit the beds of the sick, lull the cares of the sorrowful, and double the joys of the joyful. Such is the destroying fiend, such the guardian angel, woman.

SIR RICHARD STEELE (1672–1729)

The Silver Buttons

The man fell back; and a little further on Nostromo had to pull up. From the doors of the dance hall men and women emerged tottering, streaming with sweat, trembling in every limb, to lean, panting, with staring eyes and parted lips, against the wall of the structure, where the harps and guitars played on with mad speed in an incessant roll of thunder. Hundreds of hands clapped in there; voices shrieked, and then all at once would sink low, chanting in unison the refrain of a love song, with a dying fall. A red flower, flung with a good aim from somewhere in the crowd, struck the resplendent Capataz on the cheek.

He caught it as it fell, neatly, but for some time did not turn his head. When at last he condescended to look round, the throng near him had parted to make way for a pretty Morenita, her hair held up by a small golden comb, who was walking towards him in the open space.

Her arms and neck emerged plump and bare from a snowy chemisette; the blue woollen skirt, with all the fullness gathered in front, scanty on the hips and tight across the back, disclosed the provoking action of her walk. She came straight on and laid her hand on the mare's neck with a timid, coquettish look upwards out of the corner of her eyes.

'Querido,' she murmured, caressingly, 'why do you pretend not to see me when I pass?'

'Because I don't love thee any more,' said Nostromo, deliberately, after a moment of reflective silence.

The hand on the mare's neck trembled suddenly. She dropped her head before all the eyes in the wide circle formed round the generous, the terrible, the inconstant Capataz de Cargadores, and his Morenita.

Nostromo, looking down, saw tears beginning to fall down her face.

'Has it come, then, ever beloved of my heart?' she whispered. 'Is it true?'

'No,' said Nostromo, looking away carelessly. 'It was a lie. I love thee as much as ever.'

'Is that true?' she cooed, joyously, her cheeks still wet with tears.

'It is true.'

'True on the life?'

'As true as that; but thou must not ask me to swear it on the Madonna that stands in thy room.' And the Capataz laughed a little in response to the grins of the crowd.

She pouted—very pretty—a little uneasy.

'No, I will not ask for that. I can see love in your eyes.' She laid her hand on his knee. 'Why are you trembling like this? From love?' she continued, while the cavernous thundering of the gombo went on without a pause. 'But if you love her as much as that, you must give your Paquita a gold-mounted rosary of beads for the neck of her Madonna.'

'No,' said Nostromo, looking into her uplifted, begging eyes, which suddenly turned stony with surprise.

'No? Then what else will your worship give me on the day of the fiesta?' she asked, angrily; 'so as not to shame me before all these people.'

'There is no shame for thee in getting nothing from thy lover for once.'

'True! The shame is your worship's—my poor lover's,' she flared up, sarcastically.

Laughs were heard at her anger, at her retort. What an audacious spitfire she was! The people aware of this scene were calling out urgently to others in the crowd. The circle round the silver-grey mare narrowed slowly.

The girl went off a pace or two, confronting the mocking curiosity of the eyes, then flung back to the stirrup, tiptoeing, her enraged face turned up to Nostromo with a pair of blazing eyes. He bent low to her in the saddle.

'Juan,' she hissed, 'I could stab thee to the heart!'

The dreaded Capataz de Cargadores, magnificent and carelessly public in his amours, flung his arm round her neck and kissed her spluttering lips. A murmur went round.

'A knife!' he demanded at large, holding her firmly by the shoulder.

Twenty blades flashed out together in the circle. A young man in holiday attire, bounding in, thrust one in Nostromo's hand and bounded back into the ranks, very proud of himself. Nostromo had not even looked at him.

'Stand on my foot,' he commanded the girl, who, suddenly subdued, rose lightly, and when he had her up, encircling her waist, her face near to his, he pressed the knife into her little hand.

'No, Morenita! You shall not put me to shame,' he said. 'You shall have your present; and so that everyone should know who is your lover to-day, you may cut all the silver buttons off my coat.'

There were shouts of laughter and applause at this witty freak, while the girl passed the keen blade, and the impassive rider jingled in his palm the increasing hoard of silver buttons. He eased her to the ground with both her hands full. After whispering for a while with a very strenuous face, she walked away, staring haughtily, and vanished into the crowd.

JOSEPH CONRAD (1857–1924)

A Curtain Lecture

Jonathan. My dear, I wish you would lie a little longer in bed this morning.

Lætitia. Indeed I cannot; I am engaged to breakfast with Jack Strongbow.

Jonathan. I don't know what Jack Strongbow doth so often at my house. I assure you I am uneasy at it; for, though I have no suspicion of your virtue, yet it may injure your reputation in the opinion of my neighbours.

Lætitia. I don't trouble my head about my neighbours; and they shall no more tell me what company I am to keep than my husband shall.

Jonathan. A good wife would keep no company which made her husband uneasy.

Lætitia. You might have found one of those good wives, sir, if you had pleased; I had no objection to it.

Jonathan. I thought I had found one in you.

Lætitia. You did! I am very much obliged to you for thinking me so poor-spirited a creature; but I hope to convince you to the contrary. What, I suppose you took me for a raw senseless girl, who knew nothing what other married women do!

Jonathan. No matter what I took you for; I have taken you for better and worse.

Lætitia. And at your own desire too; for I am sure you never had mine. I should not have broken my heart if Mr Wild had thought proper to bestow himself on any other more happy woman. Ha, ha!

Jonathan. I hope, madam, you don't imagine that was not in my power, or that I married you out of any kind of necessity.

Lætitia. O no, sir; I am convinced there are silly women enough. And far be it from me to accuse you of any necessity for a wife. I believe you could have been very well contented with the state of a bachelor; I have no reason to complain of your necessities; but that, you know, a woman cannot tell beforehand.

Jonathan. I can't guess what you would insinuate, for I believe no woman had ever less reason to complain of her husband's want of fondness.

Lætitia. Then some, I am certain, have great reason to complain of the price they give for them. But I know better things. (*These words were spoken with a very great air, and toss of the head.*)

Jonathan. Well, my sweeting, I will make it impossible for you to wish me more fond.

Lætitia. Pray, Mr Wild, none of this nauseous behaviour, nor those odious words. I wish you were fond! I assure you, I don't know what you would pretend to insinuate of me. I have no wishes which misbecome a virtuous woman. No, nor should not, if I had married for love. And especially now, when nobody, I am sure, can suspect me of any such thing.

Jonathan. If you did not marry for love why did you marry?

Lætitia. Because it was convenient, and my parents forced me.

Jonathan. I hope, madam, at least, you will not tell me to my face you have made your convenience of me.

Lætitia. I have made nothing of you; nor do I desire the honour of making anything of you.

Jonathan. Yes, you have made a husband of me.

Lætitia. No, you made yourself so; for I repeat once more it was not my desire, but your own.

Jonathan. You should think yourself obliged to me for that desire.

Lætitia. La, sir! you was not so singular in it. I was not in despair. I have had other offers, and better too.

Jonathan. I wish you had accepted them with all my heart.

Lætitia. I must tell you, Mr Wild, this is a very brutish manner in treating a woman to whom you have such obligations; but I know how to despise it, and to despise you too for shewing it me. Indeed, I am well enough paid for the foolish preference I gave to you. I flattered myself that I should at least have been used with good manners. I thought I had married a gentleman; but I find you every way contemptible and below my concern.

Jonathan. D—n you, madam, have I not the more reason to complain when you tell me you married for your convenience only?

Lætitia. Very fine truly. Is it behaviour worthy a man to swear at a woman? Yet why should I mention what comes from a wretch whom I despise?

Jonathan. Don't repeat that word so often. I despise you as heartily as you can me. And, to tell you a truth, I married you for my convenience likewise, to satisfy a passion which I have now satisfied, and you may be d—d for anything I care.

Lætitia. The world shall know how barbarously I am treated by such a villain.

Jonathan. I need take very little pains to acquaint the world what a b—ch you are, your actions will demonstrate it.

Lætitia. Monster! I would advise you not to depend too much on my sex, and provoke me too far; for I can do you a mischief, and will, if you dare use me so, you villain!

Jonathan. Begin whenever you please, madam; but assure yourself, the moment you lay aside the woman, I will treat you as such no longer; and if the first blow is yours, I promise you the last shall be mine.

Lætitia. Use me as you will; but d—n me if ever you shall use me as a woman again; for may I be cursed if ever I enter into your bed more.

Jonathan. May I be cursed if that abstinence be not the greatest obligation you can lay upon me; for I assure you faithfully your person was all I had ever any regard for; and that I now loathe and detest as much as ever I liked it.

Lætitia. It is impossible for two people to agree better; for I always detested your person; and as for any other regard, you must be convinced I never could have any for you.

Jonathan. Why, then, since we are come to a right understanding, as we are to live together, suppose we agreed, instead of quarrelling and abusing, to be civil to each other.

Lætitia. With all my heart.

Jonathan. Let us shake hands then, and henceforwards never live like man and wife; that is, never be loving nor ever quarrel.

Lætitia. Agreed. But pray, Mr Wild, why b—ch? Why did you suffer such a word to escape you?

Jonathan. It is not worth your remembrance.

Lætitia. You agree I shall converse with whomsoever I please?

Jonathan. Without control? And I have the same liberty?

Lætitia. When I interfere may every curse you can wish attend me!

Jonathan. Let us now take a farewell kiss, and may I be hanged if it is not the sweetest you ever gave me.

Lætitia. But why b—ch? Methinks I should be glad to know why b—ch?

At which words he sprang from the bed, d—ing her temper heartily. She returned it again with equal abuse, which was continued on both sides while he was dressing. However, they agreed to continue steadfast in this new resolution; and the joy arising on that occasion at length dismissed them pretty cheerfully from each other, though Lætitia could not help concluding with the words, 'Why b—ch?'

HENRY FIELDING (1707–1754)

The Path of Excess

For this space of nine years then (from my nineteenth year, to my eight and twentieth) we lived seduced and seducing, deceived and deceiving, in divers lusts; openly, by sciences which they call liberal; secretly, with a false named religion; here proud, there superstitious, every where vain! Here, hunting after the emptiness of popular praise, down even to theatrical applauses, and poetic prizes and strifes for grassy garlands, and the follies of shows, and the intemperance of desires. There, desiring to be cleansed from these defilements, by carrying food to those who were called 'elect' and 'holy,' out of which, in the workhouse of their stomachs, they should forge for us Angels and Gods, by whom we might be cleansed. These things did I follow, and practise with my friends, deceived by me, and with me. . .

In those years I taught rhetoric, and, overcome by cupidity, made sale of a loquacity to overcome by. Yet I preferred (Lord, Thou knowest) honest scholars (as they are accounted), and these I, without artifice, taught artifices, not to be practised against the life of the guiltless, though sometimes for the life of the guilty. And Thou, O God, from afar perceivedst me stumbling in that slippery course, and amid much smoke sending out some sparks of faithfulness, which I shewed in that my guidance of *such as loved vanity*, and *sought after leasing*, myself their companion. In those years I had one,—not in that which is called lawful marriage, but whom I had found out in a wayward passion, void of understanding; yet but one, remaining faithful even to her; in whom I in my own case experienced, what difference there is betwixt the self-restraint of the marriage-covenant, for the sake of issue, and the bargain of a lustful love, where children are born against their parents' will, although, once born, they constrain love.

ST AUGUSTINE (354–430)

The Musings of a Rake

What, therefore, upon the whole, do we get by treading in these crooked paths, but danger, disgrace, and a too late repentance?

And after all, do we not frequently become the cullies of our own libertinism; sliding into the very state with those half-worn-out doxies, which perhaps we might have entered into with their ladies; at least with their superiors both in degree and fortune? And all the time lived handsomely like ourselves; not sneaking into holes and corners; and, when we crept abroad with our women, looking about us, and at every one that passed us, as if we were confessedly accountable to the censures of all honest people.

My cousin Tony Jenyns thou knewest. He had not the actively mischievous spirit that thou, Belton, Mowbray, Tourville, and *myself* have: but he imbibed the same notions we do, and carried them into practice.

How did he prate against wedlock! How did he strut about as a *wit* and a *smart*! And what a *wit* and a *smart* did all the boys and girls of our family (myself among the rest, then an urchin) think him, for the airs he gave himself! Marry! No, not for the world; what man of sense would bear the insolences, the petulances, the expensiveness of a wife! He could not for the heart of him think it tolerable, that a woman of *equal* rank and fortune, and, as it might happen, *superior* talents to his own, should look upon herself to have a right to share the benefit of that fortune which she brought him.

So, after he had fluttered about the town for two or three years, in all which time he had a better opinion of himself than anybody else had, what does he do, but enter upon an affair with his fencing master's daughter?

He succeeds; takes private lodgings for her at Hackney; visits her by stealth; both of them tender of reputations that were *extremely* tender, but which neither had quite given up; for rakes of either sex are always the last to condemn or cry down themselves: visited by nobody, nor visiting: the life of a thief, or of a man beset by creditors, afraid to look out of his own house, or to be seen abroad with her. And thus went he on for twelve years, and, though he had a good estate, hardly making both ends meet; for, though no glare, there was no economy; and besides, he had every year a child, and very fond of his children was he. But none of them lived above three years: and being now, on the death of the dozenth, grown as dully sober as if he had been a real husband, his good Mrs Thomas (for he had not permitted her to take his own name) prevailed upon him to think the loss of their children a judgment upon the parents for their wicked way of life [a time will come, Lovelace, if we live to advanced years, in which reflection will take hold of the enfeebled mind]; and then it was not difficult for his woman to induce him, by way of compounding with Heaven, to marry her. When this was done, he had leisure to sit down, and contemplate; and to recollect the many offers of persons of family and fortune which he had declined in the prime of life: his expenses *equal* at least: his reputation not only *less*, but *lost*: his enjoyments *stolen*: his partnership *unequal*, and such as he had always been ashamed of. But the women said, that after twelve or thirteen years' cohabitation, Tony did an honest thing by her. And that was all my poor cousin got by making his old mistress his new wife—not a drum, not a trumpet, not a fife, not a tabret, nor the expectation of a new joy, to animate him on!

SAMUEL RICHARDSON (1689-1761)

The Parting of the Ways

At last Gerald, resuming a suspended conversation, said as it were doggedly:

'I tell you I haven't got five francs altogether! and you can feel my pockets if you like,' added the habitual liar in him, fearing incredulity.

'Well, and what do you expect *me* to do?' Sophia inquired.

The accent, at once ironic and listless, in which she put this question, showed that strange and vital things had happened to Sophia in the four years which had elapsed since her marriage. It did really seem to her, indeed, that the Sophia whom Gerald had espoused was dead and gone, and that another Sophia had come into her body: so intensely conscious was she of a fundamental change in herself under the stress of continuous experience. And though this was but a seeming, though she was still the same Sophia more fully disclosed, it was a true seeming. Indisputably more beautiful than when Gerald had unwillingly made her his legal wife, she was now nearly twenty-four, and looked perhaps somewhat older than her age. Her frame was firmly set, her waist thicker, neither slim nor stout. The lips were rather hard, and she had a habit of tightening her mouth, on the same provocation as sends a snail into its shell. No trace was left of immature gawkiness in her gestures or of simplicity in her intonations. She was a woman of commanding and slightly arrogant charm, not in the least degree the charm of innocence and ingenuousness. Her eyes were the eyes of one who has lost her illusions too violently and too completely. Her gaze, coldly comprehending, implied familiarity with the abjectness of human nature. Gerald had begun and had finished her education. He had not ruined her, as a bad professor may ruin a fine voice, because her moral force immeasurably exceeded his; he had unwittingly produced a masterpiece, but it was a tragic masterpiece. Sophia was such a woman as, by a mere glance as she utters an opinion, will make a man say to himself, half in desire and half in alarm lest she reads him too: 'By Jove! she must have been through a thing or two. She knows what people are!'

The marriage was, of course, a calamitous folly. From the very first, from the moment when the commercial traveller had with incomparable rash fatuity thrown the paper pellet over the counter, Sophia's awakening common sense had told her that in yielding to her instinct she was sowing misery and shame for herself; but she had gone on, as if under a spell. It had needed the irretrievableness of flight from home to begin the breaking of the trance. Once fully awakened out of the trance, she had recognized her marriage for what it was. She had made neither the best nor the worst of it. She had accepted Gerald as one accepts a climate. She saw again and again that he was irreclaimably a fool and a prodigy of irresponsibleness. She tolerated him, now with sweetness, now bitterly; accepting always his caprices, and not permitting herself to have wishes of her own. She was ready to pay the price of pride and of a moment's imbecility with a lifetime of self-repression. It was high, but it was the price. She had acquired nothing but an exceptionally good knowledge of the French language (she soon learnt to scorn Gerald's glib maltreatment of the tongue), and she had conserved nothing but her dignity. She knew that Gerald was sick of her, that he would have danced for joy to be rid of her; that he was constantly unfaithful; that he had long since ceased to be excited by her beauty. She knew also that at bottom he was a little afraid of her; here was her sole moral consolation. The thing that sometimes struck her as surprising was that he had not abandoned her, simply and crudely walked off one day and forgotten to take her with him.

They hated each other, but in different ways. She loathed him, and he resented her.

'What do I expect you to do?' he repeated after her. 'Why don't you write home to your people and get some money out of them?'

Now that he had said what was in his mind, he faced her with a bullying swagger. Had he been a bigger man he might have tried the effect of physical bullying on her. One of his numerous reasons for resenting her was that she was the taller of the two.

She made no reply.

ARNOLD BENNETT (1867–1931)

An Irremediable Rupture

The time which has elapsed since the separation has been considerably more than the whole brief period of our union, and the not much longer one of our prior acquaintance. We both made a bitter mistake; but now it is over, and irrevocably so. For, at thirty-three on my part, and a few years less on yours, though it is no very extended period of life, still it is one when the habits and thought are generally so formed as to admit of no modification; and as we could not agree when younger, we should with difficulty do so now.

I say all this, because I own to you, that, notwithstanding every thing, I considered our re-union as not impossible for more than a year after the separation;—but then I gave up the hope entirely and for ever. But this very impossibility of re-union seems to me at least a reason why, on all the few points of discussion which can arise between us, we should preserve the courtesies of life, and as much of its kindness as people who are never to meet may preserve perhaps more easily than nearer connections. For my own part, I am violent, but not malignant; for only fresh provocations can awaken my resentments. To you, who are colder and more concentrated, I would just hint, that you may sometimes mistake the depth of a cold anger for dignity, and a worse feeling for duty. I assure you that I bear you *now* (whatever I may have done) no resentment whatever. Remember, that *if you have injured me* in aught, this forgiveness is something; and that, if I have *injured you*, it is something more still, if it be true, as the moralists say, that the most offending are the least forgiving.

Whether the offence has been solely on my side, or reciprocal, or on yours chiefly, I have ceased to reflect upon any but two things—viz. that you are the mother of my child, and that we shall never meet again. I think if you also consider the two corresponding points with reference to myself, it will be better for all three.

LORD BYRON (1788–1824)

Everyman—to his Mistress on going to Bed

Come, Madam, come, all rest my powers defy,
Until I labour, I in labour lie.
The foe oft-times having the foe in sight,
Is tired with standing though he never fight.
Off with that girdle, like heaven's Zone glistering,
But a far fairer world encompassing.
Unpin that spangled breastplate which you wear,
That th' eyes of busy fools may be stopt there.
Unlace yourself, for that harmonious chime
Tells me from you, that now it is bed time.
Off with that happy busk, which I envy,
That still can be, and still can stand so nigh.
Your gown going off, such beauteous state reveals,
As when from flowry meads th' hill's shadow steals.
Off with that wiry Coronet and show
The hairy Diadem which on you doth grow:
Now off with those shoes, and then safely tread
In this love's hallow'd temple, this soft bed.
In such white robes, heaven's Angels used to be
Receiv'd by men; thou Angel bring'st with thee
A heaven like Mahomet's Paradise; and though
Ill spirits walk in white, we easily know,

By this these Angels from an evil sprite,
Those set our hairs, but these our flesh upright.
  Licence my roving hands, and let them go,
Before, behind, between, above, below.
O my America! my new-found-land,
My kingdom, safeliest when with one man mann'd,
My Mine of precious stones, My Empery,
How blest am I in this discovering thee!
To enter in these bonds, is to be free;
Then where my hand is set, my seal shall be.
  Full nakedness! All joys are due to thee,
As souls unbodied, bodies uncloth'd must be,
To taste whole joys. Gems which you women use
Are like Atlanta's balls, cast in men's views,
That when a fool's eye lighteth on a Gem,
His earthly soul may covet theirs, not them.
Like pictures, or like books' gay coverings made
For lay-men, are all women thus array'd;
Themselves are mystic books, which only we
(Whom their imputed grace will dignify)
Must see reveal'd. Then since that I may know,
As liberally, as to a Midwife, show
Thyself: cast all, yea, this white linen hence,
There is no penance due to innocence.
  To teach thee, I am naked first; why then
What needst thou have more covering than a man.

JOHN DONNE (1573-1631)

The Souls Choose their Lives

'I shall tell you,' I said, 'a story, not of Alcinous, but of a valiant man, Er, son of Armenius, of the race of Pamphylia. Once upon a time he fell in battle. On the tenth day they took up the dead, who were now stinking, but his body was found fresh. They took him home, and were going to bury him when on the twelfth day he came to life as he was lying on the pyre. When he had revived, he told them what he had seen yonder. His soul, he said, departed from him, and journeyed along with a great company, until they arrived at a certain ghostly place where there were two openings in the earth side by side, and opposite them and above two openings in the heaven. In the middle sat judges.

These, when they had given their judgment, ordered the just to take the road to the right, which led upward through heaven, first binding tablets on them in front signifying their judgments. The unjust they ordered to take the road to the left, which led downward. They also had tablets signifying all that they had done bound on their backs. When it came to his turn they told him that it was laid upon him to be a messenger to men concerning the things that were there, and they ordered him to listen to and look at everything in the place. . .

'And he said that it was a sight worth seeing to behold the several souls choose their lives. And a piteous and a laughable and amazing sight it was also. The choice was mostly governed by what they had been accustomed to in their former life. He said that he saw the soul which had once been Orpheus' choosing the life of a swan; his death at the hands of women had so made him hate the whole race, that he would not consent to be born of woman. The soul of Thamyras he saw choosing the life of a nightingale. He also saw a swan turning to choose a human life, and other musical creatures doing the same. The soul that had the twentieth choice took a lion's life. It was the soul of Ajax, the son of Telamon, who refused to become a man because he remembered the judgment concerning the armour. After him came the soul of Agamemnon. He also hated the human race by reason of his sufferings, and took in exchange the life of an eagle. The soul of Atalanta obtained her choice somewhere in the middle, and catching sight of the great honours of a man who was an athlete could not pass them by, but made that her choice. After her he saw the soul of Epeus, son of Panopeus, passing into the nature of a working woman. Quite among the last he saw the soul of the ridiculous Thersites becoming a monkey. It so happened that the soul of Odysseus came forward to choose the very last of all. He remembered his former labours and had ceased from his ambition and so he spent a long time going round looking for the life of a private and obscure man. At last he found it lying about, ignored by every one else; and when he saw it he took it gladly, and said that he would have made the same choice if the lot had fallen to him first. Similarly all the other animals changed into men and into each other, the unjust into fierce, and the just into tame animals, and there were all possible combinations.

'And when all the souls had chosen their lives they went unto Lachesis in the order of their choosing. And she gave each the angel he had chosen to be a guard throughout his life and to accomplish his choice. The angel first led the soul towards Clotho, passing it under her hand and under the sweep of the whirling spindle, so ratifying the fate which the man had chosen in his turn. He touched the spindle, and then led the soul on to where Atropos was spinning, so that the threads might be made unalterable. Thence the man went without turning under the throne of Necessity, and after coming out on the other side he first waited for the others to pass through, and then all proceeded through terrible burning heat to the plain of Lethe where grew no plants nor any trees. At last they encamped at evening by the river of Forgetfulness, whose water no pitcher may hold. All had to drink a certain measure of this water, but those who were not preserved by wisdom drank more than the measure. Each as he drank it forgot everything. Then they went to sleep, and it was midnight; there was thunder and an earthquake, and at once they were carried up from thence along different ways to their birth, shooting like stars. But he himself had been forbidden to drink of the water. When or how he returned to the body he did not know, but he suddenly opened his eyes and saw it was morning and he was lying on the pyre.'

PLATO (427–347 B.C.)

Divine Knowledge

Without this divine knowledge what could men do but either become elated by the inner awareness of their past greatness, which still remains with them, or become despondent at the sight of their present weakness?

For, not seeing the whole truth, they could not attain to perfect virtue. Some considering nature as incorrupt, and others as incurable, they could not escape either pride or sloth (which are twin sources of all the vices), since [*they cannot but*] either abandon themselves thereto through cowardice, or escape therefrom through pride. For if they knew the excellence of man, they were ignorant of his corruption, with the result that they certainly avoided sloth, but lapsed into pride; and if they recognized the infirmity of nature, they knew not its dignity, with the result that they managed indeed to avoid vanity, but at the cost of yielding to despair.

Hence the various schools of philosophy: Stoics and Epicureans, dogmatists and sceptics, etc.

Only the Christian religion has been able to cure these two vices, not by expelling the one by means of the other according to the wisdom of the world, but by driving out both according to the simplicity of the Gospel. For it teaches the righteous, whom it raises even to the point of sharing in divinity, that in this sublime condition they still carry about with them the source of all corruption, which makes them subject throughout their lives to error, misery, death and sin; while it proclaims to the most ungodly that they are capable of their Redeemer's grace. Thus the Christian religion, causing those whom it justifies to tremble, and consoling those whom it condemns, so justly tempers fear with hope, through the twofold capacity for grace and sin which is common to all, that it humbles men infinitely more than reason alone can do, but without causing them to despair, and it exalts them infinitely more than natural pride, but without puffing them up. In this way it shows that it alone, being exempt from error and vice, fulfils the duty of instructing and correcting mankind.

Who then can refuse to believe and adore these heavenly lights? For is it not clearer than day that we observe within us ineffaceable marks of excellence? And is it not equally true that we continually experience the effects of our deplorable condition?

What does this chaos and monstrous confusion proclaim to us but the truth of these two states, and with a voice so powerful that it cannot be resisted?

BLAISE PASCAL (1623–1662)

How many persist in Atheism?

Come then; how shall we plead for the existence of gods dispassionately? To be sure, no man can help feeling some resentment and disgust with the parties who now, as in the past, impose the burden of the argument on us by their want of faith in the stories heard so often in earliest infancy, while still at the breast, from their mothers and nurses —stories, you may say, crooned over them, in sport and in earnest, like spells—and heard again in prayers offered over sacrifices, in conjunction with the spectacle which gives such intense delight to the eye and ear of children, as it is enacted at a sacrifice, the spectacle of our parents addressing their gods, with assured belief in their existence, in earnest prayer and supplication for themselves and their children. Then, again, at rising and setting of sun and moon, they have heard and seen the universal prostrations and devotions of mankind, Greeks and non-Greeks alike, in all the varied circumstances of evil fortune and good, with their implication that gods are no fictions, but the most certain of realities, and their being beyond the remotest shadow of a doubt. When we see all this evidence treated with contempt by the persons who are forcing us into our present argument, and that, as any man with a grain of intelligence will admit, without a single respectable reason, how, I ask, is a man to find gentle language in which to combine reproof with instruction in the initial truth about the gods—that of their existence? Still, the task is to be faced; we can never permit one party among us to run mad from lust of pleasure, and the rest equally mad from fury against them. So our dispassionate preliminary admonition to minds thus depraved shall run to this effect: (we will suppress our passion and use gentle language, imagining ourselves to be addressing a single person of the type). 'My lad, you are still young, and as time advances it will lead you to a complete reversal of many of your present convictions; you should wait for the future, then, before you undertake to judge of the supreme issues; and the greatest of these, though you now count it so trivial—is that of thinking rightly about the gods and so living well, or the reverse. I may begin with a single word of significant warning which you will assuredly find to be no mistake, and it is this. You yourself and your friends, are not the first nor the only persons to embrace this tenet as your doctrine about gods; nay, in every age there are sufferers from the malady, more or fewer. Hence I, who have had the acquaintance of many such, can assure you that no one who in early life has adopted this doctrine of the non-existence of gods has ever persisted to old age constant to that conviction, though there have been cases—not many, certainly, but still some few—of persistence in the other two attitudes, the belief that there are gods but that they are indifferent to human conduct, and again, that, though not indifferent, they are lightly placated by sacrifice and prayers.

PLATO (427–347 B.C.)

Concentrate on The Immediate

The gods are either powerless or powerful. If then they are powerless, why do you pray? But if they are powerful, why not rather pray them for the gift to fear none of these things, to desire none of them, to sorrow for none of them, rather than that any one of them should be present or absent? For surely if they can co-operate with man, they can co-operate to these ends. But perhaps you will say: 'The gods put these things in my power.' Were it not better then to use what is in your power with a free spirit rather than to be concerned for what is not in your power with a servile and abject spirit? Besides, who told you that the gods do not co-operate even in respect to what is in our power?

Begin at least to pray about these things and you will see. That man prays: 'How may I know that woman'; do *you* pray: 'How may I not desire to know her.' Another prays: 'How may I get rid of him'; do *you* pray: 'How may I not want to be rid of him.' Another: 'How may I not lose my little child'; do *you* pray: 'How may I not be afraid to lose him.' Turn your prayers round in this way generally and see what is the result.

Epicurus says: 'In illness my conversation was not about the sufferings of my body, nor used I,' he says, 'to talk to my visitors about such matters, but I continued to debate leading principles of science and to keep only to this, how the understanding while conscious of such changes in the mere flesh is yet undisturbed and preserves its own proper good. I did not even,' he goes on, 'permit the medical men to give themselves airs as though they were doing some great thing, but my life passed on happily and brightly.' Do the same then as he did, in sickness if you are sick and in any other circumstance, for it is common to every school not to desert Philosophy in any at all of the accidents of life and not to gossip with the ignorant and unlearned. Be intent only on what is now being done and on the instrument you use to do it.

MARCUS AURELIUS ANTONINUS (121–180)

... a Future Life?

'Do you believe in a future life?' asked Peter, abruptly.

'In a future life?' murmured Prince Andrew. Peter inferred a negation from his friend's answer, and having long known him to be an atheist, he went on:

'You say that you cannot see the reign of virtue and truth on earth? I do not see it either; and it is impossible to see it if you accept this life as the end of all things. On this earth there is no truth, no virtue; all is a lie; but, in the universal scheme of creation it is truth that rules. We are of course the children of this world, but in eternity we are the children of the Universe. I cannot help feeling that I am an integral atom in this immense and harmonious whole. In the numberless myriads of beings who are the manifestations of the Divinity—or, if you prefer it, of that supreme force—I feel that I am a link, that I mark a degree in the ascending scale. Seeing, as I do, that this scale, beginning at the plant, rises till it comes to me, why should I suppose that it stops at me, and rises no higher? Just as nothing in this world can ever be lost or destroyed, so can I never be lost in nothingness! I know what I have been, and shall become! I know that outside and beyond me spirits dwell, and that Truth inhabits that realm!'

'Yes, that is Herder's doctrine,' said Prince Andrew. 'But that cannot convince me. Life and death—they indeed are convincing! When we see a creature that we love, that is bound up with our life, to whom we have done wrongs that we hoped to atone for . . .' and his voice was unsteady . . . 'when that being suddenly is a victim to pain, struggles with suffering, and ceases to breathe—we wonder why! It is impossible that there should be no reply to that query, and I believe that there is one! That is what can convince a man and it convinced me.'

'But,' said Peter, 'is not that precisely what I said?'

'No. What I mean to say is that no arguments would lead me to believe in the certainty of a future life; but that when we go through life, a pair hand in hand, and suddenly our companion vanishes—drops into the void—we stand on the edge of the gulf, and look in . . . then conviction comes upon us! And I have looked in.'

'Well, then! You know that there is something else and Some One; that is to say another life and God!'

Prince Andrew made no reply. The carriage and horses had long since crossed the river, the sun was half set, and the evening chill was frosting the pools that lay at the foot of the slopes leading down to the river, while Peter and Andrew, to the great astonishment of the servants, coachmen, and passers-by, were still arguing on the ferry-steps: 'If there is a God, there must be a future life; consequently truth and virtue must exist; man's chief happiness must lie in his efforts to reach them. We must live, love, and believe that we do not exist only for the present on this speck of earth, but that we have lived, and shall live for ever in that infinitude'—and Peter pointed to the sky.

Prince Andrew listened, still leaning against the railing, and his eye lingered on the darkening waters, lighted only by a purple gleam from the dying sunset. Peter said no more. All was still, not a sound to be heard but a soft lapping against the keel of the boat which lay moored, a murmur that seemed to say, 'It is true—believe!'

LEO TOLSTOY (1828–1910)

Apocalypse—or Armageddon?

And the son of Kuntī, seeing them, all his kinsmen thus arrayed, was filled with deep compassion and, desponding, spake these words:

'Krishna, when these mine own folk I see standing before me, spoiling for the fight, my limbs give way beneath me, my mouth dries up, and trembling takes hold upon my frame: my body's hairs stand up in dread. My bow, Gāndīva, slips from my hand, My very skin is all ablaze; I cannot stand, my mind seems to wander all distraught. And portents too I see boding naught but ill. Should I strike down in battle mine own folk, no good therein see I.

'Krishna, I hanker not for victory, nor for the kingdom nor yet for things of pleasure. What use to us a kingdom, friend, what use enjoyment or life itself? Those for whose sake we covet kingdom, delights, and things of pleasure, here stand they, arrayed for battle, surrendering both wealth and life. They are our venerable teachers, fathers, sons, they too our grandsires, uncles, fathers-in-law, grand-sons, brothers-in-law, kinsmen all; these would I nowise slay though they slay me, my friend, not for dominion over the three wide worlds, how much less for this paltry earth.

'And should we slaughter Dhritarāshtra's sons, Krishna, what sweetness then is ours? Evil, and only evil, would come to dwell with us, should we slay them, hate us as they may. Therefore have we no right to kill the sons of Dhritarāshtra, our own kinsmen as they are. Should we lay low our own folk, Krishna; how could we find any joy? And even if, bereft of sense by greed, they cannot see that to ruin a family is wickedness and to break one's word (or, 'injury to a friend') a crime, how should we not be wise enough to turn aside from this evil thing?

'For the annihilation of a family we know full well is wickedness. Annihilate a family, and with it collapse the eternal laws that rule the family. Once law's destroyed, then lawlessness overwhelms all we know as family. With lawlessness triumphant, Krishna, the family's chaste women are debauched; from debauchery of the women too confusion of caste is born. Yes, caste-confusion leads to hell—the hell prepared for those who wreck The Family and for The Family so wrecked. So too their ancestors fall down to hell, cheated of their offerings of food and drink. These evil ways of men who wreck the family, these evil ways that bring on caste-confusion, these are the ways that bring caste-law to naught and the eternal family laws.

'A sure abode in hell there is for men who bring to naught the laws that rule the family: so, Krishna, have we heard. Ah, ah: so are we really bent on committing a monstrous evil deed? Coveting the sweet joys of sovereignty, look at us, all poised to slaughter our own folk! O let the sons of Dhritarāshtra, arms in hand, slay me in battle, though

I unarmed myself will offer no defence; therein were greater happiness for me!'

So saying Arjuna sat down upon the chariot-seat, though battle had begun, let slip his bow and arrows, his mind distraught with grief.

THE BHAGAVAD-GITA

The Hero Prophet

Mahomet was in his fortieth year, when having withdrawn to a cavern in Mount Hara, near Mecca, during this Ramadhan, to pass the month in prayer, and meditation on those great questions, he one day told his wife Kadijah, who with his household was with him or near him this year, That by the unspeakable special favour of Heaven he had now found it all out; was in doubt and darkness no longer, but saw it all. That all these Idols and Formulas were nothing, miserable bits of wood; that there was One God in and over all; and we must leave all Idols, and look to Him. That God is great; and that there is nothing else great! He is the Reality. Wooden Idols are not real; He is real. He made us at first, sustains us yet; we and all things are but the shadow of Him; a transitory garment veiling the Eternal Splendour. '*Allah akbar*, God is great;'—and then also '*Islam*,' That we must *submit* to God. That our whole strength lies in resigned submission to Him, whatsoever He do to us. For this world, and for the other! The thing He sends to us, were it death and worse than death, shall be good, shall be best; we resign ourselves to God.—'If this be *Islam*,' says Goethe, 'do we not all live in *Islam*?' Yes, all of us that have any moral life; we all live so. It has ever been held the highest wisdom for a man not merely to submit to Necessity,—Necessity will make him submit,—but to know and believe well that the stern thing which Necessity had ordered was the wisest, the best, the thing wanted there. To cease his frantic pretension of scanning this great God's-World in his small fraction of a brain; to know that it *had* verily, though deep beyond his soundings, a Just Law, that the soul of it was Good;—that his part in it was to conform to the Law of the Whole, and in devout silence follow that; not questioning it, obeying it as unquestionable.

I say, this is yet the only true morality known. A man is right and invincible, virtuous and on the road towards sure conquest, precisely while he joins himself to the great deep Law of the World, in spite of all superficial laws, temporary appearances, profit-and-loss calculations; he is victorious while he coöperates with that great central Law, not victorious otherwise:—and surely his first chance of coöperating with it, or getting into the course of it, is to know with his whole soul that it *is*; that it is good, and alone good! This is the soul of Islam; it is properly the soul of Christianity;—for Islam is definable as a confused form of Christianity; had Christianity not been, neither had it been.

THOMAS CARLYLE (1795-1881)

The Duties of the Believer

A believer killeth not a believer but by mischance: and whoso killeth a believer by mischance shall be bound to free a believer from slavery; and the blood-money shall be paid to the family of the slain, unless they convert it into alms. But if the slain believer be of a hostile people, then let him confer freedom on a slave who is a believer; and if he be of a people between whom and yourselves there is an alliance, then let the blood-money be paid to his family, and let him set free a slave who is a believer: and let him who hath not the means, fast two consecutive months. This is the penance enjoined by God; and God is Knowing. Wise!

But whoever shall kill a believer of set purpose, his recompense shall be hell; for ever shall he abide in it; God shall be wrathful with him, and shall curse him, and shall get ready for him a great torment.

O believers! when ye go forth to the fight for the cause of God, be discerning, and say not to every one who meeteth you with a greeting, 'Thou art not a believer' in your greed after the chance good things of this present life! With God are abundant spoils. Such hath been your wont in times past; but God hath been gracious to you. Be discerning, then, for God well knoweth what ye do.

Those believers who sit at home free from trouble, and those who do valiantly in the cause of God with their substance and their persons, shall not be treated alike. God hath assigned to those who contend earnestly with their persons and with their substance, a rank above those who sit at home. Goodly promises hath He made to all. But God hath assigned to the strenuous a rich recompense, above those who sit still at home.

THE KORAN

Breaking with the Past

We live in a transition period, when the old faiths which comforted nations, and not only so, but made nations, seem to have spent their force. I do not find the religions of men at this moment very creditable to them, but either childish and insignificant, or unmanly and effeminating. The fatal trait is the divorce between religion and morality. Here are know-nothing religions or churches that proscribe intellect; scortatory religions; slave-holding and slave-trading religions; and, even in the decent populations idolatries wherein the whiteness of the ritual covers scarlet indulgence. The lover of the old religion complains that our contemporaries, scholars as well as merchants, succumb to a great despair,—have corrupted into a timorous conservatism, and believe in nothing. In our large cities, the population is godless, materialised,—no bond, no fellow-feeling, no enthusiasm. These are not men, but hungers, thirsts, fevers, and appetites walking. How is it people manage to live on,—so aimless as they are? After their peppercorn aims are gained, it seems as if the lime in their bones alone held them together, and not any worthy purpose. There is no faith in the intellectual, none in the moral universe. There is faith in chemistry, in meat and wine, in wealth, in machinery, in the steam-engine, galvanic battery, turbine-wheels, sewing machines, and in public opinion, but not in divine causes. A silent revolution has loosed the tension of the old religious sects, and, in place of the gravity and permanence of those societies of opinion, they run into freak and extravagance. In creeds never was such levity; witness the heathenisms in Christianity, the periodic 'revivals,' the Millenium mathematics, the peacock ritualism, the retrogression to Popery, the maundering of Mormons, the squalor of Mesmerism, the deliration of rappings, the rat and mouse revelation, thumps in table-drawers, and black art. The architecture, the music, the prayer, partake of the madness; the arts sink into shift and make-believe. Not knowing what to do, we ape our ancestors; the churches stagger backward to the mummeries of the dark ages. By the irresistible maturing of the general mind, the Christian traditions have lost their hold. The dogma of the mystic offices of Christ being dropped, and he standing on his genius as a moral teacher, 'tis impossible to maintain the whole emphasis of his personality; and it recedes, as all persons must, before the sublimity of the moral laws. From this change, and in the momentary absence of any religious genius that could offset the immense material activity, there is a feeling that religion is gone. When Paul Leroux offered his article '*Dieu*' to the conductor of a leading French journal, he replied, '*La question de Dieu manque d'actualité.*' In Italy, Mr Gladstone said of the late King of Naples, 'it has been a proverb, that he has erected the negation of God into a system of government.' In this country, the like stupefaction was in the air, and the phrase 'higher law' became a political jibe. What proof of infidelity like the toleration and propagandism of slavery? What like the direction of education? What like the facility of conversion? What like the externality of churches that once sucked the roots of right and wrong, and now have perished away till they are a speck of whitewash on the wall? What proof of scepticism like the base rate at which the highest mental and moral gifts are held? Let a man attain the highest and broadest culture that any American has possessed, then let him die by sea-storm, railroad collision, or other accident, and all America will acquiesce that the best thing has happened to him; that, after the education has gone far, such is the expensiveness of America, that the best use to put a fine person to is, to drown him to save his board.

Another scar of this scepticism is the distrust in human virtue. It is believed by well-dressed proprietors that there is no more virtue than they possess; that the solid portion of society exists for the arts of comfort; that life is an affair to put somewhat between the upper and lower mandibles. How prompt the suggestion of a low motive! Certain patriots in England devoted themselves for years to creating a public opinion that should break down the corn-laws and establish free trade. 'Well,' says the man in the street, 'Cobden got a stipend out of it.' Kossuth fled hither across the ocean to try if he could rouse the New World to a sympathy with European liberty. 'Aye,' says New York, 'he made a handsome thing of it—enough to make him comfortable for life.'

RALPH WALDO EMERSON (1803–1882)

Sic transit . . .

XVII

Think, in this batter'd Caravanserai
Whose Portals are alternate Night and Day,
    How Sultán after Sultán with his Pomp
Abode his destin'd Hour, and went his way.

XVIII

They say the Lion and the Lizard keep
The Courts where Jamshyd gloried and drank deep:
    And Bahrám, that great Hunter—the Wild Ass
Stamps o'er his Head, but cannot break his Sleep.

XIX

I sometimes think that never blows so red
The Rose as where some buried Caesar bled;
　　That every Hyacinth the Garden wears
Dropt in her Lap from some once lovely Head.

XX

And this reviving Herb whose tender Green
Fledges the River-Lip on which we lean—
　　Ah, lean upon it lightly! for who knows
From what once lovely Lip it springs unseen!

EDWARD FITZGERALD (1809–1883)

The Workings of the Divine

'We scarcely know what we owe to Luther, and the Reformation in general. We are freed from the fetters of spiritual narrow-mindedness; we have, in consequence of our increasing culture, become capable of turning back to the fountain head, and of comprehending Christianity in its purity. We have, again, the courage to stand with firm feet upon God's earth, and to feel ourselves in our divinely-endowed human nature. Let mental culture go on advancing; let the natural sciences go on gaining in depth and breadth, and the human mind expand as it may—it will never go beyond the elevation and moral culture of Christianity as it glistens and shines forth in the Gospel!

'But the better we Protestants advance in our noble development, so much the more rapidly will the Catholics follow us. As soon as they feel themselves caught up by the ever-extending enlightenment of the time, they must go on, do what they will, till at last the point is reached where all is but one.

'The mischievous sectarianism of the Protestants will also cease, and with it the hatred and hostile feeling between father and son, sister and brother; for as soon as the pure doctrine and love of Christ are comprehended in their true nature, and have become a vital principle, we shall feel ourselves as human beings, great and free, and not attach special importance to a degree more or less in the outward forms of religion. Besides, we shall all gradually advance from a Christianity of words and faith, to a Christianity of feeling and action.'

The conversation turned upon the great men who had lived before

Christ—among the Chinese, the Indians, the Persians, and the Greeks; and it was remarked, that the divine power had been as operative in them as in some of the great Jews of the Old Testament. We then came to the question how far God influenced the great natures of the present world in which we live?

'To hear people speak,' said Goethe, 'you would almost believe they were of opinion God had withdrawn into silence since those old times, and man was now placed quite upon his own feet and had to see how he could get on without God and His daily invisible breath. In religious and moral matters, a divine influence is indeed still allowed; but in matters of science and art it is believed that they are merely earthy, and nothing but the product of human powers.

'Let anybody only try, with human will and human power, to produce something that may be compared with the creations that bear the names of *Mozart*, *Raphael*, or *Shakespeare*. I know very well that these three noble beings are not the only ones, and that innumerable excellent geniuses have worked in every province of art, and produced things as perfect. But if they were as great as those, they rose above ordinary human nature, and in the same proportion were as divinely endowed as they.

'And after all what does it all come to? God did not retire to rest after the well-known six days of creation, but is constantly active as on the first. It would have been for Him a poor occupation to compose this heavy world out of simple elements, and to keep it rolling in the sunbeams from year to year, if He had not had the plan of founding a nursery for a world of spirits upon this material basis. So He is now constantly active in higher natures to attract the lower ones.'

JOHANN ECKERMANN (1792–1854)

What is Philosophy?

Philosophy being nothing else but *the study of wisdom and truth*, it may with reason be expected, that those who have spent most time and pains in it should enjoy a greater calm and serenity of mind, a greater clearness and evidence of knowledge, and be less disturbed with doubts and difficulties than other men. Yet so it is, we see the illiterate bulk of mankind, that walk the high road of plain, common sense, and are governed by the dictates of nature, for the most part easy and undisturbed. To them nothing *that is familiar* appears unaccountable or difficult to comprehend. They complain not of any want of evidence in their senses, and are out of all danger of becoming *sceptics*. But no sooner do we depart from sense and instinct to follow the light of a superior principle, to reason, meditate, and reflect on the nature of things, but a thousand scruples spring up in our minds, concerning those things which before we seemed fully to comprehend. Prejudices and errors of sense do from all parts discover themselves to our view; and endeavouring to correct these by reason, we are insensibly drawn into uncouth paradoxes, difficulties, and inconsistences, which multiply and grow upon us as we advance in speculation; till at length, having wandered through many intricate mazes, we find ourselves just where we were, or, which is worse, sit down in a forlorn scepticism.

The cause of this is thought to be (1) the obscurity of things, or the natural weakness and imperfection of our understandings. It is said the faculties we have are few, and those designed by nature for the *support* and comfort (pleasure) of life, and not to penetrate into the *inward essence* and constitution of things. Besides, (2) the mind of man being finite, when it treats of things which partake of infinity, it is not to be wondered at if it run into absurdities and contradictions; out of which it is impossible it should ever extricate itself, it being of the nature of infinite not to be comprehended by that which is finite.

But perhaps we may be too partial to ourselves in placing the fault originally in our faculties, and not rather in the wrong use we make of them. *It is a hard thing to suppose, that right deductions from true principles should ever end in consequences which cannot be maintained* or made consistent. We should believe that God has dealt more bountifully with the sons of men, than to give them a strong desire for that knowledge which he had placed quite out of their reach.

GEORGE BERKELEY (1685–1753)

Of the Abuse of Words

Another great abuse of words is *inconstancy* in the use of them. It is hard to find a discourse written of any subject, especially of controversy, whereon one shall not observe, if he read with attention, the same words (and those commonly the most material in the discourse and upon which the argument turns) used sometimes for one collection of simple *ideas* and sometimes for another, which is a perfect abuse of language. Words being intended for signs of my *ideas* to make them known to others, not by any natural signification but by a voluntary imposition, it is plain cheat and abuse when I make them stand sometimes for one thing and sometimes for another, the wilful doing whereof can be imputed to nothing but great folly or greater dishonesty. And a man in his accounts with another may, with as much fairness, make the characters of numbers stand sometimes for one and sometimes for another collection of terms: v.g., this character 3 stand sometimes for three, sometimes for four, and sometimes for eight, as in his discourse or reasoning make the same words stand for different collections of simple *ideas*. If men should do so in their reckonings, I wonder who would have to do with them? One who would speak thus in the affairs and business of the world, and call 8 sometimes seven and sometimes nine, as best served his advantage, would presently have clapped upon him one of the two names men constantly are disgusted with. And yet in arguings and learned contests, the same sort of proceeding passes commonly for wit and learning; but to me it appears a greater dishonesty than the misplacing of counters in the casting up a debt, and the cheat the greater, by how much truth is of greater concernment and value than money...

Another great *abuse of words is the taking them for things*. This, though it in some degree concerns all names in general, yet more particularly affects those of substances. To this abuse those men are most subject who most confine their thoughts to any one system and give themselves up into a firm belief of the perfection of any received hypothesis: whereby they come to be persuaded that the terms of that sect are so suited to the nature of things that they perfectly correspond with their real existence. Who is there, that has been bred up in the peripatetic philosophy, who does not think the ten names, under which are ranked the ten predicaments, to be exactly conformable to the nature of things? Who is there of that school that is not persuaded that *substantial forms*, *vegetative souls*, *abhorrence of a vacuum*, *intentional species*, etc., are something real? These words men have learned from their very entrance upon knowledge and have found their masters and systems lay great stress upon them, and therefore they cannot quit the opinion that they are conformable to nature and are the representations of something that really exists. The *Platonists* have their *soul of the world*, and the *Epicureans* their *endeavour towards motion* in their atoms when at rest. There is scarce any sect in philosophy has not a distinct set of terms that others understand not. But yet this gibberish, which in the weakness of human understanding serves so well to palliate men's ignorance and cover their errors, comes by familiar use amongst those of the same tribe to seem the most important part of language, and of all other the terms the most significant; and should *aerial* and *aetherial vehicles* come once by the prevalency of that doctrine to be generally received anywhere, no doubt those terms would make impressions on men's minds so as to establish them in the persuasion of the reality of such things, as much as *peripatetic forms* and *intentional species* have heretofore done.

JOHN LOCKE (1632–1704)

Is a White Horse a Horse?

A. (You say that) a white horse is not a horse: is this (logically) admissible?

B. It is.

A. How can that be so?

B. The term 'horse' is the means by which a bodily form is named. The term 'white' is the means by which a colour is named. The naming of a colour is not the naming of a form. Therefore I say that a white horse is not a horse.

A. Since there are white horses in existence, it is not admissible to say that there are no horses in existence, (and so) it is not admissible to say that the said white horses are not horses. (If you grant that) white horses exist, how do you make out that they are not horses?

B. If you want to get a horse, a yellow horse or a black one will do perfectly well; but if you want to get a white horse, a yellow horse or a black one will not do. On the assumption that a white horse is a horse, what you are wanting to get is one thing, namely a white horse which is not different from a horse (generally). In that case, how is it that a yellow horse or a black one will do (from one point of view) and will not do (from another point of view)? If a thing both will do and will not do, its image (in the mind) is not clearly defined. The fact is, yellow horses and black ones (represent) the one-ness of horse-ness and may (logically) be used as corroborative of the fact that horses exist: but they may not (logically) be used as corroborative of the fact that white horses exist. This proves that white horses are not horses.

KUNG-SUN LUNG (fl. 250 B.C.)

Metaphysics

Human reason, in one sphere of its cognition, is called upon to consider questions, which it cannot decline, as they are presented by its own nature, but which it cannot answer, as they transcend every faculty of the mind.

It falls into this difficulty without any fault of its own. It begins with principles, which cannot be dispensed with in the field of experience, and the truth and sufficiency of which are, at the same time, insured by experience. With these principles it rises, in obedience to the laws of its own nature, to ever higher and more remote conditions. But it quickly discovers that, in this way, its labours must remain ever incomplete, because new questions never cease to present themselves; and thus it finds itself compelled to have recourse to principles which transcend the region of experience, while they are regarded by common sense without distrust. It thus falls into confusion and contradictions, from which it conjectures the presence of latent errors, which, however, it is unable to discover, because the principles it employs, transcending the limits of experience, cannot be tested by that criterion. The arena of these endless contests is called *Metaphysic*.

Time was, when she was the *queen* of all the sciences; and, if we take the will for the deed, she certainly deserves, so far as regards the high importance of her object-matter, this title of honour. Now, it is the fashion of the time to heap contempt and scorn upon her; and the matron mourns, forlorn and forsaken, like Hecuba:

> *Modo maxima rerum,*
> *Tot generis, natisque potens ...*
> *Nunc trahor exul, inops.* (Ovid, *Metamorphoses*)

At first, her government, under the administration of the *dogmatists*, was an absolute *despotism*. But, as the legislative continued to show traces of the ancient barbaric rule, her empire gradually broke up, and intestine wars introduced the reign of *anarchy*; while the *sceptics*, like nomadic tribes, who hate a permanent habitation and settled mode of living, attacked from time to time those who had organized themselves into civil communities. But their number was, very happily, small; and thus they could not entirely put a stop to the exertions of those who persisted in raising new edifices, although on no settled or uniform plan. In recent times the hope dawned upon us of seeing those disputes settled, and the legitimacy of her claims established by a kind of *physiology* of the human understanding—that of the celebrated Locke. But it was found that—although it was affirmed that this so-called queen could not refer her descent to any higher source than that of common experience, a circumstance which necessarily brought suspicion on her claims—as this *genealogy* was incorrect, she persisted in the advancement of her claims to sovereignty. Thus metaphysics necessarily fell back into the antiquated and rotten constitution of *dogmatism*, and again became obnoxious to the contempt from which efforts had been made to save it. At present, as all methods, according to the general persuasion, have been tried in vain, there reigns nought but weariness and complete *indifferentism*—the mother of chaos and night in the scientific world, but at the same time the source of, or at least the prelude to, the re-creation and reinstallation of a science, when it has fallen into confusion, obscurity, and disuse from ill-directed effort.

For it is in reality vain to profess *indifference* in regard to such inquiries, the object of which cannot be indifferent to humanity. Besides, these pretended *indifferentists*, however much they may try to disguise themselves by the assumption of a popular style and by changes in the language of the schools, unavoidably fall into metaphysical declarations and propositions, which they profess to regard with so much contempt. At the same time, this indifference, which has arisen in the world of science, and which relates to that kind of knowledge which we should wish to see destroyed the last, is a phenomenon that well deserves our attention and reflection. It is plainly not the effect of the levity, but of the matured *judgment* of the age, which refuses to be any longer entertained with illusory knowledge. It is, in fact, a call to reason, again to undertake the most laborious of all tasks—that of self-examination, and to establish a tribunal, which may secure it in its well-grounded claims, while it pronounces against all baseless assumptions and pretensions, not in an arbitrary manner, but according to its own eternal and unchangeable laws. This tribunal is nothing less than the *Critical Investigation of Pure Reason*.

I do not mean by this a criticism of books and systems, but a critical inquiry into the faculty of reason, with reference to the cognitions to which it strives to attain *without the aid of experience*; in other words, the solution of the question regarding the possibility or impossibility of Metaphysics, and the determination of the origin as well as of the extent and limits of this science.

IMMANUEL KANT (1724–1804)

The Prime Mover

The foregoing account provides a reasonable answer to our question. To reject it involves the recognition of a world derived from night, from the 'all together', from non-being. We may therefore take it as proved that there is something which is in unceasing, and therefore in circular, motion. And this is no mere theory, but is actually observed to be the case. The first heaven, then, must be eternal. Therefore there must also be something which moves it. And since that which is moved and moves is a middle term, there must be an extreme which moves without being moved, which is eternal, substance, and actuality.

The object of desire and that of thought move in this way; they move without being moved. In their primary forms these are identical. For the object of appetite is the apparent good, and the primary object of rational desire the real good. Now desire depends on thought rather than thought on desire, for thought is the starting-point. Thought is moved by its object, and the terms in the column of positives are *per se* objects of thought; in this column it is substance that comes first, and in substance that which is simple and actual. But the good and desirable belongs to the same column, and the first term in the column must be best or analogous to the best.

That the final cause may be something unchangeable is clear if we consider its various meanings. A final cause is (1) something for the good of which an action is done, and (2) something at which an action aims; of these the latter may be unchangeable, the former cannot.

The final cause, then, moves by being loved, while all other things that move do so by being moved. Now that which is moved is capable of being otherwise than it is, so that if its actual mode of existence is the primary kind of local movement, then, in so far as it is subject to change, it is capable of being otherwise in respect of place even if not in respect of substance.

The unmoved mover, on the other hand, has no contingency; it is not subject even to the minimal change (spatial motion in a circle), since this is what it originates. It exists, therefore, of necessity; its being is therefore good, and it is in this way that it is a principle of motion.

On such a principle, then, the whole physical universe depends. It is a life which is *always* such as the noblest and happiest that we can live —and live for so brief a while. Its very activity is pleasure—just as waking perceiving, thinking are most pleasant because they are activities, and hopes and memories because they are hopes and memories of these. Thought which is independent of lower faculties must be thought of what is best in itself; i.e. that which is thought in the fullest sense must be occupied with that which is best in the fullest sense. Now thought does think itself, because it shares in the intelligibility of its object. It becomes intelligible by contact with the intelligible, so that thought and object of thought are one. For that which is capable of receiving the object of thought, i.e. the essence, is thought; and it is *active* when it *possesses* this object. Therefore activity rather than potentiality is the divine element in thought—actual contemplation, the most pleasant and best of all things. If, then, God is *always* in that good state which we *sometimes* attain, this must excite our wonder; and He is in an even better state, which must inspire us with yet greater awe. God must also have life; for the actuality of thought is life, and God is that actuality. His essential actuality is life most good and eternal. God therefore is a living being, eternal, and most good; to Him belong—or rather He *is*—life and duration, continuous and eternal.

ARISTOTLE (384–322 B.C.)

The Educating of a Gentleman

The charge of the Tutor, which you shall appoint your sonne, in the choice of whom consisteth the whole substance of his education and bringing-up; on which are many branches depending, which (forasmuch as I can adde nothing of any moment to it) I will not touch at all. And for that point, wherein I presume to advise him, he may so far forth give credit unto it, as he shall see just cause. To a gentleman borne of noble parentage, and heire of a house, that aymeth at true learning, and in it would be disciplined, not so much for gaine or commoditie to himselfe (because so abject an end is far unworthie the grace and favour of the Muses, and besides, hath a regard or dependencie of others) nor for externall shew and ornament, but to adorne and enrich his inward minde, desiring rather to shape and institute an able and sufficient man, than a bare learned man.

My desire is therefore, that the parents or overseers of such a gentleman be very circumspect, and carefull in chusing his director, whom I would rather commend for having a well composed and temperate braine, than a full stuft head, yet both will doe well. And I would rather prefer wisdome, judgement, civill customes, and modest behaviour, than bare and meere literall learning; and that in his charge he hold a new course.

Some never cease brawling in their schollers eares (as if they were still pouring in a tonell) to follow their booke, yet is their charge nothing else, but to repeat, what hath beene told them before. I would have a tutor to correct this part, and that at first entrance, according to the capacitie of the wit he hath in hand, he should begin to make shew of it, making him to have a smacke of all things, and how to chuse and distinguish them, without helpe of others, sometimes opening him the way, other times leaving him to open it by himselfe. I would not have him to invent and speake alone, but suffer his disciple to speake when his turne commeth. *Socrates*, and after him *Arcesilaus*, made their schollers to speake first, and then would speake themselves. *Most commonly the authoritie of them that teach, hinders them that would learne* (Cic. *De Nat.* i.). . .

My late father, having by all the meanes and industrie, that is possible for man, sought amongst the wisest, and men of best understanding, to find a most exquisite and readie way of teaching, being advised of the inconveniences then in use; was given to understand, that the lingring while, and best part of our youth, that we imploy in learning the tongues, which cost them nothing, is the onely cause we can never attaine to that absolute perfection of skill and knowledge, of the Greekes, and Romanes. I doe not beleeve that to be the onely cause. But so it is, the expedient my father found out, was this; that being yet at nurse, and before the first loosing of my tongue, I was delivered to a Germane (who died since, a most excellent Physitian in *France*) he being then altogether ignorant of the French tongue, but exquisitely readie and skilfull in the Latine. This man, whom my Father had sent for of purpose, and to whom he gave verie great entertainment, had me continually in his armes, and was mine onely overseer. There were also joyned unto him two of his countrimen, but not so learned; whose charge was to attend, and now and then, to play with me; and all these together did never entertaine me with other than the Latine tongue. As for others of his houshold, it was an inviolable rule, that neither himselfe, nor my mother, nor man, nor maid-servant, were suffered to speake one word in my companie, except such Latine words, as every one had learned to chat and prattle with me. It were strange to tell how every one in the house profited therein. My Father and my Mother learned so much Latine, that for a need they could understand it, when they heard it spoken, even so did all the houshold servants, namely such as were neerest and most about me. To be short, we were all so Latinized, that the townes round about us had their share of it; insomuch as even at this day, many Latine names both of workmen and of their tooles, are yet in use among them. And as for my selfe, I was about six yeares old, and could understand no more French or Perigordine, than Arabike, and that without art, without bookes, rules, or grammer, without whipping or whining. I had gotten as pure a Latine tongue as my Master could speake; the rather because I could neither mingle or confound the same with other tongues. If for an Essay they would give me a Theme, whereas the fashion in Colleges is, to give it in French, I had it in bad Latine, to reduce the same into good.

MICHEL EYQUEM DE MONTAIGNE (1533–1592)

A Father to his Student Son

But although my deceased father of happy memory, Grangousier, had bent his best endeavours to make me profit in all perfection and political knowledge, and that my labour and study was fully correspondent to, yea, went beyond his desire, nevertheless, as thou mayest well understand, the time then was not so proper and fit for learning as it is at present, neither had I plenty of such good masters as thou hast had. For that time was darksome, obscured with clouds of ignorance, and savouring a little of the infelicity and calamity of the Goths, who had, wherever they set footing, destroyed all good literature, which in my age hath by the divine goodness been restored unto its former light and dignity, and that with such amendment and increase of knowledge, that now hardly should I be admitted unto the first form of the little grammar-school boys. I say, I, who in my youthful days was, and that justly, reputed the most learned of that age. Which I do not speak in vain boasting, although I might lawfully do it in writing unto thee,— in verification whereof thou hast the authority of Marcus Tullius in his book of old age, and the sentence of Plutarch, in the book intituled, How a man may praise himself without envy:—but to give thee an emulous encouragement to strive yet further.

Now it is, that the minds of men are qualified with all manner of discipline and the old sciences revived, which for many ages were extinct. Now it is, that the learned languages are to their pristine purity restored, viz., Greek, without which a man may be ashamed to account himself a scholar, Hebrew, Arabic, Chaldæan, and Latin. Printing likewise is now in use, so elegant and so correct, that better cannot be imagined, although it was found out but in my time by divine inspiration, as by a diabolical suggestion on the other side, was the invention of ordnance. All the world is full of knowing men, of most learned schoolmasters, and vast libraries; and it appears to me as a truth, that neither in Plato's time, nor Cicero's, nor Papinian's, there was ever such conveniency for studying, as we see at this day there is. Nor must any adventure henceforward to come in public or present himself in company, that hath not been pretty well polished in the shop of

Minerva. I see robbers, hangmen, free-booters, tapsters, ostlers, and such like, of the very rubbish of the people, more learned now than the doctors and preachers were in my time.

What shall I say? The very women and children have aspired to this praise and celestial manna of good learning. Yet so it is, that at the age I am now of, I have been constrained to learn the Greek tongue,—which I contemned not like Cato, but had not the leisure in my younger years to attend the study of it,—and I take much delight in the reading of Plutarch's Morals, the pleasant Dialogues of Plato, the Monuments of Pausanias, and the Antiquities of Athenæus, in waiting on the hour wherein God my Creator shall call me, and command me to depart from this earth and transitory pilgrimage. Wherefore, my son, I admonish thee to employ thy youth to profit as well as thou canst, both in thy studies and in virtue. Thou art at Paris, where the laudable examples of many brave men may stir up thy mind to gallant actions, and hast likewise, for thy tutor and pedagogue the learned Epistemon, who by his lively and vocal documents may instruct thee in the arts and sciences.

I intend, and will have it so, that thou learn the languages perfectly; first of all, the Greek, as Quintilian will have it; secondly, the Latin; and then the Hebrew, for the Holy Scripture-sake; and then the Chaldee and Arabic likewise, and that thou frame thy style in Greek in imitation of Plato; and for the Latin, after Cicero. Let there be no history which thou shalt not have ready in thy memory;—unto the prosecuting of which design, books of cosmography will be very conducible, and help thee much. Of the liberal arts of geometry, arithmetic and music, I gave thee some taste when thou wert yet little, and not above five or six years old. Proceed further in them, and learn the remainder if thou canst. As for astronomy, study all the rules thereof. Let pass, nevertheless, the divining and judicial astrology, and the art of Lullius, as being nothing else but plain abuses and vanities. As for the civil law, of that I would have thee to know the texts by heart, and then to confer them with philosophy.

Now, in matter of the knowledge of the works of nature, I would have thee to study that exactly; that so there be no sea, river, nor fountain, of which thou dost not know the fishes; all the fowls of the air; all the several kinds of shrubs and trees, whether in forest or orchards; all the sorts of herbs and flowers that grow upon the ground; all the various metals that are hid within the bowels of the earth; together with all the diversity of precious stones, that are to be seen, in the orient and south parts of the world. Let nothing of all these be hidden from thee. Then fail not most carefully to peruse the books of the Greek, Arabian, and Latin physicians, not despising the Talmudists and Cabalists; and by frequent anatomies get thee the perfect knowledge of that other world, called the microcosm, which is man. And at some of the hours of the day apply thy mind to the study of the Holy Scriptures; first, in Greek, the New Testament, with the Epistles of the Apostles; and then the Old Testament in Hebrew. In brief, let me see thee an abyss, and bottomless pit of knowledge: for from henceforward, as thou growest great and becomest a man, thou must part from this tranquillity and rest of study, thou must learn chivalry, warfare, and the exercises of the field, the better thereby to defend my house and our friends, and to succour and protect them at all their needs, against the invasion and assaults of evil doers.—Thy father, GARGANTUA.

FRANÇOIS RABELAIS (c. 1494–1553)

Humane Letters

The study of the Classics is less to be regarded as an exercise of the intellect, than as 'a discipline of humanity.' The peculiar advantage of this mode of education consists not so much in strengthening the understanding, as in softening and refining the taste. It gives men liberal views; it accustoms the mind to take an interest in things foreign to itself; to love virtue for its own sake; to prefer fame to life, and glory to riches; and to fix our thoughts on the remote and permanent, instead of narrow and fleeting objects. It teaches us to believe that there is something really great and excellent in the world, surviving all the shocks of accident and fluctuations of opinion, and raises us above that low and servile fear, which bows only to present power and upstart authority. Rome and Athens filled a place in the history of mankind, which can never be occupied again. They were two cities set on a hill, which could not be hid; all eyes have seen them, and their light shines like a mighty sea-mark into the abyss of time.

> Still green with bays each ancient altar stands,
> Above the reach of sacrilegious hands;
> Secure from flames, from envy's fiercer rage,
> Destructive war, and all-involving age.

> Hail, bards triumphant, born in happier days,
> Immortal heirs of universal praise!
> Whose honours with increase of ages grow,
> As streams roll down, enlarging as they flow!

It is this feeling, more than anything else, which produces a marked difference between the study of the ancient and modern languages, and which, from the weight and importance of the consequences attached to the former, stamps every word with a monumental firmness. By conversing with the *mighty dead*, we imbibe sentiment with knowledge; we become strongly attached to those who can no longer either hurt or serve us, except through the influence which they exert over the mind. We feel the presence of that power which gives immortality to human thoughts and actions, and catch the flame of enthusiasm from all nations and ages.

It is hard to find in minds otherwise formed, either a real love of excellence, or a belief that any excellence exists superior to their own. Everything is brought down to the vulgar level of their own ideas and pursuits. Persons without education certainly do not want either acuteness or strength of mind in what concerns themselves, or in things immediately within their observation; but they have no power of abstraction, no general standard of taste, or scale of opinion. They see their objects always near, and never in the horizon. Hence arises that egotism which has been remarked as the characteristic of self-taught men, and which degenerates into obstinate prejudice or petulant fickleness of opinion, according to the natural sluggishness or activity of their minds. For they either become blindly bigoted to the first opinions they have struck out for themselves, and inaccessible to conviction; or else (the dupes of their own vanity and shrewdness) are everlasting converts to every crude suggestion that presents itself, and the last opinion is always the true one. Each successive discovery flashes upon them with equal light and evidence, and every new fact overturns their whole system. It is among this class of persons, whose ideas never extend beyond the feeling of the moment, that we find partizans, who are very honest men, with a total want of principle, and who unite the most hardened effrontery, and intolerance of opinion, to endless inconsistency and self-contradiction.

WILLIAM HAZLITT (1778–1830)

A Father's Right!

While philosophising upon the duties of man, an event occurred which made me reflect more seriously upon my own. Thérèse became pregnant for the third time. Too honest towards myself, too proud in my heart to desire to belie my principles by my actions, I began to consider the destination of my children and my connection with their mother, in the light of the laws of nature, justice, and reason, and of that religion—pure, holy and eternal, like its author—which men have polluted, while pretending to be anxious to purify it, and which they have converted, by their formulas, into a mere religion of words, seeing that it costs men little to prescribe what is impossible, when they dispense with carrying it out in practice.

If I was wrong in my conclusions, nothing can be more remarkable than the calmness with which I abandoned myself to them. If I had been one of those low-born men, who are deaf to the gentle voice of Nature, in whose heart no real sentiment of justice or humanity ever springs up, this hardening of my heart would have been quite easy to understand. But is it possible that my warm-heartedness, lively sensibility, readiness to form attachments, the powerful hold which they exercise over me, the cruel heartbreakings I experience when forced to break them off, my natural goodwill towards all my fellow-creatures, my ardent love of the great, the true, the beautiful, and the just; my horror of evil of every kind, my utter inability to hate or injure, or even to think of it; the sweet and lively emotion which I feel at the sight of all that is virtuous, generous, and amiable; is it possible, I ask, that all these can ever agree in the same heart with the depravity which, without the least scruple, tramples underfoot the sweetest of obligations? No! I feel and loudly assert—it is impossible. Never, for a single moment in his life, could Jean-Jacques have been a man without feeling, without compassion, or an unnatural father. I may have been mistaken, never hardened. If I were to state my reasons, I should say too much. Since they were strong enough to mislead me, they might mislead many others, and I do not desire to expose young people, who may read my works, to the danger of allowing themselves to be misled by the same error. I will content myself with observing, that my error was such that, in handing over my children to the State to educate, for want of means to bring them up myself, in deciding to fit them for becoming workmen and peasants rather than adventurers and fortune-hunters, I thought that I was behaving like a citizen and a father, and considered myself a member of Plato's Republic. More than once since then, the regrets of my heart have told me that I was wrong; but, far from my reason having given me the same information, I have often blessed Heaven for having preserved them from their father's lot and from the lot which threatened them as soon as I should have been obliged to abandon them. If I had left them with Madame d'Epinay or Madame de Luxembourg, who, from friendship, generosity, or some other motive, expressed themselves willing to take charge of them, would they have been happier, would they have been brought up at least as honest men? I do not know; but I do know that they would would have been brought up to hate, perhaps to betray, their parents; it is a hundred times better that they have never known them.

My third child was accordingly taken to the Foundling Hospital, like the other two. The two next were disposed of in the same manner, for I had five altogether. This arrangement appeared to me so admirable, so rational, and so legitimate, that, if I did not openly boast of it, this was solely out of regard for the mother; but I told all who were acquainted with our relations.

JEAN-JACQUES ROUSSEAU (1712–1778)

Bygone Oxbridge

Thus young Pen, the only son of an estated country gentleman, with a good allowance, and a gentlemanlike bearing and person, looked to be a lad of much more consequence than he was really; and was held by the Oxbridge authorities, tradesmen, and under-graduates, as quite a young buck and member of the aristocracy. His manner was frank, brave, and perhaps a little impertinent, as becomes a high-spirited youth. He was perfectly generous and free-handed with his money, which seemed pretty plentiful. He loved joviality, and had a good voice for a song. Boat-racing had not risen in Pen's time to the *fureur* which, as we are given to understand, it has since attained in the University; and riding and tandem-driving were the fashions of the ingenuous youth. Pen rode well to hounds, appeared in pink, as became a young buck, and not particularly extravagant in equestrian or any other amusement, yet managed to run up a fine bill at Niles, the livery stable-keeper, and in a number of other quarters. In fact, this lucky young gentleman had almost every taste to a considerable degree. He was very fond of books of all sorts: Doctor Portman had taught him to like rare editions, and his own taste led him to like beautiful bindings. It was marvellous what tall copies, and gildings, and marbling, and blind-tooling, the booksellers and binders put upon Pen's bookshelves. He had a very fair taste in matters of art, and a keen relish for prints of a high school—none of your French Opera Dancers, or tawdry Racing Prints, such as had delighted the simple eyes of Mr Spicer, his predecessor—but your Stranges, and Rembrandt etchings, and Wilkies before the letter, with which his apartments were furnished presently in the most perfect good taste, as was allowed in the University, where this young fellow got no small reputation. We have mentioned that he exhibited a certain partiality for rings, jewellery, and fine raiment of all sorts; and it must be owned that Mr Pen, during his time at the University, was rather a dressy man, and loved to array himself in splendour. He and his polite friends would dress themselves out with as much care in order to go and dine at each other's rooms, as other folks would who were going to enslave a mistress. They said he used to wear rings over his kid gloves, which he always denies; but what follies will not youth perpetrate with its own admirable gravity and simplicity? That he took perfumed baths is a truth; and he used to say that he took them after meeting certain men of a very low set in hall.

In fact, in the course of his second year, Arthur Pendennis had become one of the men of fashion in the University. It is curious to watch that facile admiration, and simple fidelity of youth. They hang round a leader: and wonder at him, and love him, and imitate him. No generous boy ever lived, I suppose, that has not had some wonderment of admiration for another boy; and Monsieur Pen at Oxbridge had his school, his faithful band of friends, and his rivals. When the young men heard at the haberdashers' shop that Mr Pendennis of Boniface had just ordered a crimson satin cravat, you would see a couple of dozen crimson satin cravats in Main Street in the course of the week—and Simon, the jeweller, was known to sell no less than two gross of Pendennis' pins, from a pattern which the young gentleman had selected in his shop.

Now, if any person with an arithmetical turn of mind will take the trouble to calculate what a sum of money it would cost a young man to indulge freely in all the above propensities which we have said Mr Pen possessed, it will be seen that a young fellow, with such liberal tastes and amusements, must needs in the course of two or three years spend or owe a very handsome sum of money. We have said our friend Pen had not a calculating turn. No one propensity of his was outrageously extravagant: and it is certain that Paddington's tailor's account; Guttlebury's cook's bill for dinners; Dilley Tandy's bill with Finn, the printseller, for Raphael-Morghens, and Landseer proofs; and Wormall's dealings with Parkton, the great bookseller, for Aldine editions, black-letter folios, and richly illuminated Missals of the XVI. Century; and Snaffle's or Foker's score with Nile the horse-dealer, were, each and all of them, incomparably greater than any little bills which Mr Pen might run up with the above-mentioned tradesmen. But Pendennis of Boniface had the advantage over all these young gentlemen, his friends and associates, of a universality of taste: and whereas young Lord Paddington did not care twopence for the most beautiful print, or to look into any gilt frame that had not a mirror within it; and Guttlebury did not mind in the least how he was dressed, and had an aversion to horse exercise, nay a terror of it; and Snaffle never read any printed works but the *Racing Calendar* or *Bell's Life*, or cared for any manuscript except his greasy little scrawl of a betting-book:—our catholic-minded young friend occupied himself in every one of the branches of science or pleasure above mentioned, and distinguished himself tolerably in each.

WILLIAM MAKEPEACE THACKERAY (1811-1863)

Co-education the Answer

There is not, perhaps, in the kingdom, a more dogmatical, or luxurious set of men, than the pedantic tyrants who reside in colleges and preside at public schools. The vacations are equally injurious to the morals of the masters and pupils, and the intercourse, which the former keep up with the nobility, introduces the same vanity and extravagance into their families, which banish domestic duties and comforts from the lordly mansion, whose state is awkwardly aped. The boys, who live at a great expense with the masters and assistants, are never domesticated, though placed there for that purpose; for, after a silent dinner, they swallow a hasty glass of wine, and retire to plan some mischievous trick, or to ridicule the person or manners of the very people they have just been cringing to, and whom they ought to consider as the representatives of their parents.

Can it then be a matter of surprise that boys become selfish and vicious who are thus shut out from social converse? or that a mitre often graces the brow of one of these diligent pastors?

The desire of living in the same style, as the rank just above them, infects each individual and every class of people, and meanness is the concomitant of this ignoble ambition; but those professions are most debasing whose ladder is patronage; yet, out of one of these professions the tutors of youth are, in general, chosen. But, can they be expected to inspire independent sentiments, whose conduct must be regulated by the cautious prudence that is ever on the watch for preferment?

So far, however, from thinking of the morals of boys, I have heard several masters of schools argue, that they only undertook to teach Latin and Greek; and that they had fulfilled their duty, by sending some good scholars to college.

A few good scholars, I grant, may have been formed by emulation and discipline; but, to bring forward these clever boys, the health and morals of a number have been sacrificed. The sons of our gentry and wealthy commoners are mostly educated at these seminaries, and will anyone pretend to assert that the majority, making every allowance, come under the description of tolerable scholars?

It is not for the benefit of society that a few brilliant men should be brought forward at the expense of the multitude. It is true, that great men seem to start up, as great revolutions occur, at proper intervals, to restore order, and to blow aside the clouds that thicken over the face of truth; but let more reason and virtue prevail in society, and these strong winds would not be necessary. Public education, of every denomination, should be directed to form citizens. . .

I have already animadverted on the bad habits which females acquire when they are shut up together; and, I think, that the observation may fairly be extended to the other sex, till the natural inference is drawn which I have had in view throughout—that to improve both sexes they ought, not only in private families, but in public schools, to be educated together. If marriage be the cement of society, mankind should all be educated after the same model, or the intercourse of the sexes will never deserve the name of fellowship, nor will women ever fulfil the peculiar duties of their sex, till they become enlightened citizens, till they become free by being enabled to earn their own subsistence, independent of men; in the same manner, I mean, to prevent misconstruction, as one man is independent of another. Nay, marriage will never be held sacred till women, by being brought up with men, are prepared to be their companions rather than their mistresses; for the mean doublings of cunning will ever render them contemptible, whilst oppression renders them timid. So convinced am I of this truth, that I will venture to predict that virtue will never prevail in society till the virtues of both sexes are founded on reason; and, till the affections common to both are allowed to gain their due strength by the discharge of mutual duties.

Were boys and girls permitted to pursue the same studies together, those graceful decencies might early be inculcated which produce modesty without those sexual distinctions that taint the mind. Lessons of politeness, and that formulary of decorum, which treads on the heels of falsehood, would be rendered useless by habitual propriety of behaviour.

MARY WOLLSTONECRAFT (1759-1797)

Shakespeare

Others abide our question. Thou art free.
We ask and ask—Thou smilest and art still,
Out-topping knowledge. For the loftiest hill,
Who to the stars uncrowns his majesty,

Planting his steadfast footsteps in the sea,
Making the heaven of heavens his dwelling-place,
Spares but the cloudy border of his base
To the foil'd searching of mortality;

And thou, who didst the stars and sunbeams know,
Self-school'd, self-scann'd, self-honour'd, self-secure,
Didst tread on earth unguess'd at.—Better so!

All pains the immortal spirit must endure,
All weakness which impairs, all griefs which bow,
Find their sole speech in that victorious brow.

MATTHEW ARNOLD (1822-1888)

Is Chaucer a Great Poet?

If we ask ourselves wherein consists the immense superiority of Chaucer's poetry over the romance-poetry—why it is that in passing from this to Chaucer we suddenly feel ourselves to be in another world, we shall find that his superiority is both in the substance of his poetry and in the style of his poetry. His superiority in substance is given by his large, free, simple, clear yet kindly view of human life,—so unlike the total want, in the romance-poets, of all intelligent command of it. Chaucer has not their helplessness; he has gained the power to survey the world from a central, a truly human point of view. We have only to call to mind the Prologue to *The Canterbury Tales*. The right comment upon it is Dryden's: 'It is sufficient to say, according to the proverb, that *here is God's plenty*.' And again: 'He is a perpetual fountain of good sense.' It is by a large, free, sound representation of things, that poetry,

this high criticism of life, has truth of substance; and Chaucer's poetry
has truth of substance.

Of his style and manner, if we think first of the romance-poetry and
then of Chaucer's divine liquidness of diction, his divine fluidity of
movement, it is difficult to speak temperately. They are irresistible, and
justify all the rapture with which his successors speak of his 'gold dew-
drops of speech.' Johnson misses the point entirely when he finds fault
with Dryden for ascribing to Chaucer the first refinement of our numbers, and says that Gower also can show smooth numbers and easy
rhymes. The refinement of our numbers means something far more
than this. A nation may have versifiers with smooth numbers and easy
rhymes, and yet may have no real poetry at all. Chaucer is the father of
our splendid English poetry; he is our 'well of English undefiled,'
because by the lovely charm of his diction, the lovely charm of his
movement, he makes an epoch and founds a tradition. In Spenser,
Shakespeare, Milton, Keats, we can follow the tradition of the liquid
diction, the fluid movement, of Chaucer; at one time it is his liquid
diction of which in these poets we feel the virtue, and at another time it
is his fluid movement. And the virtue is irresistible.

Bounded as is my space, I must yet find room for an example of
Chaucer's virtue, as I have given examples to show the virtue of the
great classics. I feel disposed to say that a single line is enough to show
the charm of Chaucer's verse; that merely one line like this—

> O martyr souded in virginitee!

has a virtue of manner and movement such as we shall not find in all
the verse of romance-poetry;—but this is saying nothing. The virtue is
such as we shall not find, perhaps, in all English poetry, outside the
poets whom I have named as the special inheritors of Chaucer's tradition. A single line, however, is too little if we have not the strain of
Chaucer's verse well in our memory; let us take a stanza. It is from *The
Prioress's Tale*, the story of the Christian child murdered in a Jewry—

> My throte is cut unto my nekke-bone
> Saidè this child, and as by way of kinde
> I should have deyd, yea, longè time agone;
> But Jesu Christ, as ye in bookès finde,
> Will that his glory last and be in minde,
> And for the worship of his mother dere
> Yet may I sing *O Alma* loud and clere.

Wordsworth has modernized this Tale, and to feel how delicate and
evanescent is the charm of verse, we have only to read Wordsworth's
first three lines of this stanza after Chaucer's—

My throat is cut unto the bone, I trow,
Said this young child, and by the law of kind
I should have died, yea, many hours ago.

The charm is departed. It is often said that the power of liquidness and fluidity in Chaucer's verse was dependent upon a free, a licentious, dealing with language, such as is now impossible; upon a liberty, such as Burns too enjoyed, of making words like *neck*, *bird*, into a dissyllable by adding to them, and words like *cause*, *rhyme*, into a dissyllable by sounding the *e* mute. It is true that Chaucer's fluidity is conjoined with this liberty, and is admirably served by it; but we ought not to say that it was dependent upon it. It was dependent upon his talent. Other poets with a like liberty do not attain to the fluidity of Chaucer; Burns himself does not attain to it. Poets, again, who have a talent akin to Chaucer's, such as Shakespeare or Keats, have known how to attain to his fluidity without the like liberty. MATTHEW ARNOLD (1822–1888)

Walton's Book of Lives

There are no colours in the fairest sky
So fair as these. The feather, whence the pen
Was shaped that traced the lives of these good men,
Dropped from an Angel's wing. With moistened eye
We read of faith and purest charity
In Statesman, Priest, and humble Citizen:
Oh could we copy their mild virtues, then
What joy to live, what blessedness to die!
Methinks their very names shine still and bright;
Apart—like glow-worms on a summer night;
Or lonely tapers when from far they fling
A guiding ray; or seen—like stars on high,
Satellites burning in a lucid ring
Around meek Walton's heavenly memory.

WILLIAM WORDSWORTH (1770–1850)

Why Mince the Man's Meaning

Having with much ado got clear of Virgil, I have, in the next plac e to consider the genius of Lucretius, whom I have translated more happily in those parts of him which I undertook. If he was not of the best age of Roman poetry, he was at least of that which preceded it; and he himself refined it to that degree of perfection, both in the language and the thoughts, that he left an easy task to Virgil; who, as he succeeded him in time, so he copied his excellencies; for the method of the Georgics is plainly derived from him. . .

'Tis true, there is something, and that of some moment, to be objected against my englishing the *Nature of Love*, from the fourth book of Lucretius; and I can less easily answer why I translated it, than why I thus translated it. The objection arises from the obscenity of the subject; which is aggravated by the too lively and alluring delicacy of the verses. In the first place, without the least formality of an excuse, I own it pleased me: and let my enemies make the worst they can of this confession. I am not yet so secure from that passion, but that I want my author's antidotes against it. He has given the truest and most philosophical account, both of the disease and remedy, which I ever found in any author; for which reasons I translated him. But it will be asked why I turned him into this luscious English (for I will not give it a worse word). Instead of an answer, I would ask again of my supercilious adversaries whether I am not bound, when I translate an author, to do him all the right I can, and to translate him to the best advantage. If, to mince his meaning, which I am satisfied was honest and instructive, I had either omitted some part of which he said, or taken from the strength of his expression, I certainly had wronged him; and that freeness of thought and words being thus cashiered in my hands, he had no longer been Lucretius. If nothing of this kind be to be read, physicians must not study nature, anatomies must not be seen, and somewhat I could say of particular passages in books which, to avoid profaneness, I do not name. But the intention qualifies the act; and both mine and my author's were to instruct as well as please. 'Tis most certain that barefaced bawdry is the poorest pretence to wit imaginable.

JOHN DRYDEN (1631–1700)

Literary Conversation

On Saturday, July 30, Dr Johnson and I took a sculler at the Temple-stairs, and set out for Greenwich. I asked him if he really thought a knowledge of the Greek and Latin languages an essential requisite to a good education. JOHNSON. 'Most certainly, Sir; for those who know them have a very great advantage over those who do not. Nay, Sir, it is wonderful what a difference learning makes upon people even in the common intercourse of life, which does not appear to be much connected with it.' 'And yet, (said I) people go through the world very well, and carry on the business of life to good advantage, without learning.' JOHNSON. 'Why, Sir, that may be true in cases where learning cannot possibly be of any use; for instance, this boy rows us as well without learning, as if he could sing the song of Orpheus to the Argonauts, who were the first sailors.' He then called to the boy, 'What would you give, my lad, to know about the Argonauts?' 'Sir, (said the boy) I would give what I have.' Johnson was much pleased with his answer, and we gave him a double fare. Dr Johnson then turning to me, 'Sir, (said he) a desire of knowledge is the natural feeling of mankind; and every human being, whose mind is not debauched, will be willing to give all that he has, to get knowledge.'

We landed at the Old Swan, and walked to Billingsgate, where we took oars and moved smoothly along the silver Thames. It was a very fine day. We were entertained with the immense number and variety of ships that were lying at anchor, and with the beautiful country on each side of the river.

I talked of preaching, and of the great success which those called methodists have. JOHNSON. 'Sir, it is owing to their expressing themselves in a plain and familiar manner, which is the only way to do good to the common people, and which clergymen of genius and learning ought to do from a principle of duty, when it is suited to their congregations; a practice, for which they will be praised by men of sense. To insist against drunkenness as a crime, because it debases reason, the noblest faculty of man, would be of no service to the common people; but to tell them that they may die in a fit of drunkenness, and shew them how dreadful that would be, cannot fail to make a deep impression. Sir, when your Scotch clergy give up their homely manner, religion will soon decay in that country.' Let this observation, as Johnson meant it, be ever remembered.

I was much pleased to find myself with Johnson at Greenwich, which he celebrates in his 'London' as a favourite scene. I had the poem in my pocket, and read the lines aloud with enthusiasm:

> On Thames's banks in silent thought we stood,
> Where Greenwich smiles upon the silver flood:
> Pleas'd with the seat which gave ELIZA birth,
> We kneel, and kiss the consecrated earth.

He remarked that the structure of Greenwich hospital was too magnificent for a place of charity, and that its parts were too much detached, to make one great whole.

Buchanan, he said, was a very fine poet; and observed, that he was the first who complimented a lady, by ascribing to her the different perfections of the heathen goddesses; but that Johnson improved upon this, by making his lady, at the same time, free from their defects.

He dwelt upon Buchanan's elegant verses to Mary, Queen of Scots, *Nympha Caledoniæ*, &c. and spoke with enthusiasm of the beauty of Latin verse. 'All the modern languages (said he) cannot furnish so melodious a line as

Formosam resonare doces Amarillida silvas.

Afterwards he entered upon the business of the day, which was to give me his advice as to a course of study. And here I am to mention with much regret, that my record of what he said is miserably scanty. I recollect with admiration an animating blaze of eloquence, which roused every intellectual power in me to the highest pitch, but must have dazzled me so much, that my memory could not preserve the substance of his discourse; for the note which I find of it is no more than this:—'He ran over the grand scale of human knowledge; advised me to select some particular branch to excel in, but to acquire a little of every kind.' The defect of my minutes will be fully supplied by a long letter upon the subject, which he favoured me with, after I had been some time at Utrecht, and which my readers will have the pleasure to peruse in its proper place.

We walked in the evening in Greenwich Park. He asked me I suppose, by way of trying my disposition, 'Is not this very fine?' Having no exquisite relish of the beauties of Nature, and being more delighted with 'the busy hum of men,' I answered, 'Yes, Sir; but not equal to Fleet-street.' JOHNSON. 'You are right, Sir.'

I am aware that many of my readers may censure my want of taste. Let me, however, shelter myself under the authority of a very fashionable Baronet in the brilliant world, who, on his attention being called to the fragrance of a May evening in the country, observed, 'This may be very well; but for my part, I prefer the smell of a flambeau at the play-house.'

We staid so long at Greenwich, that our sail up the river, in our return to London, was by no means so pleasant as in the morning; for the night air was so cold that it made me shiver. I was the more sensible of it from having sat up all the night before recollecting and writing in my Journal what I thought worthy of preservation; an exertion, which, during the first part of my acquaintance with Johnson,

I frequently made. I remember having sat up four nights in one week, without being much incommoded in the day time.

Johnson, whose robust frame was not in the least affected by the cold, scolded me, as if my shivering had been a paltry effeminacy, saying, 'Why do you shiver?' Sir William Scott, of the Commons, told me, that when he complained of a head-ach in the post-chaise, as they were travelling together to Scotland, Johnson treated him in the same manner: 'At your age, Sir, I had no head-ach.' It is not easy to make allowance for sensations in others, which we ourselves have not at the time. We must all have experienced how very differently we are affected by the complaints of our neighbours, when we are well and when we are ill. In full health, we can scarcely believe that they suffer much; so faint is the image of pain upon our imagination: when softened by sickness, we readily sympathize with the sufferings of others.

We concluded the day at the Turk's Head coffee-house very socially. He was pleased to listen to a particular account which I gave him of my family, and of its hereditary estate, as to the extent and population of which he asked questions, and made calculations; recommending, at the same time, a liberal kindness to the tenantry, as people over whom the proprietor was placed by Providence. He took delight in hearing my description of the romantick seat of my ancestors. 'I must be there, Sir, (said he) and we will live in the old castle; and if there is not a room in it remaining, we will build one.' I was highly flattered, but could scarcely indulge a hope that Auchinleck would indeed be honoured by his presence, and celebrated by a description, as it afterwards was, in his 'Journey to the Western Islands.'

After we had again talked of my setting out for Holland, he said, 'I must see thee out of England; I will accompany you to Harwich.' I could not find words to express what I felt upon this unexpected and very great mark of his affectionate regard.

JAMES BOSWELL (1740–1795)

The Father of English Criticism

Dryden may be properly considered as the father of English criticism, as the writer who first taught us to determine upon principles the merit of composition. Of our former poets, the greatest dramatist wrote without rules, conducted through life and nature by a genius that rarely misled, and rarely deserted him. Of the rest, those who knew the laws of propriety had neglected to teach them...

The *Dialogue on the Drama* was one of his first essays of criticism, written when he was yet a timorous candidate for reputation, and therefore laboured with that diligence which he might allow himself somewhat to remit, when his name gave sanction to his positions, and his awe of the public was abated, partly by custom, and partly by success. It will not be easy to find, in all the opulence of our language, a treatise so artfully variegated with successive representations of opposite probabilities, so enlivened with imagery, so brightened with illustrations. His portraits of the English dramatists are wrought with great spirit and diligence. The account of Shakespeare may stand as a perpetual model of encomiastic criticism; exact without minuteness, and lofty without exaggeration. The praise lavished by Longinus, on the attestation of the heroes of Marathon, by Demosthenes, fades away before it. In a few lines is exhibited a character, so extensive in its comprehension, and so curious in its limitations, that nothing can be added, diminished, or reformed; nor can the editors and admirers of Shakespeare, in all their emulation of reverence, boast of much more than of having diffused and paraphrased this epitome of excellence, of having changed Dryden's gold for baser metal, of lower value though of greater bulk.

In this, and in all his other essays on the same subject, the criticism of Dryden is the criticism of a poet; not a dull collection of theorems, nor a rude detection of faults, which perhaps the censor was not able to have committed; but a gay and vigorous dissertation, where delight is mingled with instruction, and where the author proves his right of judgment by his power of performance.

SAMUEL JOHNSON (1709–1784)

Pope and Dryden Compared

[Pope] professed to have learned his poetry from Dryden, whom, whenever an opportunity was presented, he praised through his whole life with unvaried liberality; and perhaps his character may receive some illustration, if he be compared with his master.

Integrity of understanding and nicety of discernment were not allotted in a less proportion to Dryden than to Pope. The rectitude of Dryden's mind was sufficiently shown by the dismission of his poetical prejudices, and the rejection of unnatural thoughts and rugged numbers. But Dryden never desired to apply all the judgment that he had. He wrote, and professed to write, merely for the people; and when he pleased others, he contented himself. He spent no time in struggles to rouse latent powers; he never attempted to make that better which was already good, nor often to mend what he must have known to be faulty. He wrote, as he tells us, with very little consideration; when occasion or necessity called upon him, he poured out what the present moment happened to supply, and, when once it had passed the press, ejected it from his mind; for when he had no pecuniary interest, he had no further solicitude.

Pope was not content to satisfy; he desired to excel, and therefore always endeavoured to do his best: he did not court the candour, but dared the judgment of his reader, and, expecting no indulgence from others, he showed none to himself. He examined lines and words with minute and punctilious observation, and retouched every part with indefatigable diligence, till he had left nothing to be forgiven.

For this reason he kept his pieces very long in his hands, while he considered and reconsidered them. The only poems which can be supposed to have been written with such regard to the times as might hasten their publication were the two satires of *Thirty-eight*; of which Dodsley told me that they were brought to him by the author, that they might be fairly copied. 'Almost every line,' he said, 'was then written twice over; I gave him a clean transcript, which he sent some time afterwards to me for the press, with almost every line written twice over a second time.'

His declaration that his care for his works ceased at their publication was not strictly true. His parental attention never abandoned them; what he found amiss in the first edition, he silently corrected in those that followed. He appears to have revised the Iliad, and freed it from some of its imperfections; and the *Essay on Criticism* received many improvements after its first appearance. It will seldom be found that he altered without adding clearness, elegance, or vigour. Pope had perhaps the judgment of Dryden; but Dryden certainly wanted the diligence of Pope.

In acquired knowledge, the superiority must be allowed to Dryden, whose education was more scholastic, and who before he became an author had been allowed more time for study, with better means of information. His mind has a larger range, and he collects his images and illustrations from a more extensive circumference of science. Dryden knew more of man in his general nature, and Pope in his local manners. The notions of Dryden were formed by comprehensive speculation, and those of Pope by minute attention. There is more dignity in the knowledge of Dryden, and more certainty in that of Pope.

Poetry was not the sole praise of either; for both excelled likewise in prose; but Pope did not borrow his prose from his predecessor. The style of Dryden is capricious and varied; that of Pope is cautious and uniform. Dryden observes the motions of his own mind; Pope constrains his mind to his own rules of composition. Dryden is sometimes vehement and rapid; Pope is always smooth, uniform, and gentle. Dryden's page is a natural field, rising into inequalities, and diversified by the varied exuberance of abundant vegetation; Pope's is a velvet lawn, shaven by the scythe, and levelled by the roller.

Of genius, that power which constitutes a poet; that quality without which judgment is cold, and knowledge is inert; that energy which collects, combines, amplifies, and animates; the superiority must, with some hesitation, be allowed to Dryden. It is not to be inferred that of this poetical vigour Pope had only a little, because Dryden had more; for every other writer since Milton must give place to Pope; and even of Dryden it must be said, that, if he has brighter paragraphs, he has not better poems. Dryden's performances were always hasty, either excited by some external occasion, or extorted by domestic necessity; he composed without consideration, and published without correction. What his mind could supply at call, or gather in one excursion, was all that he sought, and all that he gave. The dilatory caution of Pope enabled him to condense his sentiments, to multiply his images, and to accumulate all that study might produce or chance might supply. If the flights of Dryden therefore are higher, Pope continues longer on the wing. If of Dryden's fire the blaze is brighter, of Pope's the heat is more regular and constant. Dryden often surpasses expectation, and Pope never falls below it. Dryden is read with frequent astonishment, and Pope with perpetual delight.   SAMUEL JOHNSON (1709–1784)

Mr Gibbon is pleased to Quarrel!

Lo, there is just appeared a truly classic work: a history, not majestic like Livy, nor compressed like Tacitus; not stamped with character like Clarendon; perhaps not so deep as Robertson's 'Scotland,' but a thousand degrees above his 'Charles'; not pointed like Voltaire, but as accurate as he is inexact; modest as he is *tranchant* and sly as Montesquieu without being so *recherché*. The style is as smooth as a Flemish picture, and the muscles are concealed and only for natural uses, not exaggerated like Michael Angelo's to show the painter's skill in anatomy; nor composed of the limbs of clowns of different nations, like

Dr Johnson's heterogeneous monsters. This book is Mr Gibbon's 'History of the Decline and Fall of the Roman Empire.' He is son of a foolish alderman, is a Member of Parliament, and called a whimsical one because he votes variously as his opinion leads him; and his first production was in French, in which language he shines too. I know him a little, never suspected the extent of his talents, for he is perfectly modest, or I want penetration, which I know too, but I intend to know him a great deal more—there! there is food for your residence at York.

You will be diverted to hear that Mr Gibbon has quarrelled with me. He lent me his second volume in the middle of November. I returned it with a most civil panegyric. He came for more incense, I gave it, but alas! with too much sincerity; I added, 'Mr Gibbon, I am sorry *you* should have pitched on so disgusting a subject as the Constantinopolitan History. There is so much of the Arians and Eunomians, and semi-Pelagians; and there is such a strange contrast between Roman and Gothic manners, and so little harmony between a Consul Sabinus and a Ricimer, Duke of the palace, that though you have written the story as well as it could be written, I fear few will have patience to read it.' He coloured; all his round features squeezed themselves into sharp angles; he screwed up his button-mouth, and rapping his snuff-box, said, 'It had never been put together before'—*so well* he meant to add —but gulped it. He meant *so well* certainly, for Tillemont, whom he quotes in every page, has done the very thing. Well, from that hour to this I have never seen him, though he used to call once or twice a week; nor has sent me the third volume, as he promised. I well knew his vanity, even about his ridiculous face and person, but thought he had too much sense to avow it so palpably. The 'History' is admirably written, especially in the characters of Julian and Athanasius, in both which he has piqued himself on impartiality—but the style is far less sedulously enamelled than the first volume, and there is flattery to the Scots that would choke anything but Scots, who can gobble feathers as readily as thistles. David Hume and Adam Smith are *legislators* and sages, but the homage is intended for his patron, Lord Loughborough.

HORACE WALPOLE (1717-1797)

A Tun of Man

Falstaff's wit is an emanation of a fine constitution; an exuberance of good-humour and good-nature; an overflowing of his love of laughter and good-fellowship; a giving vent to his heart's ease, and over-contentment with himself and others. He would not be in character, if he were not so fat as he is; for there is the greatest keeping in the boundless luxury of his imagination and the pampered self-indulgence of his physical appetites. He manures and nourishes his mind with jests, as he does his body with sack and sugar. He carves out his jokes, as he would a capon or a haunch of venison, where there is *cut and come again*; and pours out upon them the oil of gladness. His tongue drops fatness, and in the chambers of his brain 'it snows of meat and drink.' He keeps up perpetual holiday and open house, and we live with him in a round of invitations to a rump and dozen.—Yet we are not to suppose that he was a mere sensualist. All this is as much in imagination as in reality. His sensuality does not engross and stupify his other faculties, but 'ascends me into the brain, clears away all the dull, crude vapours that environ it, and makes it full of nimble, fiery, and delectable shapes.' His imagination keeps up the ball after his senses have done with it. He seems to have even a greater enjoyment of the freedom from restraint, of good cheer, of his ease, of his vanity, in the ideal exaggerated description which he gives of them, than in fact. He never fails to enrich his discourse with allusions to eating and drinking, but we never see him at table. He carries his own larder about with him, and he is himself 'a tun of man.' His pulling out the bottle in the field of battle is a joke to shew his contempt for glory accompanied with danger, his systematic adherence to his Epicurean philosophy in the most trying circumstances.

Again, such is his deliberate exaggeration of his own vices, that it does not seem quite certain whether the account of his hostess's bill, found in his pocket, with such an out-of-the-way charge for capons and sack with only one halfpenny-worth of bread, was not put there by himself as a trick to humour the jest upon his favourite propensities, and as a conscious caricature of himself. He is represented as a liar, a braggart, a coward, a glutton, etc. and yet we are not offended but delighted with him; for he is all these as much to amuse others as to gratify himself. He openly assumes all these characters to shew the humourous part of them. The unrestrained indulgence of his own ease, appetites, and convenience, has neither malice nor hypocrisy in it. In a word, he is an actor in himself almost as much as upon the stage, and we no more object to the character of Falstaff in a moral point of view than we should think of bringing an excellent comedian, who should represent him to the life, before one of the police offices.

We only consider the number of pleasant lights in which he puts certain foibles (the more pleasant as they are opposed to the received rules and necessary restraints of society) and do not trouble ourselves about the consequences resulting from them, for no mischievous consequences do result. Sir John is old as well as fat, which gives a melancholy retrospective tinge to the character; and by the disparity between his inclinations and his capacity for enjoyment, makes it still more ludicrous and fantastical.

The secret of Falstaff's wit is for the most part a masterly presence of mind, an absolute self-possession, which nothing can disturb. His repartees are involuntary suggestions of his self-love; instinctive evasions of every thing that threatens to interrupt the career of his triumphant jollity and self-complacency. His very size floats him out of all his difficulties in a sea of rich conceits; and he turns round on the pivot of his convenience, with every occasion and at a moment's warning. His natural repugnance to every unpleasant thought or circumstance, of itself makes light of objections, and provokes the most extravagant and licentious answers in his own justification. His indifference to truth puts no check upon his invention, and the more improbable and unexpected his contrivances are, the more happily does he seem to be delivered of them, the anticipation of their effect acting as a stimulus to the gaiety of his fancy. The success of one adventurous sally gives him spirits to undertake another: he deals always in round numbers, and his exaggerations and excuses are 'open, palpable, monstrous as the father that begets them.'

WILLIAM HAZLITT (1778–1830)

A Painter Dies Young

Having spoken upon these questions of art, possibly at greater length than was necessary, I will now return to Raphael. A great friend of his, Bernardo Divizio, cardinal of Bibbiena, had for many years urged him to take a wife. Raphael had not definitely refused, but had temporised, saying he would wait for three or four years. At the end of this time, when he did not expect it, the cardinal reminded him of his promise. Feeling obliged to keep his word, Raphael accepted a niece of the cardinal for wife. But being very ill-content with this arrangement, he kept putting things off, so that many months passed without the marriage taking place. This was not done without a purpose, because he had served the court so many years, and Leo was his debtor for a good sum, so that he had received an intimation that, on completing the room which he was doing, the Pope would give him the red hat for his labours and ability, as it was proposed to create a good number of cardinals, some of less merit than Raphael.

Meanwhile Raphael continued his secret pleasures beyond all measure. After an unusually wild debauch he returned home with a severe fever, and the doctors believed him to have caught a chill. As he did not confess the cause of his disorder the doctors imprudently let blood, thus enfeebling him when he needed restoratives. Accordingly he made his will, first sending his mistress out of the house, like a Christian, leaving her the means to live honestly. He then divided his things among his pupils, Giulio Romano, of whom he was always very fond, Gio. Francesco of Florence, called 'il Fattore,' and some priest of Urbino, a relation. He ordained and left a provision that one of the antique tabernacles in S. Maria Rotonda should be restored with new stones, and an altar erected with a marble statue of the Madonna. This was chosen for his tomb after his death. He left all his possessions to Giulio and Gio. Francesco, making M. Baldassare da Pescia, then the Pope's datary, his executor. Having confessed and shown penitence, he finished the course of his life on the day of his birth, Good Friday, aged thirty-seven. We may believe that his soul adorns heaven as his talent has embellished the earth. At the head of the dead man, in the room where he worked, they put the Transfiguration, which he had done for the Cardinal de' Medici. The sight of the dead and of this living work filled all who saw them with poignant sorrow. The picture was placed by the cardinal in S. Pietro a Montorio, at the high altar, and was always prized for its execution. The body received honoured burial, as befitted so noble a spirit, for there was not an artist who did not grieve or who failed to accompany it to the tomb.

GIORGIO VASARI (1511–1574)

A Carver Sculptor

This day, I first acquainted his Majesty with that incomparable young man, Gibbon, whom I had lately met with in an obscure place by mere accident, as I was walking near a poor solitary thatched house, in a field in our parish, near Sayes Court. I found him shut in; but looking in at the window, I perceived him carving that large cartoon, or crucifix, of Tintoretto, a copy of which I had myself brought from Venice, where the original painting remains. I asked if I might enter; he opened the door civilly to me, and I saw him about such a work as for the curiosity of handling, drawing, and studious exactness, I never had before seen in all my travels. I questioned him why he worked in such an obscure and lonesome place; he told me it was that he might apply himself to his profession without interruption, and wondered not a little how I found him out. I asked if he was unwilling to be made known to some great man, for that I believed it might turn to his profit; he answered, he was yet but a beginner, but would not be sorry to sell off that piece; on demanding the price, he said £100. In good earnest, the very frame was worth the money, there being nothing in nature so tender and delicate as the flowers and festoons about it, and yet the work was very strong; in the piece was more than one hundred figures of men, &c. I found he was likewise musical, and very civil, sober, and discreet in his discourse. There was only an old woman in the house. So, desiring leave to visit him sometimes, I went away.

Of this young artist, together with my manner of finding him out, I acquainted the King, and begged that he would give me leave to bring him and his work to Whitehall, for that I would adventure my reputation with his Majesty that he had never seen anything approach it, and that he would be exceedingly pleased, and employ him. The King said he would himself go see him. This was the first notice his Majesty ever had of Mr Gibbon.

I caused Mr Gibbon to bring to Whitehall his excellent piece of carving, where being come, I advertised his Majesty, who asked me where it was; I told him in Sir Richard Browne's (my father-in-law) chamber, and that if it pleased his Majesty to appoint whither it should be brought, being large and though of wood heavy, I would take care for it. 'No,' says the King, 'show me the way, I'll go to Sir Richard's chamber,' which he immediately did, walking along the entries after me; as far as the ewry, till he came up into the room, where I also lay. No sooner was he entered and cast his eye on the work, but he was astonished at the curiosity of it; and having considered it a long time, and discoursed with Mr Gibbon, whom I brought to kiss his hand, he commanded it should be immediately carried to the Queen's side to show her. It was carried up into her bed-chamber, where she and the King looked on and admired it again; the King, being called away, left us with the Queen, believing she would have bought it, it being a crucifix; but, when his Majesty was gone, a French peddling woman, one Madame de Boord, who used to bring petticoats and fans, and baubles, out of France to the ladies, began to find fault with several things in the work, which she understood no more than an ass, or a monkey, so as in a kind of indignation, I caused the person who brought it to carry it back to the chamber, finding the Queen so much governed by an ignorant Frenchwoman, and this incomparable artist had his labour only for his pains, which not a little displeased me; and he was fain to send it down to his cottage again; he not long after sold it for 80*l.*, though well worth 100*l.*, without the frame, to Sir George Viner.

His Majesty's Surveyor, Mr Wren, faithfully promised me to employ him. I having also bespoke his Majesty for his work at Windsor, which my friend, Mr May, the architect there, was going to alter, and repair universally; for, on the next day, I had a fair opportunity of talking to his Majesty about it, in the lobby next the Queen's side, where I presented him with some sheets of my history. I thence walked with him through St James's Park to the garden, where I both saw and heard a very familiar discourse between . . . . . and Mrs Nelly, as they called an impudent comedian, she looking out of her garden on a terrace at the top of the wall, and . . . . . standing on the green walk under it. I was heartily sorry at this scene. Thence the King walked to the Duchess of Cleveland, another lady of pleasure, and curse of our nation.

JOHN EVELYN (1620–1706)

A Poet's Illustrator

'Since we are talking of Mephistopheles,' continued Goethe, 'I will show you something Coudray has brought me from Paris. What do you think of it?'

He laid before me a lithograph, representing the scene where Faust and Mephistopheles, on their way to free Margaret from prison, are rushing by the gallows at night on two horses. Faust rides a black horse; which gallops with all its might, and seems, like its rider, afraid of the spectres under the gallows. They ride so fast that Faust can scarcely keep his seat; the wind has blown off his cap, which, fastened by straps about his neck, flies far behind him. He has turned his fearful inquiring face to Mephistopheles, to whom he listens. Mephistopheles, on the contrary, sits undisturbed, like a being of a higher order: he rides no living horse, for he loves not what is living; indeed, he does not need it, for his will moves him with the swiftness he requires. He has a horse merely because he must look as if he were riding, and it has been quite enough for him to take a beast that is a mere bag of bones, from the first field he came to. It is of a bright colour, and seems to be phosphorescent in the darkness of night. It is neither bridled nor saddled. The supernatural rider sits easily and negligently, with his face turned towards Faust in conversation. The opposing element of air does not exist for him; neither he nor his horse feels anything of it. Not a hair of either is stirred.

We expressed much pleasure at this ingenious composition. 'I confess,' said Goethe, 'I myself did not think it out so perfectly. Here is another. What say you to this?'

I saw a representation of the wild drinking scene in Auerbach's cellar, at the all-important moment when the wine sparkles up into flames and the brutality of the drinkers is shown in the most varied ways. All is passion and movement; Mephistopheles alone maintains his usual composure. The wild cursing and screaming, and the drawn knife of the man who stands next him, are to him nothing. He has seated himself on a corner of the table, dangling his legs. His upraised finger is enough to subdue flame and passion.

The longer this excellent design was looked at, the greater seemed the intelligence of the artist; who made no figure like another, but in each one expressed some different part of the action.

'M. Delacroix,' said Goethe, 'is a man of great talent, who found in *Faust* his proper aliment. The French censure his wildness, but it suits him well here. He will, I hope, go through all *Faust*, and I anticipate a special pleasure from the witches' kitchen and the scenes on the Brocken. We can see he has a good knowledge of life, for which a city like Paris has given him the best opportunity.'

I observed that these designs greatly conduce to the comprehension of a poem.

'Undoubtedly,' said Goethe; 'for the more perfect imagination of such an artist constrains us to think the situations as beautiful as he conceived them himself. And if I must confess that M. Delacroix has in some scenes surpassed my own notions, how much more will the reader find all in full life and surpassing his imagination!'

JOHANN ECKERMANN (1792–1854)

Artist and Model

No sooner had I dismounted than one of those good folks who take pleasure in seeing one's misfortunes, came to tell me that Pagolo Micceri had taken a house for that little baggage Caterina and her mother, and that he was always paying her visits; also that when he spoke of me, it was with contempt, as: 'Benvenuto set the cat to watch the cream, and thought it would not lap it. Now all he can do is to swagger, thinking I am afraid of him. But I have girt myself with this sword and this dagger, to let him see that mine can cut as well as his; that I am a Florentine as much as he, and of the Micceri, a much better house than the Cellini.' The rascal's story had such an effect on me that I was seized with a sudden fever—fever it was: I do not speak in figures. And this mad passion might have brought me to my death, had not I given vent to it as the opportunity occurred, and according to my instinct of the moment. So I told my Ferrarese workman Chioccia to come with me, and ordered a servant to follow with my horse.

Having reached the villain's house, we found the door ajar. I went in and saw him with his sword and dagger by his side, seated on a chest, with his arm round Caterina's neck. Just as I came in, I heard him and her mother joking about my affairs. Pushing the door open, I seized my sword and pointed it at his throat, giving him no time to bethink himself that he too was armed. 'Base coward!' I shouted. 'Recommend yourself to God, for you are a dead man!' Too terrified to move, he called out thrice, 'O mother mine, help me!' I had meant to kill him on the spot; but hearing him utter these foolish words, half my anger passed away.

Meanwhile I had ordered my apprentice, Chioccia, not to let either the mother or daughter out of the house; for when I had punished the man, I meant to do as much to the two worthless jades. So I kept the point of my sword at his throat, now and then giving him a little prick, and raining threats on him the while. But when I saw that he did nothing to defend himself, I did not know what more to do; and it looked as if I might go on threatening him for ever. So another idea came into my head. What better could I do than force them to marry? I could wait for my revenge. Having made up my mind, I said, 'Take that ring you have on your finger, coward, and marry her, that I may pay you out as you deserve.' He answered at once, 'If only you do not kill me, I will do anything you please.' Then I said, 'Put that ring on her finger.' I withdrew the sword a little from his throat, and he did as I told him. 'This is not enough,' I added. 'I wish two notaries to be fetched, that it may be a real contract.' I told Chioccia to go for the notaries; and then, turning to Caterina and her mother, and speaking in French, I said, 'Notaries and witnesses have been sent for. The first of you who lets out this business I will kill; indeed, I will kill the three of you. Keep that in mind.' To Pagolo I said in Italian, 'If you hinder my purpose, at the least word I shall tear your guts out with my dagger.'

He answered, 'If you only do not kill me, I will do whatever you like.'
The notaries and witnesses came and drew up the contract in proper
form. Then the heat of the fever passed out of me; and after I had paid
the notaries' fees I took myself off. . .

If I did not own that in some of these incidents I did wrong, my
account of the others, in which I know I did well, would be suspect.
So I own I made a mistake in revenging myself so violently on Pagolo
Micceri. Had I known him to be such a weak creature, it would never
have come into my head to shame him by such a vengeance. For it
was not enough for me that I had made him take to wife this wicked
hussy. Over and above that, to complete my scheme of vengeance, I
made her pose to me as a model, naked, for thirty soldi a day. I paid
her in advance and fed her well; but I used her for my pleasure out of
revenge, and then cast this insult in her husband's teeth and her own.
Moreover, I forced her to pose in an uncomfortable position hour after
hour, which annoyed her as much as it delighted me; for her form was
very lovely, and did me much credit.

BENVENUTO CELLINI (1500–1571)

The Picturesque and the Beautiful

'I perceive,' said Mr Milestone, after they had walked a few paces,
'these grounds have never been touched by the finger of taste.'

'The place is quite a wilderness,' said Squire Headlong: 'for, during
the latter part of my father's life, while I was *finishing* my *education*, he
troubled himself about nothing but the cellar, and suffered everything
else to go to rack and ruin. A mere wilderness, as you see, even now in
December; but in summer a complete nursery of briers, a forest of
thistles, a plantation of nettles, without any live stock but goats, that
have eaten up all the bark of the trees. Here you see is the pedestal of
a statue, with only half a leg and four toes remaining: there were many
here once. When I was a boy, I used to sit every day on the shoulders
of Hercules: what became of *him* I have never been able to ascertain.
Neptune has been lying these seven years in the dust-hole; Atlas had
his head knocked off to fit him for propping a shed; and only the day
before yesterday we fished Bacchus out of the horse-pond.

'My dear sir,' said Mr Milestone, 'accord me your permission to
wave the wand of enchantment over your grounds. The rocks shall be
blown up, the trees shall be cut down, the wilderness and all its goats
shall vanish like mist. Pagodas and Chinese bridges, gravel walks and

shrubberies, bowling-greens, canals, and clumps of larch, shall rise upon its ruins. One age, sir, has brought to light the treasures of ancient learning; a second has penetrated into the depths of metaphysics; a third has brought to perfection the science of astronomy; but it was reserved for the exclusive genius of the present times, to invent the noble art of picturesque gardening, which has given, as it were, a new tint to the complexion of nature, and a new outline to the physiognomy of the universe!'

'Give me leave,' said Sir Patrick O'Prism, 'to take an exception to that same. Your system of levelling, and trimming, and clipping, and docking, and clumping, and polishing, and cropping, and shaving, destroys all the beautiful intricacies of natural luxuriance, and all the graduated harmonies of light and shade, melting into one another, as you see them on that rock over yonder. I never saw one of your improved places, as you call them, and which are nothing but big bowling-greens, like sheets of green paper, with a parcel of round clumps scattered over them, like so many spots of ink, flicked at random out of a pen, and a solitary animal here and there looking as if it were lost, that I did not think it was for all the world like Hounslow Heath, thinly sprinkled over with bushes and highwaymen.'

'Sir,' said Mr Milestone, 'you will have the goodness to make a distinction between the picturesque and the beautiful.'

'Will I?' said Sir Patrick, 'och! but I won't. For what is beautiful? That what pleases the eye. And what pleases the eye? Tints variously broken and blended. Now, tints variously broken and blended constitute the picturesque.'

'Allow me,' said Mr Gall. 'I distinguish the picturesque and the beautiful, and I add to them, in the laying out of grounds, a third and distinct character, which I call *unexpectedness*.'

'Pray, sir,' said Mr Milestone, 'by what name do you distinguish this character, when a person walks round the grounds for the second time?'

THOMAS LOVE PEACOCK (1785-1866)

The Genius of Jewry

'You never observe a great intellectual movement in Europe in which the Jews do not greatly participate. The first Jesuits were Jews: that mysterious Russian diplomacy which so alarms Western Europe is organised and principally carried on by Jews; that mighty revolution which is at this moment preparing in Germany, and which will be in fact a second and greater Reformation, and of which so little is as yet known in England, is entirely developing under the auspices of Jews, who almost monopolise the professorial chairs of Germany. Neander, the founder of Spiritual Christianity, and who is Regius Professor of Divinity in the University of Berlin, is a Jew. Benary, equally famous, and in the same university, is a Jew. Wehl, the Arabic Professor of Heidelberg, is a Jew. Years ago, when I was in Palestine, I met a German student who was accumulating materials for the history of Christianity, and studying the genius of the place; a modest and learned man. It was Wehl; then unknown, since become the first Arabic scholar of the day, and the author of the life of Mahomet. But for the German professors of this race, their name is legion. I think there are more than ten at Berlin alone.

'I told you just now that I was going up to town to-morrow, because I always made it a rule to interpose when affairs of state were on the carpet. Otherwise, I never interfere. I hear of peace and war in newspapers, but I am never alarmed, except when I am informed that the sovereigns want treasure; then I know that monarchs are serious.

'A few years back we were applied to by Russia. Now there has been no friendship between the Court of St Petersburg and my family. It has Dutch connections which have generally supplied it, and our representations in favour of the Polish Hebrews, a numerous race, but the most suffering and degraded of all the tribes, has not been very agreeable to the czar. However circumstances drew to an approximation between the Romanoffs and the Sidonias. I resolved to go myself to St Petersburg. I had on my arrival an interview with the Russian Minister of Finance, Count Cancrin; I beheld the son of a Lithuanian Jew. The loan was connected with the affairs of Spain; I resolved on repairing to Spain from Russia. I travelled without intermission. I had an audience immediately on my arrival with the Spanish minister, Senor Mendizabel; I beheld one like myself, the son of a Nuovo Christiano, a Jew of Arragon. In consequence of what transpired at Madrid, I went straight to Paris to consult the President of the French Council; I beheld the son of a French Jew, a hero, an imperial marshal, and very properly so, for who should be military heroes if not those who worship the Lord of Hosts?'

'And is Soult a Hebrew!'

'Yes, and others of the French marshals, and the most famous; Massena, for example; his real name was Manasseh: but to my anecdote. The consequence of our consultations was that some northern power should be applied to in a friendly and mediative capacity. We fixed on Prussia, and the President of the Council made an application to the Prussian minister, who attended a few days after our conference. Count Arnim entered the cabinet, and I beheld a Prussian Jew. So you see, my dear Coningsby, that the world is governed by very different personages to what is imagined by those who are not behind the scenes.'

'You startle, and deeply interest me.'

'You must study physiology, my dear child. Pure races of Caucasus may be persecuted, but they cannot be despised, except by the brutal ignorance of some mongrel breed, that brandishes faggots and howls exterminations, but is itself exterminated without persecutions by that irresistible law of Nature which is fatal to curs.'

'But I come also from Caucasus,' said Coningsby.

'Verily; and thank your Creator for such a destiny: and your race is sufficiently pure. You come from the shores of the Northern Sea, land of the blue eye, and the golden hair, and the frank brow; 'tis a famous breed, with whom we Arabs have contended long; from whom we have much suffered; but these Goths, and Saxons, and Normans, were doubtless great men.'

'But so favoured by Nature, why has not your race produced great poets, great orators, great writers?'

'Favoured by Nature and by Nature's God we produced the lyre of David; we gave you Isaiah and Ezekiel; they are our Olynthians, our Philippics. Favoured by Nature we still remain: but in exact proportion as we have been favoured by Nature we have been persecuted by man. After a thousand struggles; after acts of heroic courage that Rome has never equalled; deeds of divine patriotism that Athens, and Sparta, and Carthage have never excelled; we have endured fifteen hundred years of supernatural slavery, during which, every device that can degrade or destroy man has been the destiny that we have sustained and baffled. The Hebrew child has entered adolescence only to learn that he was the pariah of that ungrateful Europe that owes to him the best part of its laws, a fine portion of its literature, all its religion. Great poets require a public; we have been content with the immortal melodies that we sung more than two thousand years ago by the waters of Babylon and wept. They record our triumphs; they solace our affliction. Great orators are the creatures of popular assemblies; we were permitted only by stealth to meet even in our temples. And as for great writers the catalogue is not blank. What are all the schoolmen, Aquinas himself, to Maimonides; and as for modern philosophy, all springs from Spinoza.

'But the passionate and creative genius that is the nearest link to divinity, and which no human tyranny can destroy, though it can divert it; that should have stirred the hearts of nations by its inspired sympathy, or governed senates by its burning eloquence, has found a medium for its expression, to which, in spite of your prejudices and your evil passions, you have been obliged to bow. The ear, the voice, the fancy teeming with combinations, the imagination fervent with picture and emotion, that came from Caucasus and which we have preserved unpolluted, have endowed us with almost the exclusive privilege of MUSIC; that science of harmonious sounds which the ancients recognised as most divine, and deified in the person of their most beautiful creation. I speak not of the past, though were I to enter into the history of the lords of melody, you would find it the annals of Hebrew genius. But at this moment even, musical Europe is ours. There is not a company of singers, not an orchestra in a single capital, that are not crowded with our children under the feigned names which they adopt to conciliate the dark aversion which your posterity will some day disclaim with shame and disgust. Almost every great composer, skilled musician, almost every voice that ravishes you with its transporting strains, spring from our tribes. The catalogue is too vast to enumerate; too illustrious to dwell for a moment on secondary names, however eminent. Enough for us that the three great creative minds to whose exquisite inventions all nations at this moment yield; Rossini, Meyerbeer, Mendelssohn; are of Hebrew race: and little do your men of fashion, your 'muscadins' of Paris and your dandies of London, as they thrill into raptures at the notes of a Pasta or a Grisi, little do they suspect that they are offering their homage to the sweet singers of Israel!'

LORD BEACONSFIELD (1804–1881)

The Sphynx

And near the Pyramids, more wondrous and more awful than all else in the land of Egypt, there sits the lonely Sphynx. Comely the creature is, but the comeliness is not of this world: the once worshipped beast is a deformity and a monster to this generation; and yet you can see that those lips, so thick and heavy, were fashioned according to some ancient mould of beauty—some mould of beauty now forgotten—

forgotten because that Greece drew forth Cytherea from the flashing foam of the Ægean, and in her image created new forms of beauty, and made it a law among men that the short and proudly-wreathed lip should stand for the sign and the main condition of loveliness through all generations to come. Yet still there lives on the race of those who were beautiful in the fashion of the elder world; and Christian girls of Coptic blood will look on you with the sad, serious gaze, and kiss you your charitable hand with the big pouting lips of the very Sphynx.

Laugh and mock if you will at the worship of stone idols; but mark ye this, ye breakers of images, that in one regard, the stone idol bears awful semblance of Deity—unchangefulness in the midst of change—the same seeming will and intent for ever and ever inexorable! Upon ancient dynasties of Ethiopian and Egyptian kings—upon Greek and Roman, upon Arab and Ottoman conquerors—upon Napoleon dreaming of an Eastern empire—upon battle and pestilence—upon the ceaseless misery of the Egyptian race—upon keen-eyed travellers—Herodotus yesterday, and Warburton to-day—upon all and more this unworldly Sphynx has watched, and watched like a Providence with the same earnest eyes, and the same sad, tranquil mien. And we, we shall die, and Islam will wither away; and the Englishman, straining far over to hold his loved India, will plant a firm foot on the banks of the Nile and sit in the seats of the Faithful, and still that sleepless rock will lie watching and watching the works of the new busy race, with those same sad earnest eyes, and the same tranquil mien everlasting. You dare not mock at the Sphynx.

ALEXANDER WILLIAM KINGLAKE (1809–1891)

Washing for Gold

Went and waited on the Dooty, and presented him with five bars of amber, and two of beads, requesting his permission to go and look at the gold-mines, which I understood were in the vicinity. Having obtained his permission, I hired a woman to go with me, and agreed to pay her a bar of amber if she would show me a grain of gold. We travelled about half a mile west of the town, when we came to a small meadow spot of about four or five acres' extent, in which were several holes dug resembling wells. They were in general about ten or twelve feet deep; towards the middle of the meadow spot the holes were deepest, and shallower towards the sides. Their number was about thirty, besides many old ones which had sunk down. Near the mouths of these pits were several other shallow pits, lined with clay, and full of rain-water: between the mine pits and these wash pits laid several heaps of sandy gravel. On the top of each was a stone; some of the stones white, others red, others black, etc. These serve to distinguish each person's property. I could see nothing peculiar in this gravel; some silicious pebbles as large as a pigeon's egg, pieces of white and reddish quartz, iron stone, and killow, and a soft friable yellow stone, which crumbled to pieces by the fingers, were the chief minerals that I could distinguish. Besides the above there was a great portion of sand, and a yellow earth resembling *till*.

The woman took about half a pound of gravel with one hand from the heap, which I suppose belonged to her; and having put it into a large calabash, threw a little water on it with a small calabash; which two calabashes are all that are necessary for washing gold. The quantity of water was only sufficient to cover the sand about one inch. She then crumbled the sand to pieces, and mixt it with the water; this she did not in a rotatory manner, but by pulling her hands towards herself.

She then threw out all the large pebbles, looking on the ground where she threw them, for fear of throwing out a piece of gold. Having done this, she gave the sand and water a rotatory motion, so as to make a part of the sand and water fly over the brim of the calabash. While she did this with her *right* hand, with her *left* she threw out of the centre of the vortex a portion of sand and water at every revolution. She then put in a little fresh water, and as the quantity of sand was now much diminished, she held the calabash in an oblique direction, and made the sand move slowly round, while she constantly agitated it with a quick motion.

I now observed a quantity of black matter, resembling gunpowder, which she told me was *gold rust*; and before she had moved the sand one quarter round the calabash, she pointed to a yellow speck, and said, *sanoo affilli*, see the gold. On looking attentively I saw a portion of pure gold, and took it out. It would have weighed about *one grain*. The whole of the washing, from the first putting in of the sand till she showed me the gold, did not exceed the space of *two minutes*. I now desired her to take a larger portion. She put in, as nearly as I could guess, about two pounds; and having washed it in the same manner, and nearly in the same time, found no fewer than *twenty-three* particles; some of them were very small. In both cases I observed that the quantity of *sanoo mira*, or *gold rust*, was at least forty times greater than the quantity of gold. She assured me that they sometimes found pieces of gold as large as her fist.

MUNGO PARK (1771–1806)

The Gardens of Iztapalapan

But the pride of Iztapalapan, on which its lord had freely lavished his care and his revenues, was its celebrated gardens. They covered an immense tract of land; were laid out in regular squares, and the paths intersecting them were bordered with trellises, supporting creepers and aromatic shrubs, that loaded the air with their perfumes. The gardens were stocked with fruit-trees, imported from distant places, and with the gaudy family of flowers which belong to the Mexican Flora, scientifically arranged, and growing luxuriant in the equable temperature of the table-land. The natural dryness of the atmosphere was counteracted by means of aqueducts and canals, that carried water into all parts of the grounds.

In one quarter was an aviary, filled with numerous kinds of birds, remarkable in this region both for brilliancy of plumage and of song. The gardens were intersected by a canal communicating with the lake of Tezcuco, and of sufficient size for barges to enter from the latter. But the most elaborate piece of work was a huge reservoir of stone, filled to a considerable height with water, well supplied with different sorts of fish. This basin was sixteen hundred paces in circumference, and was surrounded by a walk, made also of stone, wide enough for four persons to go abreast. The sides were curiously sculptured, and a flight of steps led to the water below, which fed the aqueducts above noticed, or, collected into fountains, diffused a perpetual moisture.

Such are the accounts transmitted of these celebrated gardens, at a period when similar horticultural establishments were unknown in Europe; and we might well doubt their existence in this semi-civilised land, were it not a matter of such notoriety at the time, and so explicitly attested by the invaders. But a generation had scarcely passed after the Conquest before a sad change came over these scenes so beautiful. The town itself was deserted, and the shore of the lake was strewed with the wreck of buildings which once were its ornament and its glory. The gardens shared the fate of the city. The retreating waters withdrew the means of nourishment, converting the flourishing plains into a foul and unsightly morass, the haunt of loathsome reptiles;

and the water-fowl built her nest in what had once been the palaces of princes!

WILLIAM HICKLING PRESCOTT (1796–1859)

The Naturalist must travel

Among the scenes which are deeply impressed on my mind, none exceed in sublimity the primeval forests undefaced by the hand of man; whether those of Brazil, where the powers of Life are predominant, or those of Tierra del Fuego, where Death and Decay prevail. Both are temples filled with the varied productions of the God of Nature:—no one can stand in these solitudes unmoved, and not feel that there is more in man than the mere breath of his body. In calling up images of the past, I find that the plains of Patagonia frequently cross before my eyes; yet these plains are pronounced by all wretched and useless. They can be described only by negative characters; without habitations, without water, without trees, without mountains, they support merely a few dwarf plants. Why then, and the case is not peculiar to myself, have these arid wastes taken so firm a hold on my memory? Why have not the still more level, the greener and more fertile Pampas, which are serviceable to mankind, produced an equal impression? I can scarcely analyze these feelings: but it must be partly owing to the free scope given to the imagination. The plains of Patagonia are boundless, for they are scarcely passable, and hence unknown: they bear the stamp of having lasted, as they are now, for ages, and there appears no limit to their duration through future time. If, as the ancients supposed, the flat earth was surrounded by an impassable breadth of water, or by deserts heated to an intolerable excess, who would not look at these last boundaries to man's knowledge with deep but ill-defined sensations?

Lastly, of natural scenery, the views from lofty mountains, though certainly in one sense not beautiful, are very memorable. When looking down from the highest crest of the Cordillera, the mind, undisturbed by minute details, was filled with the stupendous dimensions of the surrounding masses.

Of individual objects, perhaps nothing is more certain to create astonishment than the first sight in his native haunt of a barbarian,—of man in his lowest and most savage state. One's mind hurries back over past centuries, and then asks, could our progenitors have been men like these?—men, whose very signs and expressions are less intelligible to us than those of the domesticated animals; men, who do not possess the instinct of those animals, nor yet appear to boast of human reason, or at least of arts consequent on that reason. I do not believe it is possible to describe or paint the difference between savage and civilized man. It is the difference between a wild and tame animal: and part of the interest in beholding a savage, is the same which would lead every one to desire to see the lion in his desert, the tiger tearing his prey in the jungle, or the rhinoceros wandering over the wild plains of Africa.

Among the other most remarkable spectacles which we have beheld, may be ranked the Southern Cross, the cloud of Magellan, and the other constellations of the southern hemisphere—the water-spout—the glacier leading its blue stream of ice, overhanging the sea in a bold precipice—a lagoon-island raised by the reef-building corals—an active volcano—and the overwhelming effects of a violent earthquake. These latter phenomena, perhaps, possess for me a peculiar interest, from their intimate connexion with the geological structure of the world. The earthquake, however, must be to every one a most impressive event: the earth, considered from our earliest childhood as the type of solidity, has oscillated like a thin crust beneath our feet; and in seeing the laboured works of man in a moment overthrown, we feel the insignificance of his boasted power.

It has been said, that the love of the chase is an inherent delight in man—a relic of an instinctive passion. If so, I am sure the pleasure of living in the open air, with the sky for a roof and the ground for a table, is part of the same feeling; it is the savage returning to his wild and native habits. I always look back to our boat cruises, and my land journeys, when through unfrequented countries, with an extreme delight, which no scenes of civilization could have created. I do not doubt that every traveller must remember the glowing sense of happiness which he experienced, when he first breathed in a foreign clime, where the civilized man had seldom or never trod.

There are several other sources of enjoyment in a long voyage, which are of a more reasonable nature. The map of the world ceases to be a blank; it becomes a picture full of the most varied and animated figures. Each part assumes its proper dimensions: continents are not looked at in the light of islands, or islands considered as mere specks, which are, in truth, larger than many kingdoms of Europe. Africa, or North and South America, are well-sounding names, and easily pronounced; but it is not until having sailed for weeks along small portions of their shores, that one is thoroughly convinced what vast spaces on our immense world these names imply.

From seeing the present state, it is impossible not to look forward with high expectations to the future progress of nearly an entire hemisphere. The march of improvement, consequent on the introduction of Christianity throughout the South Sea, probably stands by itself in the records of history. It is the more striking when we remember that only sixty years since, Cook, whose excellent judgment none will dispute, could foresee no prospect of a change. Yet these changes have now been effected by the philanthropic spirit of the British nation.

In the same quarter of the globe Australia is rising, or indeed may be said to have risen, into a grand centre of civilization, which, at some not very remote period, will rule as empress over the southern hemisphere. It is impossible for an Englishman to behold these distant colonies, without a high pride and satisfaction. To hoist the British flag, seems to draw with it as a certain consequence, wealth, prosperity, and civilization.

In conclusion, it appears to me that nothing can be more improving to a young naturalist, than a journey in distant countries. It both sharpens, and partly allays that want and craving, which, as Sir J. Herschel remarks, a man experiences although every corporeal sense be fully satisfied. The excitement from the novelty of objects, and the chance of success, stimulate him to increased activity. Moreover, as a number of isolated facts soon become uninteresting, the habit of comparison leads to generalization. On the other hand, as the traveller stays but a short time in each place, his descriptions must generally consist of mere sketches, instead of detailed observations. Hence arises, as I have found to my cost, a constant tendency to fill up the wide gaps of knowledge, by inaccurate and superficial hypotheses.

But I have too deeply enjoyed the voyage, not to recommend any naturalist, although he must not expect to be so fortunate in his companions as I have been, to take all chances, and to start, on travels by land if possible, if otherwise on a long voyage. He may feel assured, he will meet with no difficulties or dangers, excepting in rare cases, nearly so bad as he beforehand anticipates. In a moral point of view, the effect ought to be, to teach him good-humoured patience, freedom from selfishness, the habit of acting for himself, and of making the best of every occurrence. In short, he ought to partake of the characteristic qualities of most sailors. Travelling ought also to teach him distrust; but at the same time he will discover, how many truly kind-hearted people there are, with whom he never before had, or ever again will have any further communication, who yet are ready to offer him the most disinterested assistance.

CHARLES DARWIN (1809–1882)

The Philosophy of an American Farmer

As you are the first enlightened European I have ever had the pleasure of being acquainted with, you will not be surprised that I should, according to your earnest desire and my promise, appear anxious of preserving your friendship and correspondence. By your accounts, I observe a material difference subsists between your husbandry, modes, and customs, and ours; everything is local; could we enjoy the advantages of the English farmer, we should be much happier, indeed, but this wish, like many others, implies a contradiction; and could the English farmer have some of those privileges we possess, they would be the first of their class in the world. Good and evil I see is to be found in all societies, and it is in vain to seek for any spot where those ingredients are not mixed. I therefore rest satisfied, and thank God that my lot is to be an American farmer, instead of a Russian boor, or an Hungarian peasant. I thank you kindly for the idea, however dreadful, which you have given me of their lot and condition; your observations have confirmed me in the justness of my ideas, and I am happier now than I thought myself before. It is strange that misery, when viewed in others, should become to us a sort of real good, though I am far from rejoicing to hear that there are in the world men so thoroughly wretched; they are no doubt as harmless, industrious, and willing to work as we are. Hard is their fate to be thus condemned to a slavery worse than that of our negroes. Yet when young I entertained some thoughts of selling my farm. I thought it afforded but a dull repetition of the same labours and pleasures. I thought the former tedious and heavy, the latter few and insipid; but when I came to consider myself as divested of my farm, I then found the world so wide, and every place so full, that I began to fear lest there would be no room for me. My farm, my house, my barn, presented to my imagination objects from which I adduced quite new ideas; they were more forcible than before. Why should not I find myself happy, said I, where my father was before? He left me no good books it is true, he gave me no other education than the art of reading and writing; but he left me a good farm, and his experience; he left me free from debts, and no kind of difficulties to struggle with.—I married, and this perfectly reconciled me to my situation; my wife rendered my house all at once cheerful and pleasing; it no longer appeared gloomy and solitary as before; when I went to work in my fields I worked with more alacrity and sprightliness; I felt that I did not work for myself alone, and this encouraged me much. My wife would often come with her knitting in her hand, and sit under the shady trees, praising the straightness of my furrows, and the docility of my horses; this swelled my heart and made everything light and pleasant, and I regretted that I had not married before.

I felt myself happy in my new situation, and where is that station which can confer a more substantial system of felicity than that of an American farmer, possessing freedom of action, freedom of thoughts, ruled by a mode of government which requires but little from us? I owe nothing, but a pepper corn to my country, a small tribute to my king, with loyalty and due respect; I know no other landlord than the lord of all land, to whom I owe the most sincere gratitude. My father left me three hundred and seventy-one acres of land, forty-seven of which are good timothy meadow, an excellent orchard, a good house, and a substantial barn. It is my duty to think how happy I am that he lived to build and to pay for all these improvements; what are the labours which I have to undergo, what are my fatigues when compared to his, who had everything to do, from the first tree he felled to the finishing of his house? Every year I kill from 1,500 to 2,000 weight of pork, 1,200 of beef, half a dozen of good wethers in harvest: of fowls my wife has always a great stock: what can I wish more? My negroes are tolerably faithful and healthy; by a long series of industry and honest dealings, my father left behind him the name of a good man; I have but to tread his paths to be happy and a good man like him. I know enough of the law to regulate my little concerns with propriety, nor do I dread its power; these are the grand outlines of my situation, but as I can feel much more than I am able to express, I hardly know how to proceed.

When my first son was born, the whole train of my ideas were suddenly altered; never was there a charm that acted so quickly and powerfully; I ceased to ramble in imagination through the wide world; my excursions since have not exceeded the bounds of my farm, and all my principal pleasures are now centred within its scanty limits: but at the same time there is not an operation belonging to it in which I do not find some food for useful reflections. This is the reason, I suppose, that when you was here, you used, in your refined style, to denominate me the farmer of feelings; how rude must those feelings be in him who daily holds the axe or the plough, how much more refined on the contrary those of the European, whose mind is improved by education, example, books, and by every acquired advantage! Those feelings, however, I will delineate as well as I can, agreeably to your earnest request.

When I contemplate my wife, by my fire-side, while she either spins, knits, darns, or suckles our child, I cannot describe the various emotions of love, of gratitude, of conscious pride, which thrill in my heart and often overflow in involuntary tears. I feel the necessity, the sweet pleasure of acting my part, the part of an husband and father, with an attention and propriety which may entitle me to my good fortune. It is true these pleasing images vanish with the smoke of my pipe, but though they disappear from my mind, the impression they have made on my heart is indelible. When I play with the infant, my warm imagination runs forward, and eagerly anticipates his future temper and constitution. I would willingly open the book of fate, and know in which page his destiny is delineated; alas! where is the father who in those moments of paternal ecstasy can delineate one half of the thoughts which dilate his heart? I am sure I cannot; then again I fear for the health of those who are become so dear to me, and in their sicknesses I severely pay for the joys I experienced while they were well. Whenever I go abroad it is always involuntary. I never return home without feeling some pleasing emotion, which I often suppress as useless and foolish. The instant I enter on my own land, the bright idea of property, of exclusive right, of independence exalt my mind. Precious soil, I say to myself, by what singular custom of law is it that thou wast made to constitute the riches of the freeholder? What should we American farmers be without the distinct possession of that soil? It feeds, it clothes us, from it we draw even a great exuberancy, our best meat, our richest drink, the very honey of our bees comes from this privileged spot. No wonder we should thus cherish its possession, no wonder that so many Europeans who have never been able to say that such portion of land was theirs, cross the Atlantic to realise that happiness. This formerly rude soil has been converted by my father into a pleasant farm, and in return it has established all our rights; on it is founded our rank, our freedom, our power as citizens, our importance as inhabitants of such a district. These images I must confess I always behold with pleasure, and extend them as far as my imagination can reach: for this is what may be called the true and the only philosophy of an American farmer.

MICHEL-GUILLAUME JEAN DE CRÈVECŒUR (1735–1813)

Currency Lasses

That low-lived Englishman who, in the pride of his John Bull breed, and of his condition as paymaster to an exiled marching regiment, distinguished the Emigrant from the Native population of New South Wales, by nicknaming the one Sterling, and the other Currency, was, no doubt, a man of taste, according to his station and habits. Colonial money being at the time below par with reference to British money, he intended to depreciate the Native colonists with reference to true-born British colonists; as if, forsooth, there were a pin to choose between colonists, in point of rank. But, probably, he was an admirer of cherry cheeks, purple arms, thick legs, and a nutmeg-grater skin, in the one sex, and of bulk, high cheek-bones, and red whiskers in the other—all characteristic, perhaps, of the regimental paymaster and his tramping wife. If so, no wonder that he should think meanly of the Native Australians. But, if an Englishman of refined taste had been compelled to express his opinion of the two races by terms signifying measures of value, he would, I believe, have given the higher denomination to the Australians, who, as they differ from a vulgar Englishman's idea of perfection, approach to that of Flaxman and Byron.

'Tous les goûts sont dans la nature; celui qu'on a est le meilleur.' In English, 'everyone to his taste, as the old woman said when she kissed her cow.' Nevertheless, in spite of the many proverbs which declare that there is no standard of taste, the same human form which more than two thousand years ago was embodied by Phidias and Praxiteles, is still considered the model of perfection by all refined Europeans. Where does that form most commonly breathe? In Greece, and even in the very Cyprus, where Adonis was conceived, and where the Goddess of Beauty had two temples. You may laugh or sneer; but the latitude of Sydney corresponds exactly with that of Paphos; and it is no less true that the native Australians bear a stronger resemblance to the modern Greeks than to any other people. They have been described as lank, sallow and relaxed, like the Americans; but I have seen the Apollo and the Venus, some thousands of breathing Greeks, and some millions of Americans; and I assert the description to be false. The Australian youth are neither chubby, ruddy, and strongly knit, like the English, whose otherwise variable climate is almost constantly wet; nor fat, white, thick-skinned, and shapeless, like the Dutch, whose climate is one fog, dripping or frozen; nor indescribable, like the mongrel French, whose climate is neither one thing nor the other: and they are still less like the Americans, whose climate, more variable than that of England, is always in extremes, blowing burning hot and biting cold with the same breath; but they resemble the Castilians, the sea-coast Italians, and more especially the island Greeks, which last enjoy, like them, perpetual summer upon a soil not alluvial.

As to form and mien you shall judge for yourself. The young men of Australia, like Alfieri and Mr Hope's Modern Greek, are passionately fond of horses. If you would see one of them, look in Flaxman's illustrations of the Iliad, at the figure of Diomed returning with the spoils of Rhesus. The Australian girls, like the girls of Genoa, Naples and the Archipelago, are passionately fond of swimming. If you would see a group of them, look at Flaxman's sea nymphs obeying the command of Thetis—

Ye sister Nereids, to your deeps descend.

But Flaxman's outlines represent only form and mien. How shall I paint the rest? As for the young men, I cannot help feeling envious and jealous of their personal beauty: so I shall not mention it again; and you may fancy what you please, or get a woman of observation to take their picture for you. But the girls—oh! that is quite another thing; and I will write for my own pleasure, whether you read or not. And let me ask, by the by, whether, if the women of a country be generally beautiful, the men, likewise, will not be handsome? Why is the highest class in England better looking than the others? Because, I imagine, it obtains a constant accession of beautiful women;—men of rank having the largest choice, and marrying to please their eyes; whilst young men of wealth, aspiring to rank, marry girls of condition, the daughters of beauty, and of rank, whose mother was beauty. Thus, not only does the highest class pick out the beauties of two or three classes, but it also keeps its own beauties. Supposing you to agree with me that both sexes of the English highest class, do generally excel in person both sexes of the other classes, it would seem to follow that if the female colonists, generally, are beautiful, beauty in both sexes will be a colonial attribute. However, infer what you like. Here is the fact.

You remember that Genoese girl before whom you trembled and I became faint, though she only handed us some grapes. Do you remember that, having recovered ourselves, we measured her eyelashes? Do you remember how long they were, and how she laughed? Do you remember that bright laugh, and how I patted her cheek, and told her that it was softer than her country's velvet? And how she blushed —do you remember that?—to the tips of her fingers and the roots of her hair? And then how —— do you remember how, peasant as she was, and but just fifteen, she tossed her head and stamped her little foot, with the air of a Queen? And then how, on a sudden, her large eyes were filled with tears; and the grace with which she folded her arms across that charming bosom; and the tone—I hear it now—the deep, grave, penetrating tone in which, half angry, half afraid, she at once threatened us with her 'Berto' and implored our respect? We did not care much for Mr Berto, certainly; but did we not swear, both together, that not a hair of her head should be hurt? And when, flattered by our involuntary devotion, she departed with a healthy lively step, showing her small smooth ancles, and now and then turning her profile to us, and laughing as before—did we not, dashing blades as we thought ourselves, snuffle and blow our noses, and shake hands without the least motive, like two fools? And afterwards, notwithstanding that gratuitous fit of friendship, did we not feel jealous of each other for three days, though neither of us could hope to see the little angel again?—Yes, you remember it all. Well, just such another girl as that brings fruit to my door every morning.

I do not pretend, however, that *all* the girls of Australia are equally beautiful; but I do declare, what you know to be true of the Ligurian girls, that three out of four of them would be considered beauties in Mayfair.

EDWARD GIBBON WAKEFIELD (1796–1862)

Journalist's Risk

'Those men mean mischief,' said I to my friend D——, of the *Morning Chronicle*, who at this moment joined me; 'and depend upon it, that if they are ordered they will commence firing, caring nothing whom they hit,—but what can those cavalry fellows behind them mean, who are evidently of the other opinion by their shouting; why don't they charge at once this handful of foot people and overturn them? Once down, the crowd would wrest from them their muskets in a moment. You are a liberal, which I am not; why do you not go to that silly young man who commands the horse, and give him a word of counsel in time?'

D—— turned upon me his broad, red good-humoured English countenance, with a peculiarly arch look, as much as to say . . . (whatever you think most applicable, gentle reader,) then taking me by the arm, 'Let us get,' said he, 'out of this crowd and mount to some window, where I can write down what is about to take place, for I agree with you that mischief is meant.' Just opposite the post office was a large house, in the topmost storey of which we beheld a paper displayed, importing that apartments were to let; whereupon we instantly ascended the common stair, and having agreed with the mistress of the *étage* for the use of the front room for the day, we bolted the door, and the reporter, producing his pocket-book and pencil, prepared to take notes of the coming events, which were already casting their shadow before.

What most extraordinary men are these reporters of newspapers in general—I mean English newspapers; surely if there be any class of individuals who are entitled to the appellation of cosmopolites, it is these; who pursue their avocation in all countries indifferently, and accommodate themselves at will to the manners of all classes of society: their fluency of style as writers is only surpassed by their facility of language in conversation, and their attainments in classical and polite literature only by their profound knowledge of the world, acquired by an early introduction into its bustling scenes. The activity, energy, and courage which they occasionally display in the pursuit of information, are truly remarkable. I saw them during the three days at Paris, mingled with canaille and gamins behind the barriers, whilst the mitraille was flying in all directions, and the desperate cuirassiers were dashing their fierce horses against the seemingly feeble bulwarks. There they stood, dotting down their observations in their pocketbooks as unconcernedly as if reporting the proceedings of a reform meeting in Covent Garden or Finsbury Square; whilst in Spain, several of them accompanied the Carlist and Christino guerillas in some of their most desperate raids and expeditions, exposing themselves to the danger of hostile bullets, the inclemency of winter, and the fierce heat of the summer sun.

We had scarcely been five minutes at the window, when we suddenly heard the clattering of horses' feet hastening down the street called the Calle de Carretas. The house in which we had stationed ourselves was, as I have already observed, just opposite to the post office, at the left of which this street debouches from the north into the Puerta del Sol: as the sounds became louder and louder, the cries of the crowd below diminished, and a species of panic seemed to have fallen upon all; once or twice, however, I could distinguish the words, Quesada! Quesada! The foot soldiers stood calm and motionless, but I observed that the cavalry, with the young officer who commanded them, displayed both confusion and fear, exchanging with each other some hurried words; all of a sudden that part of the crowd which stood near the mouth of the Calle de Carretas fell back in great disorder, leaving a considerable space unoccupied, and the next moment Quesada, in complete general's uniform, and mounted on a bright bay thoroughbred English horse, with a drawn sword in his hand, dashed at full gallop into the area, in much the same manner as I have seen a Manchegan bull rush into the amphitheatre when the gates of his pen are suddenly flung open.

He was closely followed by two mounted officers, and at a short distance by as many dragoons. In almost less time than is sufficient to relate it, several individuals in the crowd were knocked down and lay sprawling upon the ground beneath the horses of Quesada and his two friends, for as to the dragoons, they halted as soon as they had entered the Puerta del Sol. It was a fine sight to see three men, by dint of valour and good horsemanship, strike terror into at least as many thousands: I saw Quesada spur his horse repeatedly into the dense masses of the crowd, and then extricate himself in the most masterly manner. The rabble were completely awed and gave way, retiring by the Calle del Comercio and the street of Alcala. All at once, Quesada singled out two nationals, who were attempting to escape, and setting spurs to his horse, turned them in a moment, and drove them in another direction striking them in a contemptuous manner with the flat of his sabre. He was crying out, 'Long live the absolute queen!' when, just beneath me, amidst a portion of the crowd which had still maintained its ground, perhaps from not having the means of escaping, I saw a small gun glitter for a moment, then there was a sharp report, and a bullet had nearly sent Quesada to his long account, passing so near to the countenance of the general as to graze his hat. I had an indistinct view for a moment of a well-known foraging cap just about the spot from whence the gun had been discharged, then there was a rush of the crowd, and the shooter, whoever he was, escaped discovery amidst the confusion which arose.

As for Quesada, he seemed to treat the danger from which he had escaped with the utmost contempt. He glared about him fiercely for a moment, then leaving the two nationals, who sneaked away like whipped hounds, he went up to the young officer who commanded the cavalry, and who had been active in raising the cry of the constitution, and to him he addressed a few words with an air of stern menace; the youth evidently quailed before him, and probably in obedience to his orders, resigned the command of the party, and rode slowly away with a discomfited air; whereupon Quesada dismounted, and walked slowly backwards and forwards before the Casa de Postas with a mien which seemed to bid defiance to mankind.

This was the glorious day of Quesada's existence, his glorious and last day. I call it the day of his glory, for he certainly never before appeared under such brilliant circumstances, and he never lived to see another sun set. No action of any conqueror or hero on record is to be compared with this closing scene of the life of Quesada, for who, by his single desperate courage and impetuosity, ever before stopped a revolution in full course? Quesada did: he stopped the revolution at Madrid for one entire day, and brought back the uproarious and hostile mob of a huge city to perfect order and quiet. His burst into the Puerta del Sol was the most tremendous and successful piece of daring ever witnessed. I admired so much the spirit of the 'brute bull' that I frequently, during his wild onset shouted, 'Viva Quesada!' for I wished him well. Not that I am of *any* political party or system. No, no! I have lived too long with Rommany Chals and Petulengres to be of any politics save gipsy politics: and it is well known that, during elections, the children of Roma side with both parties so long as the event is doubtful, promising success to each; and then when the fight is done, and the battle won, invariably range themselves in the ranks of the victorious. But I repeat that I wished well to Quesada, witnessing, as I did, his stout heart and good horsemanship. Tranquillity was restored to Madrid throughout the remainder of the day; the handful of infantry bivouacked in the Puerta del Sol. No more cries of 'Long live the Constitution' were heard; and the revolution in the capital seemed to have been effectually put down.

GEORGE BORROW (1803–1881)

A Debt of Honour

The next moment he crossed the threshold. There was a leap, a stifled cry, an instantaneous struggle; and before Colonel Geraldine could spring to his aid, the Prince held the man, disarmed and helpless, by the shoulders.

'Dr Noel,' he said, 'you will be so good as to re-light the lamp.'

And relinquishing the charge of his prisoner to Geraldine and Brackenbury, he crossed the room and set his back against the chimney-piece. As soon as the lamp had kindled, the party beheld an unaccustomed sternness on the Prince's features. It was no longer Florizel, the careless gentleman; it was the Prince of Bohemia, justly incensed and full of deadly purpose, who now raised his head and addressed the captive President of the Suicide Club.

'President,' he said, 'you have laid your last snare, and your own feet are taken in it. The day is beginning; it is your last morning. You have just swum the Regent's Canal; it is your last bathe in this world. Your old accomplice, Dr Noel, so far from betraying me, has delivered you into my hands for judgment. And the grave you had dug for me this afternoon shall serve, in God's almighty providence, to hide your own just doom from the curiosity of mankind. Kneel and pray, sir, if you have a mind that way; for your time is short, and God is weary of your iniquities.'

The President made no answer either by word or sign; but continued to hang his head and gaze sullenly on the floor, as though he were conscious of the Prince's prolonged and unsparing regard.

'Gentlemen,' continued Florizel, resuming the ordinary tone of his conversation, 'this is a fellow who has long eluded me, but whom, thanks to Dr Noel, I now have tightly by the heels. To tell the story of his misdeeds would occupy more time than we can now afford; but if the canal had contained nothing but the blood of his victims, I believe the wretch would have been no drier than you see him. Even in an affair of this sort I desire to preserve the forms of honour. But I make you the judges, gentlemen—this is more an execution than a duel; and to give the rogue his choice of weapons would be to push too far a point of etiquette. I cannot afford to lose my life in such a business,' he continued, unlocking the case of swords; 'and as a pistol-bullet travels so often on the wings of chance, and skill and courage may fall by the most trembling marksman, I have decided, and I feel sure you will approve my determination, to put this question to the touch of swords.'

When Brackenbury and Major O'Rooke, to whom these remarks were particularly addressed, had each intimated his approval, 'Quick, sir,' added Prince Florizel to the President, 'choose a blade and do not keep me waiting; I have an impatience to be done with you for ever.'

For the first time since he was captured and disarmed the President raised his head, and it was plain that he began instantly to pluck up courage.

'Is it to be stand up?' he asked eagerly, 'and between you and me?'

'I mean so far to honour you,' replied the Prince.

'Oh, come!' cried the President. 'With a fair field, who knows how things may happen? I must add that I consider it handsome behaviour on your Highness's part; and if the worst comes to the worst I shall die by one of the most gallant gentlemen in Europe.'

And the President, liberated by those who had detained him, stepped up to the table and began, with minute attention, to select a sword.

He was highly elated, and seemed to feel no doubt that he should issue victorious from the contest. The spectators grew alarmed in the face of so entire a confidence, and adjured Prince Florizel to reconsider his intention.

'It is but a farce,' he answered; 'and I think I can promise you, gentlemen, that it will not be long a-playing.'

'Your Highness will be careful not to over-reach,' said Colonel Geraldine.

'Geraldine,' returned the Prince, 'did you ever know me fail in a debt of honour? I owe you this man's death, and you shall have it.'

The President at last satisfied himself with one of the rapiers, and signified his readiness by a gesture that was not devoid of a rude nobility. The nearness of peril, and the sense of courage, even in this obnoxious villain lent an air of manhood and a certain grace.

The Prince helped himself at random to a sword.

'Colonel Geraldine and Dr Noel,' he said, 'will have the goodness to await me in this room. I wish no personal friend of mine to be involved in this transaction. Major O'Rooke, you are a man of some years and a settled reputation—let me recommend the President to your good graces. Lieutenant Rich will be so good as to lend me his attentions: a young man cannot have too much experience in such affairs.'

'Your Highness,' replied Brackenbury, 'it is an honour I shall prize extremely.'

'It is well,' returned Prince Florizel; 'I shall hope to stand your friend in more important circumstances.'

And so saying he led the way out of the apartment and down the kitchen stairs.

The two men who were thus left alone threw open the window and leaned out, straining every sense to catch an indication of the tragical events that were about to follow. The rain was now over; day had almost come, and the birds were piping in the shrubbery and on the forest trees of the garden. The Prince and his companions were visible for a moment as they followed an alley between two flowering thickets; but at the first corner a clump of foliage intervened, and they were again concealed from view. This was all that the Colonel and the physician had an opportunity to see, and the garden was so vast, and the place of combat evidently so remote from the house, that not even the noise of sword-play reached their ears.

'He has taken him towards the grave,' said Dr Noel, with a shudder.

'God,' cried the Colonel, 'God defend the right!'

And they awaited the event in silence, the Doctor shaking with fear, the Colonel in an agony of sweat. Many minutes must have elasped, the day was sensibly broader, and the birds were singing more heartily in the garden before a sound of returning footsteps recalled their glances towards the door. It was the Prince and the two Indian officers who entered. God had defended the right.

'I am ashamed of my emotion,' said Prince Florizel. 'I feel it is a weakness unworthy of my station, but the continued existence of that hound of hell had begun to pray upon me like a disease, and his death has more refreshed me than a night of slumber. Look, Geraldine,' he continued, throwing his sword upon the floor, 'there is the blood of the man who killed your brother. It should be a welcome sight. And yet,' he added, 'see how strangely we men are made! my revenge is not yet five minutes old, and already I am beginning to ask myself if even revenge be attainable on this precarious stage of life. The ill he did, who can undo it? The career in which he amassed a huge fortune (for the house itself in which we stand belonged to him)—that career is now a part of the destiny of mankind for ever; and I might weary myself making thrusts in carte until the crack of judgment, and Geraldine's brother would be none the less dead, and a thousand other innocent persons would be none the less dishonoured and debauched! The existence of a man is so small a thing to take, so mighty a thing to employ! Alas!' he cried, 'is there anything in life so disenchanting as attainment?'

'God's justice has been done,' replied the Doctor. 'So much I behold. The lesson, your Highness, has been a cruel one for me; and I await my own turn with deadly apprehension.'

'What was I saying?' cried the Prince. 'I have punished, and here is the man beside us who can help me to undo. Ah, Dr Noel! you and I have before us many a day of hard and honourable toil; and perhaps, before we have done, you may have more than redeemed your early errors.'

'And in the meantime,' said the Doctor, 'let me go and bury my oldest friend.'

ROBERT LOUIS STEVENSON (1850–1894)

The Descending Pendulum

All this I saw indistinctly and by much effort—for my personal condition had been greatly changed during slumber. I now lay upon my back, and at full length, on a species of low framework of wood. To this I was securely bound by a long strap resembling a surcingle. It passed in many convolutions about my limbs and body, leaving at liberty only my head, and my left arm to such extent, that I could, by dint of much exertion, supply myself with food from an earthen dish which lay by my side on the floor. I saw, to my horror, that the pitcher had been removed. I say to my horror—for I was consumed with intolerable thirst. This thirst it appeared to be the design of my persecutors to stimulate—for the food in the dish was meat pungently seasoned.

Looking upward, I surveyed the ceiling of my prison. It was some thirty or forty feet overhead, and constructed much as the side walls. In one of its panels a very singular figure riveted my whole attention. It was the painted figure of Time as he is commonly represented, save that, in lieu of a scythe, he held what, at a casual glance, I supposed to be the pictured image of a huge pendulum, such as we see on antique clocks. There was something, however, in the appearance of this machine which caused me to regard it more attentively. While I gazed directly upward at it (for its position was immediately over my own) I fancied that I saw it in motion. In an instant afterward the fancy was confirmed. Its sweep was brief, and of course slow. I watched it for some minutes somewhat in fear, but more in wonder. Wearied at length with observing its dull movement, I turned my eyes upon the other objects in the cell.

A slight noise attracted my notice, and, looking to the floor, I saw several enormous rats traversing it. They had issued from the well which lay just within view to my right. Even then, while I gazed, they came up in troops, hurriedly, with ravenous eyes, allured by the scent of the meat. From this it required much effort and attention to scare them away.

It might have been half an hour, perhaps even an hour (for I could take but imperfect note of time), before I again cast my eyes upward. What I then saw confounded and amazed me. The sweep of the pendulum had increased in extent by nearly a yard. As a natural consequence its velocity was also much greater. But what mainly disturbed me was the idea that it had perceptibly *descended*. I now observed—with what horror it is needless to say—that its nether extremity was formed of a crescent of glittering steel, about a foot in length from horn to horn; the horns upward, and the under edge evidently as keen as that of a razor. Like a razor also, it seemed massive and heavy, tapering from the edge into a solid and broad structure above. It was appended to a weighty rod of brass, and the whole *hissed* as it swung through the air.

I could no longer doubt the doom prepared for me by monkish ingenuity in torture. My cognisance of the pit had become known to the inquisitorial agents—*the pit*, whose horrors had been destined for so bold a recusant as myself—*the pit*, typical of hell and regarded by rumour as the Ultima Thule of all their punishments. The plunge into this pit I had avoided by the merest of accidents, and I knew that surprise, or entrapment into torment, formed an important portion of all the grotesquerie of these dungeon deaths. Having failed to fall, it was no part of the demon plan to hurl me into the abyss; and thus (there being no alternative) a different and a milder destruction awaited me. Milder! I half smiled in my agony as I thought of such application of such a term.

What boots it to tell of the long, long hours of horror more than mortal, during which I counted the rushing oscillations of the steel! Inch by inch—line by line—with a descent only appreciable at intervals that seemed ages—down and still down it came! Days passed—it might have been that many days passed—ere it swept so closely over me as to fan me with its acrid breath. The odour of the sharp steel forced itself into my nostrils. I prayed—I wearied heaven with my prayer for its more speedy descent. I grew frantically mad, and struggled to force myself upward against the sweep of the fearful scimitar. And then I fell suddenly calm, and lay smiling at the glittering death, as a child at some rare bauble.

There was another interval of utter insensibility; it was brief; for upon again lapsing into life, there had been no perceptible descent in the pendulum. But it might have been long—for I knew there were demons who took note of my swoon, and who could have arrested the vibration at pleasure. Upon my recovery, too, I felt very—oh! inexpressibly—sick and weak, as if through long inanition. Even amid the agonies of that period the human nature craved food. With painful effort I outstretched my left arm as far as my bonds permitted, and took possession of the small remnant which had been spared me by the rats. As I put a portion of it within my lips, there rushed to my mind a half-formed thought of joy—of hope. Yet what business had *I* with hope? It was, as I say, a half-formed thought—man has many such, which are never completed. I felt that it was of joy—of hope; but I felt also that it had perished in its formation. In vain I struggled to perfect —to regain it. Long suffering had nearly annihilated all my ordinary powers of mind. I was an imbecile—an idiot.

The vibration of the pendulum was at right angles to my length. I saw that the crescent was designed to cross the region of the heart. It would fray the serge of my robe—it would return and repeat its operations—again—and again. Notwithstanding its terrifically wide sweep (some thirty feet or more), and the hissing vigour of its descent, sufficient to sunder these very walls of iron, still the fraying of my robe would be all that, for several minutes, it would accomplish. And at this thought I paused. I dared not go further than this reflection. I dwelt upon it with a pertinacity of attention—as if, in so dwelling, I could arrest *here* the descent of the steel. I forced myself to ponder upon the sound of the crescent as it should pass across the garment—upon the peculiar thrilling sensation which the friction of cloth produces on the nerves. I pondered over all this frivolity until my teeth were on edge.

Down—steadily down it crept. I took a frenzied pleasure in contrasting its downward with its lateral velocity. To the right—to the left—far and wide—with the shriek of a damned spirit! to my heart, with the stealthy pace of the tiger! I alternately laughed and howled, as the one or the other idea grew predominant.

Down—certainly, relentlessly down! It vibrated within three inches of my bosom! I struggled violently—furiously—to free my left arm. This was free only from the elbow to the hand. I could reach the latter, from the platter beside me, to my mouth, with great effort, but no farther. Could I have broken the fastenings above the elbow, I would have seized and attempted to arrest the pendulum. I might as well have attempted to arrest an avalanche!

Down—still unceasingly—still inevitably down! I gasped and struggled at each vibration. I shrunk convulsively at its every sweep. My eyes followed its outward or upward whirls with the eagerness of the most unmeaning despair; they closed themselves spasmodically at the descent, although death would have been a relief, oh, how unspeakable! Still I quivered in every nerve to think how slight a sinking of the machinery would precipitate that keen, glistening axe upon my bosom. It was *hope* that prompted the nerve to quiver—the frame to shrink. It was *hope*—the hope that triumphs on the rack—that whispers to the death-condemned even in the dungeons of the Inquisition.

I saw that some ten or twelve vibrations would bring the steel in actual contact with my robe—and with this observation there suddenly came over my spirit all the keen, collected calmness of despair. For the first time during many hours—or perhaps days—I *thought*. It now occurred to me, that the bandage, or surcingle, which enveloped me, was *unique*. I was tied by no separate cord. The first stroke of the razor-like crescent athwart any portion of the band would so detach it that it might be unwound from my person by means of my left hand. But how fearful, in that case, the proximity of the steel! The result of the slightest struggle, how deadly! Was it likely, moreover, that the minions of the torturer had not foreseen and provided for this possibility? Was it probable that the bandage crossed my bosom in the track of the pendulum? Dreading to find my faint and, as it seemed, my last hope frustrated, I so far elevated my head as to obtain a distinct view of my breast. The surcingle enveloped my limbs and body close in all directions—*save in the path of the destroying crescent.*

Scarcely had I dropped my head back into its original position, when there flashed upon my mind what I cannot better describe than as the unformed half of that idea of deliverance to which I have previously alluded, and of which a moiety only floated indeterminately through my brain when I raised food to my burning lips. The whole thought was now present—feeble, scarcely sane, scarcely definite—but still entire. I proceeded at once, with the nervous energy of despair, to attempt its execution.

For many hours the immediate vicinity of the low framework upon which I lay had been literally swarming with rats. They were wild, bold, ravenous—their red eyes glaring upon me as if they waited but for motionlessness on my part to make them their prey. 'To what food,' I thought, 'have they been accustomed in the well?'

They had devoured, in spite of all my efforts to prevent them, all but a small remnant of the contents of the dish. I had fallen into an habitual see-saw or wave of the hand about the platter; and, at length, the unconscious uniformity of the movement deprived it of effect. In their voracity, the vermin frequently fastened their sharp fangs in my fingers. With the particles of the oily and spicy viand which now remained, I thoroughly rubbed the bandage wherever I could reach it; then, raising my hand from the floor, I lay breathlessly still.

At first, the ravenous animals were startled and terrified at the change—at the cessation of movement. They shrank alarmedly back; many sought the well. But this was only for a moment. I had not counted in vain upon their voracity. Observing that I remained without motion, one or two of the boldest leaped upon the framework, and smelt at the surcingle. This seemed the signal for a general rush. Forth from the well they hurried in fresh troops. They clung to the wood—they overran it, and leaped in hundreds upon my person. The measured movement of the pendulum disturbed them not at all. Avoiding its strokes, they busied themselves with the anointed bandage. They pressed—they swarmed upon me in ever accumulating heaps. They writhed upon my throat; their cold lips sought my own; I was half stifled by their thronging pressure; disgust, for which the world has no name, swelled my bosom, and chilled, with a heavy clamminess, my heart. Yet one minute, and I felt that the struggle would be over. Plainly I perceived the loosening of the bandage. I knew that in more than one place it must be already severed. With a more than human resolution I lay *still*.

Nor had I erred in my calculations—nor had I endured in vain. I at length felt that I was *free*. The surcingle hung in ribands from my body. But the stroke of the pendulum already pressed upon my bosom. It had divided the serge of the robe. It had cut through the linen beneath. Twice again it swung, and a sharp sense of pain shot through every nerve. But the moment of escape had arrived. At a wave of my hand my deliverers hurried tumultuously away. With a steady movement—cautious, sidelong, shrinking, and slow—I slid from the embrace of the bandage and beyond the reach of the scimitar. For the moment, at least, *I was free*.

EDGAR ALLAN POE (1809–1849)

A Sixteen-Dollar Piece is offered

It drew near the close of day. Suddenly he came to a halt by the bulwarks, and inserting his bone leg into the auger-hole there, and with one hand grasping a shroud, he ordered Starbuck to send everybody aft.

'Sir!' said the mate, astonished at an order seldom or never given on shipboard except in some extraordinary case.

'Send everybody aft,' repeated Ahab. 'Mastheads, there! come down!'

When the entire ship's company were assembled, and with curious and not wholly unapprehensive faces, were eyeing him, for he looked not unlike the weather horizon when a storm is coming up, Ahab, after rapidly glancing over the bulwarks, and then darting his eyes among the crew, started from his standpoint; and as though not a soul were nigh him resumed his heavy turns upon the deck. With bent head and half-slouched hat he continued to pace, unmindful of the wondering whispering among the men; till Stubb cautiously whispered to Flask, that Ahab must have summoned them there for the purpose of witnessing a pedestrian feat. But this did not last long. Vehemently pausing he cried—

'What do ye do when ye see a whale, men?'

'Sing out for him!' was the impulsive rejoinder from a score of clubbed voices.

'Good!' cried Ahab, with a wild approval in his tones; observing the hearty animation into which his unexpected question had so magnetically thrown them.

'And what do ye next, men?'

'Lower away, and after him!'

'And what tune is it ye pull to, men?'

'A dead whale or a stove boat!'

More and more strangely and fiercely glad and approving grew the countenance of the old man at every shout; while the mariners began to gaze curiously at each other, as if marvelling how it was that they themselves became so excited at such seemingly purposeless questions.

But, they were all eagerness again, as Ahab, now half-revolving in his pivot-hole, with one hand reaching high up a shroud, and tightly, almost convulsively grasping it, addressed them thus—

'All ye mastheaders have before now heard me give orders about a white whale. Look ye! d'ye see this Spanish ounce of gold?'—holding up a broad bright coin to the sun—'it is a sixteen dollar piece, men. D'ye see it? Mr Starbuck, hand me yon top-maul.'

While the mate was getting the hammer, Ahab, without speaking, was slowly rubbing the gold piece against the skirts of his jacket, as if to heighten its lustre, and without using any words was meanwhile lowly humming to himself, producing a sound so strangely muffled and inarticulate that it seemed the mechanical humming of the wheels of his vitality in him.

Receiving the top-maul from Starbuck, he advanced towards the mainmast with the hammer uplifted in one hand, exhibiting the gold with the other, and with a high raised voice exclaiming: 'Whosoever of ye raises me a white-headed whale with a wrinkled brow and a crooked jaw; whosoever of ye raises me that white-headed whale, with three holes punctured in his starboard fluke—look ye, whosoever of ye raises me that same white whale, he shall have this gold ounce, my boys!'

'Huzza! huzza!' cried the seamen, as with swinging tarpaulins they hailed the act of nailing the gold to the mast.

'It's a white whale, I say,' resumed Ahab, as he threw down the top-maul; 'a white whale. Skin your eyes for him, men; look sharp for white water; if ye see but a bubble, sing out.'

HERMAN MELVILLE (1819–1891)

The Winning of Olwen

Said Arthur, 'Is there any of the marvels still unobtained?' Said one of the men, 'There is: the blood of the Black Witch, daughter of the White Witch, from the head of the Valley of Grief in the uplands of Hell.' Arthur set out for the North and came to where the hag's cave was. And it was the counsel of Gwyn son of Nudd and Gwythyr son of Greidawl that Cacamwri and Hygwydd his brother be sent to fight with the hag. And as they came inside the cave the hag grabbed at them, and caught Hygwydd by the hair of his head and flung him to the floor beneath her. And Cacamwri seized her by the hair of her head, and dragged her to the ground off Hygwydd, but she then turned on Cacamwri and dressed them down both and disarmed them, and drove them out squealing and squalling. And Arthur was angered to see his two servants well nigh slain, and he sought to seize the cave. And then Gwyn and Gwythyr told him, 'It is neither seemly nor pleasant for us to see thee scuffling with a hag. Send Long Amren and Long Eiddil into the cave.' And they went. But if ill was the plight of the first two, the plight of those two was worse, so that God knows not one of the whole four could have stirred from the place, but for the way they were all four loaded on Llamrei, Arthur's mare. And then Arthur seized the entrance to the cave, and from the entrance he took aim at the hag with Carnwennan his knife, and struck her across the middle until she was as two tubs. And Cadw of Prydein took the witch's blood and kept it with him.

And then Culhwch set forth, and Goreu son of Custennin with him, and every one that wished ill to Ysbaddaden Chief Giant, and those marvels with them to his court. And Cadw of Prydein came to shave his beard, flesh and skin to the bone, and his two ears outright. And Culhwch said, 'Hast had thy shave, man?' 'I have,' said he. 'And is thy daughter mine now?' 'Thine,' said he. 'And thou needst not thank me for that, but thank Arthur who has secured her for thee. Of my own free will thou shouldst never have had her. And it is high time to take away my life.' And then Goreu son of Custennin caught him by the hair of his head and dragged him behind him to the mound, and cut off his head, and set it on the bailey-stake. And he took possession of his fort and his dominions.

And that night Culhwch slept with Olwen, and she was his only wife so long as he lived. And the hosts of Arthur dispersed, every one to his country.

And in this wise did Culhwch win Olwen daughter of Ysbaddaden Chief Giant.

THE MABINOGION

The Burial of Guenever

Then Sir Launcelot rose up or day, and told the hermit. It were well done, said the hermit, that ye made you ready, and that you disobey not the advision. Then Sir Launcelot took his seven fellows with him, and on foot they yede from Glastonbury to Almesbury, the which is little more than thirty mile. And thither they came within two days, for they were weak and feeble to go. And when Sir Launcelot was come to Almesbury within the nunnery, Queen Guenever died but half an hour afore. And the ladies told Sir Launcelot that Queen Guenever told them all or she passed, that Sir Launcelot had been priest near a twelvemonth, And hither he cometh as fast as he may to fetch my corpse; and beside my lord, King Arthur, he shall bury me. Wherefore the queen said in hearing of them all: I beseech Almighty God that I may never have power to see Sir Launcelot with my worldly eyen; and thus, said all the ladies, was ever her prayer these two days, till she was dead. Then Sir Launcelot saw her visage, but he wept not greatly, but sighed. And so he did all the observance of the service himself, both the dirge at night, and on the morn he sang mass. And there was ordained an horse bier; and so with an hundred torches ever burning about the corpse of the queen, and ever Sir Launcelot with his seven fellows went about the horse bier, singing and reading many an holy orison, and frankincense upon the corpse incensed. Thus Sir Launcelot and his seven fellows went on foot from Almesbury unto Glastonbury. And when they were come to the chapel and the hermitage, there she had a dirge, with great devotion. And on the morn the hermit that sometime was Bishop of Canterbury sang the mass of *requiem* with great devotion. And Sir Launcelot was the first that offered, and then also his seven fellows. And then she was wrapped in cered cloth of Raines, from the top to the toe, in thirtyfold; and after she was put in a web of lead, and then in a coffin of marble. And when she was put in the earth

Sir Launcelot swooned, and lay long still, while the hermit came and awaked him, and said: Ye be to blame, for ye displease God with such manner of sorrow making. Truly, said Sir Launcelot, I trust I do not displease God, for He knoweth mine intent. For my sorrow was not, nor is not, for any rejoicing of sin, but my sorrow may never have end. For when I remember of her beauty, and of her noblesse, that was both with her king and with her, so when I saw his corpse and her corpse so lie together, truly mine heart would not serve to sustain my careful body. Also when I remember me how by my default, mine orgulity and my pride, that they were both laid full low, that were peerless that ever was living of Christian people, wit you well, said Sir Launcelot, this remembered, of their kindness and mine unkindness, sank so to mine heart, that I might not sustain myself.

SIR THOMAS MALORY (c. 1400–1470)

The Three Hundred

So the allies, when Leonidas ordered them to retire, obeyed him and forthwith departed. Only the Thespians and the Thebans remained with the Spartans; and of these the Thebans were kept back by Leonidas as hostages, very much against their will. The Thespians, on the contrary, stayed entirely of their own accord, refusing to retreat, and declaring that they would not forsake Leonidas and his followers. So they abode with the Spartans, and died with them. Their leader was Demophilus, the son of Diadromes.

At sunrise Xerxes made libations, after which he waited until the time when the forum is wont to fill, and then began his advance. Ephialtes had instructed him thus as the descent of the mountain is much quicker, and the distance much shorter, than the way round the hills, and the ascent. So the barbarians under Xerxes began to draw nigh; and the Greeks under Leonidas, as they now went forth determined to die, advanced much further than on previous days, until they reached the more open portion of the pass. Hitherto they had held their station within the wall, and from this had gone forth to fight at the point where the pass was the narrowest. Now they joined battle beyond the defile, and carried slaughter among the barbarians, who fell in heaps. Behind them the captains of the squadrons, armed with whips, urged their men forward with continual blows. Many were thrust into the sea, and there perished; a still greater number were trampled to death by their own soldiers; no one heeded the dying. For the Greeks, reckless of their own safety and desperate, since they knew that, as the mountain had been crossed, their destruction was nigh at hand, exerted themselves with the most furious valour against the barbarians.

By this time the spears of the greater number were all shivered, and with their swords they hewed down the ranks of the Persians; and here, as they strove, Leonidas fell fighting bravely, together with many other famous Spartans, whose names I have taken care to learn on account of their great worthiness, as indeed I have those of all the three hundred. There fell too at the same time very many famous Persians: among them, two sons of Darius, Abrocomes and Hyperanthes, his children by Phrataguné, the daughter of Artanes. Artanes was brother of King Darius, being a son of Hystaspes, the son of Arsames; and when he gave his daughter to the king, he made him heir likewise of all his substance; for she was his only child.

Thus two brothers of Xerxes here fought and fell. And now there arose a fierce struggle between the Persians and the Lacedæmonians over the body of Leonidas, in which the Greeks four times drove back the enemy, and at last by their great bravery succeeded in bearing off the body. This combat was scarcely ended when the Persians with Ephialtes approached; and the Greeks, informed that they drew nigh, made a change in the manner of their fighting. Drawing back into the narrowest part of the pass, and retreating even behind the cross wall, they posted themselves upon a hillock, where they stood all drawn up together in one close body, except only the Thebans. The hillock whereof I speak is at the entrance of the straits, where the stone lion stands which was set up in honour of Leonidas. Here they defended themselves to the last, such as still had swords using them, and the others resisting with their hands and teeth; till the barbarians, who in part had pulled down the wall and attacked them in front, in part had gone round and now encircled them upon every side, overwhelmed and buried the remnant which was left beneath showers of missile weapons.

HERODOTUS (c.483–c.425 B.C.)

Vercingetorix Capitulates

After this second disastrous repulse, the Gauls held a council of war, and, by calling in men familiar with the neighbourhood, they learned the positions and strength of our camps on the surrounding heights. It had been impossible to encircle Mont Réa, on the north, because of its huge circumference, and we had been obliged to establish a camp there at the foot of a gentle slope which would give an assailant some small advantage. It was occupied by two legions commanded respectively by Gaius Antistius Reginus and Gaius Caninius Rebilus. Following patrol reconnaissance of the locality, the enemy commanders agreed in secret on their objective and plan of action, and detailed 60,000 men from the most warlike tribes to launch an attack at noon under Vercassivellaunus. Leaving camp an hour or so after sunset, he completed his march just before daybreak and ordered his troops to rest under cover of Mont Réa. As zero hour approached, he began moving on the Roman camp while the Gallic cavalry advanced towards our circumvallation and infantry paraded in strength outside their encampment.

Vercingetorix saw these movements from the citadel of Alesia: he had faggots, poles, mantlets, grappling-hooks, and other apparatus brought out in readiness for an assault on our fortifications. There was fighting along the whole line, and the Gauls made desperate efforts to overwhelm the weaker points in the defence. My troops found difficulty in meeting these simultaneous attacks: they were unnerved, too, by the shouting in their rear, which impressed them with a sense of their utter dependence on the courage of others; for it is generally the invisible that is most alarming.

Standing on the north-west slope of Flavigny, I could see the whole battle-field, and was thus able to send up reinforcements wherever they were needed. Both sides realized that the crisis demanded a supreme effort: the Gauls knew that everything depended on their smashing through our fortifications, while the legions foresaw an end of all their labours if they could only hold their ground. The fighting was most bitter at Mont Réa, where the enemy's downhill thrust told heavily against us: some of them flung javelins while others advanced under locked shields, the entire force being constantly relieved by fresh waves of men. Earth was heaped against the fortifications at all points, enabling them to climb the rampart and at the same time covering the traps which we had laid. I received word that the men were tiring and short of ammunition. Six battalions were therefore sent to their relief under Labienus, who had orders to stand his ground unless and until the position became absolutely untenable, in which case he was to regroup and fight his way out. I then visited other parts of the field to encourage the exhausted troops with a reminder that to give way now would undo all their former victories.

Vercingetorix had realized by this time the hopelessness of trying to break through our defences in the plain: he now decided to storm the contravallation where it crossed the heights of Flavigny, and accordingly moved his assault apparatus over to that sector. The defenders were forced from their towers under a hail of missiles, the trenches filled in with faggots and earth, the rampart and breastwork torn down with grappling-hooks. Several battalions led by young Brutus were ordered to reinforce the position, then more under Gaius Fabius; finally, as the struggle grew more desperate, I took up a fresh detachment in person. The balance was restored and the enemy fell back.

I then started for Mont Réa, taking five battalions from the nearest redoubt. One detachment of cavalry was ordered to accompany us while another rode round the circumvallation to take the enemy's rear. The trenches and rampart had failed against the Gallic assault; fortunately, however, Labienus had been able to concentrate eleven battalions from the redoubts in his sector, and he now sent to warn me of his next move. I hurried forward to be present at this engagement.

The enemy recognized my scarlet cloak, and then saw my combined force moving down the slopes, which were clearly visible from Mont Réa. As they joined battle both sides raised a cheer which was taken up by the soldiers on the rampart and along the whole line of fortifications. The legionaries dispensed with pikes, and had got to work with their swords when the Gauls suddenly beheld our mounted squadrons in their rear as fresh battalions of infantry closed in from the south. They broke and fled, but were intercepted by the cavalry and mown down. Sedulius, chief magistrate and commander of the Lemovices, was killed; Vercassivellaunus was taken prisoner in the rout; and I was presented with seventy-four Gallic standards. Very few of that great army got back safely to camp.

Vercingetorix witnessed the rout and slaughter of his countrymen: he gave up all hope, and withdrew once again into Alesia, while the camp on Mussy-la-Fosse was hurriedly abandoned. Were it not for the fact that our men were tired out after a long day's work, in the line or in reserve, the entire enemy force might well have been annihilated. As it was, the cavalry went out just after midnight and overtook their rearguard, many of whom were cut down or taken prisoner. The survivors made for home.

On the following day Vercingetorix addressed a meeting of the chiefs, and explained that he had embarked upon this war not for private ends, but in his country's cause. 'Now,' he said, 'I must bow to the decrees of Fate.' He then invited the assembly to palliate the wrath of Rome in whatever way they chose, either by putting him to death or by delivering him up alive. A deputation having referred the matter to me, they were ordered to surrender their weapons together with their leading men; and seated on the entrenchments before my camp, I received the capitulation of Alesia. The chieftains were marched out, Vercingetorix was handed over, and all their arms were stacked.

JULIUS CAESAR (C. 102–44 B.C.)

Seven Feet of English Ground

King Harald Godwinsson had come with an immense army, both of cavalry and infantry. Now King Harald Sigurdson rode around his array, to see how every part was drawn up. He was upon a black horse, and the horse stumbled under him, so that the king fell off. He got up in haste, and said, 'A fall is lucky for a traveller.'

The English king Harald said to the Northmen who were with him, 'Do ye know the stout man who fell from his horse, with the blue kirtle and the beautiful helmet?'

'That is the king himself,' said they.

The English king said, 'A great man, and of stately appearance is he; but I think his luck has left him.'

Twenty horsemen rode forward from the Thing-men's troops against the Northmen's array; and all of them, and likewise their horses, were clothed in armour.

One of the horsemen said, 'Is Earl Toste in this army?'

The earl answered, 'It is not to be denied that ye will find him here.'

The horseman says, 'Thy brother King Harald sends thee salutation, with the message that thou shalt have the whole of Northumberland; and rather than thou shouldst not submit to him, he will give thee the third part of his kingdom to rule over along with himself.'

The earl replies, 'This is something different from the enmity and scorn he offered last winter; and if this had been offered then it would have saved many a man's life who now is dead and it would have been better for the kingdom of England. But if I accept of this offer, what will he give King Harald Sigurdson for his trouble?'

The horseman replied, 'He has also spoken of this; and will give him seven feet of English ground, or as much more as he may be taller than other men.'

'Then,' said the earl, 'go now and tell King Harald to get ready for battle; for never shall the Northmen say with truth that Earl Toste left King Harald Sigurdson to join his enemy's troops, when he came to fight west here in England. We shall rather all take the resolution to die with honour, or to gain England by a victory.'

Then the horsemen rode back.

King Harald Sigurdson said to the earl, 'Who was the man who spoke so well?'

The earl replied, 'That was King Harald Godwinsson.'

Then said King Harald Sigurdson, 'That was by far too long concealed from me; for they had come so near to our army, that this Harald should never have carried back the tidings of our men's slaughter.'

Then said the earl, 'It was certainly imprudent for such chiefs, and it may be as you say; but I saw he was going to offer me peace and a great dominion, and that, on the other hand, I would be his murderer if I betrayed him; and I would rather he should be my murderer than I his, if one of us two be to die.'

SNORRI STURLUSON (1178-1241)

To Quell Mutiny

The lenity of the emperor confirmed the insolence of the troops; the legions imitated the example of the guards, and defended their prerogative of licentiousness with the same furious obstinacy. The administration of Alexander was an unavailing struggle against the corruption of his age. In Illyricum, in Mauritania, in Armenia, in Mesopotamia, in Germany, fresh mutinies perpetually broke out; his officers were murdered, his authority was insulted, and his life at last sacrificed to the fierce discontents of the army. One particular fact well deserves to be recorded, as it illustrates the manners of the troops, and exhibits a singular instance of their return to a sense of duty and obedience. Whilst the emperor lay at Antioch, in his Persian expedition, the particulars of which we shall hereafter relate, the punishment of some soldiers, who had been discovered in the baths of women, excited a sedition in the legion to which they belonged. Alexander ascended his tribunal, and with a modest firmness represented to the armed multitude, the absolute necessity as well as his inflexible resolution of correcting the vices introduced by his impure predecessor, and of maintaining the discipline, which could not be relaxed without the ruin of the Roman name and empire. Their clamours interrupted his mild expostulation. 'Reserve your shouts,' said the undaunted emperor, 'till you take the field against the Persians, the Germans, and the

Sarmatians. Be silent in the presence of your sovereign and benefactor, who bestows upon you the corn, the clothing, and the money of the provinces; Be silent, or I shall no longer style you soldiers, but *citizens*, if those indeed who disclaim the laws of Rome deserve to be ranked among the meanest of the people.' His menaces inflamed the fury of the legion, and their brandished arms already threatened his person. 'Your courage,' resumed the intrepid Alexander, 'would be more nobly displayed in the field of battle; *me* you may destroy, you cannot intimidate; and the severe justice of the republic would punish your crime, and revenge my death.' The legion still persisted in clamorous sedition, when the emperor pronounced, with a loud voice, the decisive sentence, '*Citizens!* lay down your arms, and depart in peace to your respective habitations.' The tempest was instantly appeased; the soldiers, filled with grief and shame, silently confessed the justice of their punishment and the power of discipline, yielded up their arms and military ensigns, and retired in confusion, not to their camp, but to the several inns of the city. Alexander enjoyed, during thirty days, the edifying spectacle of their repentance; nor did he restore them to their former rank in the army, till he had punished with death those tribunes whose connivance had occasioned the mutiny. The grateful legion served the emperor, whilst living, and revenged him when dead.

EDWARD GIBBON (1737–1794)

Sir Richard Grenville

But to returne to the fight, the Spanish ships which attempted to bord the Revenge, as they were wounded and beaten off, so always others came in their places, she having never lesse then two mighty Gallions by her sides, and aboard her: So that ere the morning, from three of the clocke the day before, there had fifteene severall Armadas assayled her; and all so ill approved their entertainment, as they were by the breake of day, far more willing to harken to a composition, then hastily to make any more assaults or entries. But as the day encreased, so our men decreased: and as the light grew more and more, by so much more grewe our discomforts. For none appeared in sight but enemies, saving one small ship called the Pilgrim, commaunded by Jacob Whiddon, who hovered all night to see the successe: but in the morning bearing with the Revenge, was hunted like a hare amongst many ravenous houndes, but escaped.

All the powder of the Revenge to the last barrell was now spent, all her pikes broken, fortie of her best men slaine, and the most part of the rest hurt. In the beginning of the fight shee had but one hundreth free from sicknes, and fourescore & ten sicke, laid in hold upon the Ballast. A small troup to man such a ship, & a weake garrison to resist so mighty an army. By those hundred al was susteined, the voleis, boordings, and entrings of fifteen ships of warre, besides those which beat her at large. On the contrary, the Spanish were always supplied with souldiers brought from every squadron: all maner of Armes and powder at will. Unto ours there remained no comfort at all, no hope, no supply either of ships, men, or weapons; the Mastes all beaten over boord, all her tackle cut asunder, her upper worke altogether rased, and in effect evened shee was with the water, but the very foundation or bottome of a ship, nothing being left over head either for flight or defence. Sir Richard finding himselfe in this distresse, and unable any longer to make resistance, having endured in this fifteene houres fight, the assault of fifteene severall Armadas, all by turnes aboord him, and by estimation eight hundred shotte of great Artillerie, besides many assaults and entries; and that himselfe and the shippe must needes be possessed by the enemy, who were now all cast in a ring round about him. (The Revenge not able to moove one way or other, but as she was moved with the waves and billow of the sea) commaunded the Master gunner, whom hee knew to be a most resolute man, to split and sinke the shippe; that thereby nothing might remaine of glory or victory to the Spaniards: seeing in so many houres fight, and with so great a Navie they were not able to take her, having had fifteene houres time, above ten thousand men, & fiftie and three saile of men of warre to performe it withall: and perswaded the company, or as many as hee could induce, to yeelde themselves unto God, and to the mercie of none else; but as they had, like valiant resolute men, repulsed so many enemies, they should not nowe shorten the honour of their Nation, by prolonging their owne lives for a few houres, or a fewe dayes. The Master gunner readily condescended and divers others; but the Captaine and the Master were of another opinion, and besought Sir Richard to have care of them: alleaging that the Spaniard would be as ready to entertaine a composition, as they were willing to offer the same: and that there being divers sufficient and valiant men yet living, and whose wounds were not mortal, they might do their Countrey and prince acceptable service hereafter. And whereas Sir Richard had alleaged that the Spaniards should never glory to have taken one shippe of her Majestie, seeing they had so long and so notably defended themselves; they answered, that the shippe had sixe foote water in holde, three shot under water, which were so weakely stopped, as with the first working of the sea, she must needs sinke, and was besides so crusht and brused, as shee could never be removed out of the place.

And as the matter was thus in dispute, and Sir Richard refusing to hearken to any of those reasons: the Master of the Revenge (while the Captaine wanne unto him the greater party) was convoyd aboord the Generall Don Alfonso Baçan. Who (finding none over hastie to enter the Revenge againe, doubting least Sir Richard would have blowne them up and himselfe, and perceiving by the report of the Master of the Revenge his dangerous disposition) yeelded that all their lives should be saved, the company sent for England, & the better sort to pay such reasonable ransome as their estate would beare, and in the meane season to be free from Gally or imprisonment. To this he so much the rather condescended as wel, as I have said, for feare of further losse and mischiefe to themselves, as also for the desire he had to recover Sir Richard Greenvil; whom for his notable valure he seemed greatly to honour and admire.

When this answere was returned, and that safetie of life was promised, the common sort being now at the ende of their perill, the most drew backe from Sir Richard and the Master gunner, being no hard matter to disswade men from death to life. The Master gunner finding himselfe and Sir Richard thus prevented and mastered by the greater number, would have slaine himselfe with a sword, had he not bene by force with-held and locked into his Cabben. Then the Generall sent many boates aboord the Revenge, and divers of our men fearing Sir Richards disposition, stole away aboord the Generall and other shippes. Sir Richard thus over-matched, was sent unto by Alfonso Baçan to remoove out of the Revenge, the shippe being marveilous unsavorie, filled with blood and bodies of dead, and wounded men like a slaughter house. Sir Richard answered that hee might doe with his body what he list, for hee esteemed it not, and as he was carried out of the shippe hee swounded, and reviving againe desired the company to pray for him. The Generall used Sir Richard with all humanitie, and left nothing unattempted that tended to his recoverie, highly commending his valour and worthinesse, and greatly bewailing the danger wherein he was, being unto them a rare spectacle, and a resolution sildome approoved, to see one shippe turne toward so many enemies, to endure the charge and boording of so many huge Armadas, and to resist and repell the assaults and entries of so many souldiers.

SIR WALTER RALEIGH (1552–1618)

Defeat

By five in the evening the defeat was total. More than a hundred field-pieces had fallen into the hands of the French. All Przebichewsky's corps had laid down their arms; the others having lost more than half their number, retired in disorder. The remains of the divisions under Langeron and Dokhtourow were crowded in confusion round the pools and sluices of the village of Auguest. By six the enemy's fire was directed on this point only; they had posted their batteries half-way up the heights of Pratzen, and were firing on the allies as they retreated.

Dokhtourow and some others of the rear pulled their regiments together, reformed their battalions, and turned against the French cavalry, who were pursuing them.

It was now dusk. The narrow mill dam of Auguest—where for a long course of peaceful years the good old miller had dropped his fishing-line into the pool, while his grandchild, with his shirt-sleeves rolled up, plunged his bare arms into the water-can among the wriggling silver fish—where the Moravian farmer in his fur cap and dark-blue coat had followed the huge, slow waggons carrying heavy sheaves of wheat to the mill, and returning with full sacks of fine white flour, filling the air with light dust—was now packed with a scared and bewildered crowd, pushing, falling, to be crushed by the hoofs of horses, or the wheels of waggons and gun-carriages, or trampling the dead under foot merely to be killed in their turn a little further on.

Every few seconds a ball or a shell came hurtling and bursting in the midst of this compact mass of human beings, killing and bespattering all within range. Dologhow, who had already gained his promotion, himself wounded in the hand, with ten men and his colonel, were the sole survivors of their regiment. Carried on by the stream, they had forced their way to the end of the mill dam, where they were stopped by a horse in a gun-carriage, which had been killed, and which had to be cut from the harness. A ball killed a man behind them, and another fell in front and sprinkled Dologhow over with blood. Then the mass rushed forward desperately a few paces, and had to stop again.

'A hundred yards farther, and there is safety! To stop here another two minutes is death!' This was what everyone was saying.

Dologhow, who had been shoved back into the middle, got as far as the edge of the mill-pool, and ran across the thin ice that coated the water.

'Look here, come this way!' he cried to the gunner. 'The ice will bear.'

The ice in fact did not break under his weight, but it cracked and yielded, and it was quite evident that even without the weight of the gun and of the mass of men it would give way under him. The men looked at him, and crowded on the bank, but could not make up their minds to follow him. The general in command, who was on horseback, raised his arm, and had just opened his lips to speak, when a ball crashed past, so low down over the terrified heads, that all bent low—and something fell. It was the general, who sank in a pool of blood. No one looked round at him; no one could think of picking him up.

'On the ice! Don't you hear? On the ice! Turn round, turn!' shouted several; most of the men had no idea themselves why they shouted this.

One of the gun-carriages made the venture; the crowd rushed on to the ice, which cracked under one of the fugitives; his foot was in the water, and in trying to get it out, he fell in to the waist. The men who were nearest to him held back; the gunner stopped his horse, while behind them the shouts rose louder than ever: 'Get on to the ice; go on, push on!' and shrieks of terror sounded on every side.

The soldiers gathered round the cannon, tugging and beating the horses to get them on. The poor beasts started, the ice gave way in one sheet, and forty men sank. The cannon-balls did not cease whistling and pelting with hideous steadiness, falling sometimes on the ice, and sometimes in the water, decimating the living mass that swarmed on the dyke, on the pools, and on the shore.

LEO TOLSTOY (1828–1910)

A Roundhead Officer

He was of a middle stature, of a slender and exactly well-proportioned shape in all parts, his complexion fair, his hair of light brown, very thick set in his youth, softer than the finest silk, and curling into loose great rings at the ends; his eyes of a lively grey, well-shaped and full of life and vigour, graced with many becoming motions; his visage thin, his mouth well made, and his lips very ruddy and graceful, although the nether chap shut over the upper, yet it was in such a manner as was not unbecoming; his teeth were even and white as the purest ivory; his chin was something long, and the mould of his face; his forehead was not very high; his nose was raised and sharp; but withal he had a most amiable countenance, which carried in it something of magnanimity and majesty mixed with sweetness, that at the same time bespoke love and awe in all that saw him; his skin was smooth and white, his legs and feet excellently well-made; he was quick in his pace and turns, nimble and active and graceful in all his motions; he was apt for any bodily exercise, and any that he did became him; he could dance admirably well, but neither in youth nor riper years made any practice of it; he had skill in fencing, such as became a gentleman; he had a great love of music, and often diverted himself with a viol, on which he played masterly; and he had an exact ear and judgment in other music; he shot excellently in bows and guns, and much used them for his exercise; he had great judgment in paintings, graving, sculpture, and all liberal arts, and had many curiosities of value in all kinds; he took great delight in perspective glasses, and for his other rarities was not so much affected with the antiquity as the merit of the work; he took much pleasure in improvement of grounds, in planting groves, and walks, and fruit-trees, in opening springs and making fish-ponds; of country recreations he loved none but hawking, and in that was very eager and much delighted for the time he used it, but soon left it off; he was wonderfully neat, cleanly, and genteel in his habit, and had a very good fancy in it, but he left off very early the wearing of anything that was costly, yet in his plainest negligent habit appeared very much a gentleman; he had more address than force of body, yet the courage of his soul so supplied his members that he never wanted strength when he found occasion to employ it; his conversation was very pleasant, for he was naturally cheerful, had a ready wit and apprehension; he was eager in everything he did, earnest in dispute, but withal very rational, so that he was seldom overcome; everything that it was necessary for him to do he did with delight, free and unconstrained; he hated ceremonious compliment, but yet had a natural civility and complaisance to all people; he was of a tender constitution, but through the vivacity of his spirit could undergo labours, watchings, and journeys, as well as any of stronger compositions; he was rheumatic, and had a long sickness and distemper occasioned thereby, two or three years after the war ended, but else, for the latter half of his life, was healthy though tender; in his youth and childhood he was sickly, much troubled with weakness and toothaches, but then his spirits carried him through them; he was very patient under sickness or pain, or any common accidents, but yet, upon occasions, though never without just ones, he would be very angry, and had even in that such a grace as made him to be feared, yet he was never outrageous in passion; he had a very good faculty in persuading, and would speak very well, pertinently, and effectually without premeditation upon the greatest occasions that could be offered, for indeed, his judgment was so nice, that he could never frame any speech beforehand to please himself; but his invention was so ready, and wisdom so habitual in all his speeches, that he never had reason to repent himself of speaking at any time without ranking the words beforehand; he was not talkative, yet free of discourse; of a very spare diet, not given to sleep, and an early riser when in health; he never was at any time idle, and hated to see any one else so; in all his natural and ordinary inclinations and composure, there was something extraordinary and tending to virtue, beyond what I can describe, or can be gathered from a bare dead description; there was a life of spirit and power in him that is not to be found in any copy drawn from him. To sum up, therefore, all that can be said of his outward frame and disposition, we must truly conclude, that it was a very handsome and well furnished lodging prepared for the reception of that prince, who in the administration of all excellent virtues reigned there a while, till he was called back to the palace of the universal emperor.

LUCY HUTCHINSON (1620–?1680)

Napoleon when First Consul

At length the two human hedges were finally formed, the door of the audience chamber was thrown wide open with a commanding crash, and a vivacious officer, sentinel, or I know not what, nimbly descended the three steps into our apartment, and placing himself at the side of the door, with one hand spread as high as possible above his head, and the other extended horizontally, called out in a loud and authoritative voice: 'Le Premier Consul!'

You will easily believe nothing more was necessary to obtain attention; not a soul either spoke or stirred as he and his suite passed along, which was so quickly that, had I not been placed so near the door, and had not all about me facilitated my standing foremost, and being least crowd-obstructed, I could hardly have seen him. As it was, I had a view so near, though so brief, of his face, as to be very much struck by it. It is of a deeply impressive cast, pale even to sallowness, while not only in the eye but in every feature—care, thought, melancholy, and meditation are strongly marked, with so much of character, nay, genius, and so penetrating a seriousness, or rather sadness, as powerfully to sink into an observer's mind.

Yet, though the busts and medallions I have seen are, in general, such good resemblances that I think I should have known him untold, he has by no means the look to be expected from Bonaparte, but rather that of a profoundly studious and contemplative man, who 'o'er books consumes' not only the 'midnight oil' but his own daily strength, 'and wastes the puny body to decay' by abstruse speculation and theoretic plans, or rather visions, ingenious but not practicable. But the look of the commander who heads his own army, who fights his own battles, who conquers every difficulty by personal exertion, who executes all he plans, who performs even all he suggests; whose ambition is of the most enterprising, and whose bravery is of the most daring cast—this, which is the look to be expected from his situation, and the exploits which have led to it, the spectator watches for in vain. The plainness, also, of his dress, so conspicuously contrasted by the finery of all around him, conspires forcibly with his countenance, so 'sicklied o'er with the pale hue of thought,' to give him far more the air of a student than a warrior. . .

Bonaparte, mounting a beautiful and spirited white horse, closely encircled by his glittering aides-de-camp, and accompanied by his generals, rode round the ranks, holding his bridle indifferently in either hand, and seeming utterly careless of the prancing, rearing, or other freaks of his horse, insomuch as to strike some who were near me with a notion of his being a bad horseman. I am the last to be a *judge* upon this subject; but as a *remarker*, he only appeared to me a man who knew so well he could manage the animal when he pleased, that he did not deem it worth his while to keep constantly in order what he knew, if urged or provoked, he could subdue in a moment.

FANNY BURNEY (1752–1840)

A Natural Leader

His ship was full of young midshipmen, of whom there were not less than thirty on board: and happy were they whose lot it was to be placed with such a captain. If he perceived that a boy was afraid at first going aloft, he would say to him, in a friendly manner: 'Well, sir, I am going a race to the mast-head, and beg that I may meet you there.' The poor little fellow instantly began to climb, and got up how he could,—Nelson never noticed in what manner; but, when they met in the top, spoke cheerfully to him; and would say, how much any person was to be pitied who fancied that getting up was either dangerous or difficult. Every day he went into the schoolroom, to see that they were pursuing their nautical studies; and at noon he was always the first on deck with his quadrant. Whenever he paid a visit of ceremony some of these youths accompanied him: and when he went to dine with the governor at Barbadoes, he took one of them in his hand and presented him, saying, 'Your Excellency must excuse me for bringing one of my midshipmen. I make it a rule to introduce them to all the good company I can, as they have few to look up to, besides myself, during the time they are at sea.'

To his midshipmen he ever showed the most winning kindness, encouraging the diffident, tempering the hasty, counselling and befriending both. 'Recollect,' he used to say, 'that you must be a seaman to be an officer; and also, that you cannot be a good officer without being a gentleman.' A lieutenant wrote to him, to say that he was dissatisfied with his captain. Nelson's answer was in that spirit of perfect wisdom and perfect goodness which regulated his whole conduct toward those who were under his command. 'I have just received your letter, and I am truly sorry that any difference should arise between your captain, who has the reputation of being one of the bright officers of the service, and yourself, a very young man, and a very young officer, who must naturally have much to learn: therefore the chance is that you are perfectly wrong in the disagreement. However, as your present situation must be very disagreeable, I will certainly take an early opportunity of removing you, provided your conduct to your present captain be such that another may not refuse to receive you.'..

The gentleness and benignity of his disposition never made him forget what was due to discipline. Being on one occasion applied to, to save a young officer from a court-martial which he had provoked by his misconduct, his reply was: 'That he would do everything in his power to oblige so gallant and good an officer as Sir John Warren,' in whose name the intercession had been made: 'But what,' he added, 'would he do if he were here?—Exactly what I have done, and am still willing to do. The young man must write such a letter of contrition as would be an acknowledgment of his great fault; and with a sincere promise, if his captain will intercede to prevent the impending court-martial, never to so misbehave again. On his captain's inclosing me such a letter, with a request to cancel the order for the trial, I might be induced to do it: but the letters and reprimand will be given in the public order-book of the fleet, and read to all the officers. The young

man has pushed himself forward to notice, and he must take the consequence. It was upon the quarter-deck, in the face of the ship's company, that he treated his captain with contempt; and I am in duty
bound to support the authority and consequence of every officer under
my command. A poor ignorant seaman is for ever punished for contempt to *his* superiors.'

ROBERT SOUTHEY (1774–1843)

Dame Fortune

It is not unknown to me how many men have had, and still have, the
opinion that the affairs of the world are in such wise governed by
Fortune and by God that men with their wisdom cannot direct them
and that no one can even help them; and because of this they would
have us believe that it is not necessary to labour much in affairs, but
to let chance govern them. This opinion has been more credited in our
times because of the great changes in affairs which have been seen,
and may still be seen, every day, beyond all human conjecture.
Sometimes pondering over this, I am in some degree inclined
to their opinion. Nevertheless, not to extinguish our free will, I hold
it to be true that Fortune is the arbiter of one-half of our actions,
but that she still leaves us to direct the other half, or perhaps a little
less.

I compare her to one of those raging rivers, which when in flood
overflows the plains, sweeping away trees and buildings, bearing away
the soil from place to place; everything flies before it, all yield to its
violence, without being able in any way to withstand it; and yet,
though its nature be such, it does not follow therefore that men, when
the weather becomes fair, shall not make provision, both with defences
and barriers, in such a manner that, rising again, the waters may pass
away by canal, and their force be neither so unrestrained nor so dangerous. So it happens with Fortune, who shows her power where valour
has not prepared to resist her, and thither she turns her forces where
she knows that barriers and defences have not been raised to constrain
her.

And if you will consider Italy, which is the seat of these changes,
and which has given to them their impulse, you will see it to be an open
country without barriers and without any defence. For if it had been
defended by proper valour, as are Germany, Spain, and France, either
this invasion would not have made the great changes it has made or it

would not have come at all. And this I consider enough to say concerning resistance to fortune in general.

But confining myself more to the particular, I say that a prince may be seen happy to-day and ruined to-morrow without having shown any change of disposition or character. This, I believe, arises firstly from causes that have already been discussed at length, namely, that the prince who relies entirely upon fortune is lost when it changes. I believe also that he will be successful who directs his actions according to the spirit of the times, and that he whose actions do not accord with the times will not be successful. Because men are seen, in affairs that lead to the end which every man has before him, namely, glory and riches, to get there by various methods; one with caution, another with haste; one by force, another by skill; one by patience, another by its opposite; and each one succeeds in reaching the goal by a different method. One can also see of two cautious men the one attain his end, the other fail; and similarly, two men by different observances are equally successful, the one being cautious, the other impetuous; all this arises from nothing else than whether or not they conform in their methods to the spirit of the times. This follows from what I have said, that two men working differently bring about the same effect, and of two working similarly, one attains his object and the other does not.

Changes in estate also issue from this, for if, to one who governs himself with caution and patience, times and affairs converge in such a way that his administration is successful, his fortune is made; but if times and affairs change, he is ruined if he does not change his course of action. But a man is not often found sufficiently circumspect to know how to accommodate himself to the change, both because he cannot deviate from what nature inclines him to, and also because, having always prospered by acting in one way, he cannot be persuaded that it is well to leave it; and, therefore, the cautious man, when it is time to turn adventurous, does not know how to do it, hence he is ruined; but had he changed his conduct with the times fortune would not have changed.

Pope Julius II went to work impetuously in all his affairs, and found the times and circumstances conform so well to that line of action that he always met with success. Consider his first enterprise against Bologna, Messer Giovanni Bentivogli being still alive. The Venetians were not agreeable to it, nor was the King of Spain, and he had the enterprise still under discussion with the King of France; nevertheless he personally entered upon the expedition with his accustomed boldness and energy, a move which made Spain and the Venetians stand irresolute and passive, the latter from fear, the former from desire to recover all the kingdom of Naples; on the other hand, he drew after him the King of France, because that king, having observed the movement, and desiring to make the pope his friend so as to humble the Venetians, found it impossible to refuse him soldiers without manifestly offending him. Therefore Julius with his impetuous action accomplished what no other pontiff with simple human wisdom could have done; for if he had waited in Rome until he could get away, with his plans arranged and everything fixed, as any other pontiff would have done, he would never have succeeded. Because the King of France would have made a thousand excuses, and the others would have raised a thousand fears.

I will leave his other actions alone, as they were all alike, and they all succeeded, for the shortness of his life did not let him experience the contrary; but if circumstances had arisen which required him to go cautiously, his ruin would have followed, because he would never have deviated from those ways to which nature inclined him.

I conclude therefore that, fortune being changeful and mankind steadfast in their ways, so long as the two are in agreement men are successful, but unsuccessful when they fall out. For my part I consider that it is better to be adventurous than cautious, because Fortune is a woman, and if you wish to keep her under it is necessary to beat and ill use her; and it is seen that she allows herself to be mastered by the adventurous rather than by those who go to work more coldly. She is, therefore, always, woman-like, a lover of young men, because they are less cautious, more violent, and with more audacity command her.

NICCOLO MACHIAVELLI (1469-1527)

The Vice-Consul's Petticoats

Every one was in a fury except Jack, who did nothing but laugh. The captain wanted to return to obtain Miss Hicks, Gascoigne to obtain Azar, and the vice-consul to obtain his liberty—but the wind was foul for their return, and Jack soon gained the captain on his side. He pointed out to him that, in the first place, if he presumed to return, he would forfeit his charter bond; in the second, he would have to pay for all the bullocks that died; in the third, that if he wished to take Miss Hicks as his wife, he must not first injure her character by having her on board before the solemnity; and lastly, that he could always go and marry her whenever he pleased; the brother could not prevent him. All this was very good advice, and the captain became quite calm and rational, and set his studding-sails below and aloft.

As for Gascoigne, it was no use reasoning with him, so it was agreed that he should have satisfaction as soon as they could get on shore again. Mr Hicks was the most violent; he insisted that the vessel should return, while both Jack and the captain refused, although he threatened them with the whole foreign office. He insisted upon having his clothes, but Jack replied that they had tumbled overboard as they pulled from the shore. He then commanded the mate and men to take the vessel back, but they laughed at him and his woman's clothes.

'At all events, I'll have you turned out of the service,' said he to our hero in his fury.

'I shall be extremely obliged to you,' said Jack—and Captain Hogg was so much amused with the vice-consul's appearance in his sister's clothes, that he quite forgot his own disappointment in laughing at his intended brother-in-law. He made friends again with Jack, who regained his ascendancy, and ordered out the porter on the capstern-head. They had an excellent dinner, but Mr Hicks refused to join them, which however did not spoil the appetite of Jack or the captain: as for Gascoigne, he could not eat a mouthful, but he drank to excess, looking over the rim of his tumbler, as if he could devour our hero, who only laughed the more. Mr Hicks had applied to the men to lend him some clothes, but Jack had foreseen that, and he was omnipotent. There was not a jacket or a pair of trousers to be had for love or money. Mr Hicks then considered it advisable to lower his tone, and he applied to Captain Hogg, who begged to be excused without he consented to his marriage with his sister, to which Mr Hicks gave an indignant negative. He then applied to Gascoigne, who told him in a very surly tone to go to h—ll. At last he applied to our hero, who laughed, and said that he would see him d—d first. So Mr Hicks sat down in his petticoats and vowed revenge. Gascoigne, who had drunk much and eaten nothing, turned in and went to sleep—while Captain Hogg and our hero drank porter on the capstern.

Thus passed the first day, and the wind was famously fair—the bullocks lowed, the cocks crew, the sheep baa'd, and the *Mary Ann* made upwards of two hundred miles. Jack took possession of the other berth in the cabin, and his Majesty's representative was obliged to lie down in his petticoats upon a topsail which lay between decks, with a bullock on each side of him, who every now and then made a dart at him with their horns, as if they knew that it was to him that they were indebted for their embarkation and being destined to drive the scurvy out of the Toulon fleet.

We cannot enter into the details of the passage, which, as the wind was fair, was accomplished in ten days without the loss of a bullock. During this time Mr Hicks condescended to eat without speaking, imagining that the hour of retribution would come when they joined the admiral. Gascoigne gradually recovered himself, but did not speak to our hero, who continued to laugh and drink porter. On the eleventh morning they were in the midst of the Toulon fleet, and Mr Hicks smiled exultingly as he passed our hero in his petticoats, and wondered that Jack showed no signs of trepidation.

The fleet hove-to, Jack ran under the admiral's stern, lowered down his boat, and went on board, showed his credentials, and reported his bullocks. The general signal was made, there was a fair division of the spoil, and then the admiral asked our hero whether the master of the transport had any other stock on board. Jack replied that he had not; but that, having been told by the governor of Malta that they might be acceptable, he had bought a few sheep and some dozen of fowls, which were much at his service, if he would accept of them. The admiral was much obliged to the governor, and also to Jack, for thinking of him, but would not, of course, accept of the stock without paying for them. He requested him to send all of them on board that he could spare, and then asked Jack to dine with him, for Jack had put on his best attire, and looked very much of a gentleman.

'Mr Easy,' said the flag-captain, who had been looking at the transport with his glass, 'is that the master's wife on board?'

'No, sir,' replied Jack; 'it's the vice-consul.'

'What, in petticoats! the vice-consul?'

'Yes, the vice-consul of Tetuan. He came on board in that dress when the brig was under way, and I considered it my duty not to delay, being aware how very important it was that the fleet should be provided with fresh beef.'

'What is all this, Mr Easy?' said the admiral; 'there has been some trick here. You will oblige me by coming into the cabin.'

Easy followed the admiral and flag-captain into the cabin, and then boldly told the whole story how he tricked them all. It was impossible for either of them to help laughing, and when they began to laugh, it was almost as impossible to stop.

'Mr Easy,' said the admiral at last, 'I do not altogether blame you; it appears that the captain of the transport would have delayed sailing because he was in love—and that Mr Gascoigne would have stayed behind because he was infatuated, independent of the ill-will against the English which would have been excited by the abduction of the girl. But I think you might have contrived to manage all that without putting the vice-consul in petticoats.'

'I acted to the best of my judgment, sir,' replied Jack, very humbly.

'And altogether you have done well. Captain Malcolm, send a boat for the vice-consul.'

Mr Hicks was too impatient to tell his wrongs to care for his being in his sister's clothes: he came on board, and although the tittering was great, he imagined that it would soon be all in his favour, when it was known that he was a diplomatic. He told his story, and waited for the decision of the admiral, which was to crush our hero, who stood with the midshipmen on the lee side of the deck; but the admiral replied, 'Mr Hicks, in the first place, this appears to me to be a family affair concerning the marriage of your sister, with which I have nothing to do. You went on board of your own free will in woman's clothes. Mr Easy's orders were positive, and he obeyed them. It was his duty to sail as soon as the transport was ready. You may forward your complaint if you please, but, as a friend, I tell you that it will probably occasion your dismissal; for these kind of pranks are not understood at the foreign office.'

FREDERICK MARRYAT (1792–1848)

How to Hang a Picture

You never saw such a commotion up and down a house in all your life, as when my Uncle Podger undertook to do a job. A picture would have come home from the frame-maker's, and be standing in the dining-room, waiting to be put up; and Aunt Podger would ask what was to be done with it, and Uncle Podger would say:

'Oh, you leave that to *me*. Don't you, any of you, worry yourselves about that. *I'll* do all that.'

And then he would take off his coat, and begin. He would send the girl out for sixpen'orth of nails, and then one of the boys after her to tell her what size to get; and, from that, he would gradually work down, and start the whole house.

'Now you go and get me my hammer, Will,' he would shout; 'and you bring me the rule, Tom; and I shall want the stepladder, and I had better have a kitchen-chair, too; and Jim! you run round to Mr

Goggles, and tell him, "Pa's kind regards and hopes his leg's better; and will he lend him his spirit-level?" And don't you go, Maria, because I shall want somebody to hold me the light; and when the girl comes back she must go out again for a bit of picture-cord; and Tom!—where's Tom?—Tom, you come here; I shall want you to hand me up the picture.'

And then he would lift up the picture, and drop it, and it would come out of the frame, and he would try to save the glass, and cut himself; and then he would spring round the room, looking for his handkerchief. He could not find his handkerchief, because it was in the pocket of the coat he had taken off, and he did not know where he had put the coat, and all the house had to leave off looking for his tools, and start looking for his coat; while he would dance round and hinder them.

'Doesn't anybody in the whole house know where my coat is? I never came across such a set in all my life—upon my word I didn't. Six of you!—and you can't find a coat that I put down not five minutes ago! Well, of all the——'

Then he'd get up, and find that he had been sitting on it, and would call out:

'Oh, you can give it up! I've found it myself now. Might just as well ask the cat to find anything as expect you people to find it.'

And when half an hour had been spent in tying up his finger, and a new glass had been got, and the tools, and the ladder, and the chair, and the candle had been brought, he would have another go, the whole family, including the girl, and the charwoman, standing round in a semicircle, ready to help. Two people would have to hold the chair, and a third would help him up on it, and hold him there, and a fourth would hand him a nail, and a fifth would pass him up the hammer, and he would take hold of the nail, and drop it.

'There!' he would say, in an injured tone, 'now the nail's gone.'

And we would all have to go down on our knees and grovel for it, while he would stand on the chair, and grunt, and want to know if he was to be kept there all the evening.

The nail would be found at last, but by that time he would have lost the hammer.

'Where's the hammer? What did I do with the hammer? Great heavens! Seven of you, gaping round there, and you don't know what I did with the hammer!'

We would find the hammer for him, and then he would have lost sight of the mark he had made on the wall, where the nail was to go in, and each of us had to get up on the chair beside him, and see if we could find it; and we would each discover it in a different place, and he would call us all fools, one after another, and tell us to get down. And he would take the rule, and remeasure, and find that he wanted half thirty-one and three-eighths inches from the corner and would try to do it in his head, and go mad.

And we would all try to do it in our heads, and all arrive at different results, and sneer at one another. And in the general row, the original number would be forgotten, and Uncle Podger would have to measure it again.

He would use a bit of string this time, and at the critical moment, when the old fool was leaning over the chair at an angle of forty-five, and trying to reach a point three inches beyond what was possible for him to reach, the string would slip, and down he would slide on to the piano, a really fine musical effect being produced by the suddenness with which his head and body struck all the notes at the same time.

And Aunt Maria would say that she would not allow the children to stand round and hear such language.

At last, Uncle Podger would get the spot fixed again, and put the point of the nail on it with his left hand, and take the hammer in his right hand. And, with the first blow, he would smash his thumb, and drop the hammer, with a yell, on somebody's toes.

Aunt Maria would mildly observe that, next time Uncle Podger was going to hammer a nail into the wall, she hoped he'd let her know in time, so that she could make arrangements to go and spend a week with her mother while it was being done.

'Oh! you women, you make such a fuss over everything,' Uncle Podger would reply, picking himself up. 'Why, I *like* doing a little job of this sort.'

And then he would have another try, and, at the second blow, the nail would go clean through the plaster, and half the hammer after it, and Uncle Podger be precipitated against the wall with force nearly sufficient to flatten his nose.

Then we had to find the rule and the string again, and a new hole was made; and, about midnight, the picture would be up—very crooked and insecure, the wall for yards round looking as if it had been smoothed down with a rake, and everybody dead beat and wretched —except Uncle Podger.

'There you are,' he would say, stepping heavily off the chair on to the charwoman's corns, and surveying the mess he had made with evident pride. 'Why, some people would have had a man in to do a little thing like that!'

JEROME K. JEROME (1859–1927)

The Bottle Neck

And many thousands of people stood watching the balloon, the old maid watching with the rest; she stood at her open window in the attic, where the cage hung with the little linnet which then had no bird-bath but had to make do with a cup. On the window-sill itself stood a myrtle-tree, which had been moved to one side so as not to get pushed out when the old maid leant forward to watch. As she did so she clearly saw the balloonist drop the rabbit by parachute, drink a toast to the crowd, and then throw the bottle up into the air; but little did she think that she had seen that very same bottle fly into the air for herself and her friend on that happy day in the green woods, in the time of her youth.

The bottle had no time to think, it found itself so suddenly and unexpectedly at the height of its career. Roof-tops and towers lay far away below and the people looked so very tiny.

And then it began to fall, but at an altogether different speed from the rabbit, turning somersaults in the air and feeling so young and so mad with joy: it was half full of wine, though not for very long. What a journey! The sun shone on the bottle and all the people were watching it; the balloon was gone—and soon the bottle was gone too. It had fallen on to one of the roofs and had been smashed. But there was so much kick in the bits that they wouldn't lie down but skipped and danced till they got down to the yard and lay in even smaller bits. Only the bottle neck held together, looking just as if it had been cut with a diamond.

'It would do for a bird-bath!' said the cellar-man. But he himself had neither bird nor cage and it would have been too much to get himself these because he happened to have found the bottle neck that could be used as a bath; it would come in for the old maid in the attic, he thought. And so the bottle neck went up there, got a cork in it, was turned upside-down in the way things often happen when changes are made, was filled with fresh water, and was hung up in front of the cage for the little bird, which sang away for very joy.

'Yes, *you* can sing!' was what the bottle neck said. And the bottle neck was a strange thing, because it had been up in a balloon. Nothing else was known of its history. And now it hung there as a bird-bath, where it could hear people clattering and pattering in the street below and the old maid talking in the room within. There happened just then to be a visitor, a lady friend of her own age, and they were talking not of the bottle neck but of the myrtle that stood in the window.

'You certainly shouldn't give five shillings for a wedding bouquet for your daughter,' the old maid was saying; 'you shall have a nice little one from me, quite full of blossom! Look how beautifully it grows. You know, it was a cutting from the myrtle which you gave me the day after my engagement, the one that I was to make my own wedding bouquet from at the end of the year. Only the day never came! The eyes that were to have brightened my life in gladness and joy were closed. He sleeps peacefully on the ocean bed, my angel dear! The plant grew into an old plant, but I grew older still; and when it withered away I took the last fresh branch and planted it in the ground; and now the branch has grown into a really big plant and is going to a wedding after all, as a wedding bouquet for your daughter!'

And there were tears in the old maid's eyes as she spoke of the friend of her youth and the engagement in the woods, and thought of the toast that had been drunk and of the first kiss: only she said nothing of all this, as she was an old maid. She thought of so many things, but she never thought that just outside her window there was another memory of that time: the neck of the bottle that had said 'plop' when the cork had flown off before the toast.

HANS ANDERSEN (1805–1875)

An Uninvited Guest

There was a table set out under a tree in front of the house, and the March Hare and the Hatter were having tea at it: a Dormouse was sitting between them, fast asleep, and the other two were resting their elbows on it, and talking over its head. 'Very uncomfortable for the Dormouse,' thought Alice; 'only, as it's asleep, I suppose it doesn't mind.'

The table was a large one, but the three were all crowded together at one corner of it. 'No room! No room!' they cried out when they saw Alice coming. 'There's *plenty* of room!' said Alice indignantly, and she sat down in a large arm-chair at one end of the table.

'Have some wine,' the March Hare said in an encouraging tone.

Alice looked all round the table, but there was nothing on it but tea. 'I don't see any wine,' she remarked.

'There isn't any,' said the March Hare.

'Then it wasn't very civil of you to offer it,' said Alice angrily.

'It wasn't very civil of you to sit down without being invited,' said the March Hare.

'I didn't know it was *your* table,' said Alice; 'it's laid for a great many more than three.'

'Your hair wants cutting,' said the Hatter. He had been looking at Alice for some time with great curiosity, and this was his first speech.

'You shouldn't make personal remarks,' Alice said with some severity; 'it's very rude.'

The Hatter opened his eyes very wide on hearing this; but all he *said* was, 'Why is a raven like a writing-desk?'

'Come, we shall have some fun now!' thought Alice. 'I'm glad they've begun asking riddles.—I believe I can guess that,' she added aloud.

'Do you mean that you think you can find out the answer to it?' said the March Hare.

'Exactly so,' said Alice.

'Then you should say what you mean,' the March Hare went on.

'I do,' Alice hastily replied; 'at least—at least I mean what I say— that's the same thing, you know.'

'Not the same thing a bit!' said the Hatter. 'You might just as well say that "I see what I eat" is the same thing as "I eat what I see"!'

'You might just as well say,' added the March Hare, 'that "I like what I get" is the same thing as "I get what I like"!'

'You might just as well say,' added the Dormouse, who seemed to be talking in his sleep, 'that "I breathe when I sleep" is the same thing as "I sleep when I breathe"!'

'It *is* the same thing with you,' said the Hatter, and here the conversation dropped, and the party sat silent for a minute, while Alice thought over all she could remember about ravens and writing-desks, which wasn't much.

The Hatter was the first to break the silence. 'What day of the month is it?' he said, turning to Alice: he had taken his watch out of his pocket, and was looking at it uneasily, shaking it every now and then, and holding it to his ear.

Alice considered a little, and then said, 'The fourth.'

'Two days wrong!' sighed the Hatter. 'I told you butter wouldn't suit the works!' he added, looking angrily at the March Hare.

'It was the *best* butter,' the March Hare meekly replied.

'Yes, but some crumbs must have got in as well,' the Hatter grumbled: 'you shouldn't have put it in with the bread-knife.'

The March Hare took the watch and looked at it gloomily: then he dipped it into his cup of tea, and looked at it again: but he could think of nothing better to say than his first remark, 'It was the *best* butter, you know.'

Alice had been looking over his shoulder with some curiosity. 'What a funny watch!' she remarked. 'It tells the day of the month, and doesn't tell what o'clock it is!'

'Why should it?' muttered the Hatter. 'Does *your* watch tell you what year it is?'

'Of course not,' Alice replied very readily: 'but that's because it stays the same year for such a long time together.'

'Which is just the case with *mine*,' said the Hatter.

LEWIS CARROLL (1832–1898)

£20 in Parachikka Chlorates

Carrie has several times recently called attention to the thinness of my hair at the top of my head, and recommended me to get it seen to. I was this morning trying to look at it by the aid of a small hand-glass, when somehow my elbow caught against the edge of the chest of drawers and knocked the glass out of my hand and smashed it. Carrie was in an awful way about it, as she is rather absurdly superstitious. To make matters worse, my large photograph in the drawing-room fell during the night, and the glass cracked.

Carrie said: 'Mark my words, Charles, some misfortune is about to happen.'

I said: 'Nonsense, dear.'

In the evening Lupin arrived home early, and seemed a little agitated. I said: 'What's up, my boy?' He hesitated a good deal, and then said: 'You know those Parachikka Chlorates I advised you to invest £20 in?' I replied: 'Yes, they are all right, I trust?' He replied: 'Well, no! To the surprise of everybody, they have utterly collapsed.'

My breath was so completely taken away, I could say nothing. Carrie looked at me, and said: 'What did I tell you?' Lupin, after a while, said: 'However, you are specially fortunate. I received an early tip, and sold out yours immediately, and was fortunate to get £2 for them. So you get something after all.'

I gave a sigh of relief. I said: 'I was not so sanguine as to suppose, as you predicted, that I should get six or eight times the amount of my investment; still a profit of £2 is a good percentage for such a short time.' Lupin said, quite irritably: 'You don't understand. I sold your £20 shares for £2; you therefore lose £18 on the transaction, whereby Cummings and Gowing will lose the whole of theirs.'

Lupin, before going to town, said: 'I am very sorry about those Parachikka Chlorates; it would not have happened if the boss, Job Cleanands, had been in town. Between ourselves, you must not be surprised if something goes wrong at our office. Job Cleanands has not been seen the last few days, and it strikes me several people *do* want to see him very particularly.'

In the evening Lupin was just on the point of going out to avoid a collision with Gowing and Cummings, when the former entered the room, without knocking, but with his usual trick of saying, 'May I come in?'

He entered, and to the surprise of Lupin and myself, seemed to be in the very best of spirits. Neither Lupin nor I broached the subject to him, but he did so of his own accord. He said: 'I say, those Parachikka Chlorates have gone an awful smash! You're a nice one, Master Lupin. How much do you lose?' Lupin, to my utter astonishment, said 'Oh! I had nothing in them. There was some informality in my application—I forgot to enclose the cheque or something, and I didn't get any. The Guv. loses £18.' I said: 'I quite understood you were in it, or nothing would have induced me to speculate.' Lupin replied: 'Well, it can't be helped; you must go double on the next tip.' Before I could reply, Gowing said: 'Well, I lose nothing, fortunately. From what I heard, I did not quite believe in them, so I persuaded Cummings to take my £15 worth, as he had more faith in them than I had.'

Lupin burst out laughing, and, in the most unseemly manner, said: 'Alas, poor Cummings! He'll lose £35.' At that moment there was a ring at the bell. Lupin said: 'I don't want to meet Cummings.' If he had gone out of the door he would have met him in the passage, so as quickly as possible Lupin opened the parlour window and got out. Gowing jumped up suddenly, exclaiming: 'I don't want to see him either!' and, before I could say a word, he followed Lupin out of the window.

For my own part, I was horrified to think my own son and one of my most intimate friends should depart from the house like a couple of interrupted burglars. Poor Cummings was very upset, and of course was naturally very angry both with Lupin and Gowing. I pressed him to have a little whisky, and he replied that he had given up whisky; but would like a little 'Unsweetened,' as he was advised it was the most healthy spirit. I had none in the house, but sent Sarah round to Lockwood's for some.

The first thing that caught my eye on opening the *Standard* was—'Great Failure of Stock and Share Dealers! Mr Job Cleanands Absconded!' I handed it to Carrie and she replied: 'Oh! perhaps it's for Lupin's good. I never did think it a suitable situation for him.' I thought the whole affair very shocking.

Lupin came down to breakfast, and seeing he looked painfully distressed, I said: 'We know the news, my dear boy, and feel very sorry for you.' Lupin said: 'How did you know? Who told you?' I handed him the *Standard*. He threw the paper down, and said: 'Oh I don't care a button for that! I expected that, but I did not expect this.' He then read a letter from Frank Mutlar, announcing, in a cool manner, that Daisy Mutlar is to be married next month to Murray Posh. I exclaimed, 'Murray Posh! Is not that the very man Frank had the impudence to bring here last Tuesday week?' Lupin said: 'Yes; the "*Posh's-three-shilling-hats*" chap.'

We all then ate our breakfast in dead silence.

In fact, I could eat nothing. I was not only too worried, but I cannot and will not eat cushion of bacon. If I cannot get streaky bacon, I will do without anything.

When Lupin rose to go I noticed a malicious smile creep over his face. I asked him what it meant. He replied: 'Oh! only a little consolation—still it *is* a consolation. I have just remembered that, by *my* advice, Mr Murray Posh has invested £600 in Parachikka Chlorates?'

GEORGE (1847–1912) AND WEEDON (1853–1919) GROSSMITH

Twelve Sous

The man who either disdains or fears to walk up a dark entry, may be an excellent good man, and fit for a hundred things; but he will not do to make a good sentimental traveller. I count little of the many things I see pass at broad noon-day, in large and open streets. Nature is shy, and hates to act before spectators; but in such an unobserved corner you sometimes see a single short scene of hers, worth all the sentiments of a dozen French plays compounded together. And yet they are *absolutely* fine; and whenever I have a more brilliant affair upon my hands than common, as they suit a preacher just as well as a hero, I generally make my sermon out of 'em, and for the text: 'Cappadocia, Pontus and Asia, Phrygia and Pamphylia' is as good as any one in the Bible.

There is a long dark passage issuing out from the opera comique into a narrow street; 'tis trod by a few who humbly wait for a *fiacre*, or wish to get off quietly o'foot when the opera is done. At the end of it, towards the theatre, 'tis lighted by a small candle, the light of which is almost lost before you get half-way down, but near the door. 'Tis more for ornament than use: you see it as a fix'd star of the least magnitude; it burns, but does little good to the world, that we know of.

In returning along this passage, I discern'd, as I approach'd within five or six paces of the door, two ladies standing arm in arm with their backs against the wall, waiting, as I imagined, for a *fiacre*. As they were next the door, I thought they had a prior right; so edged myself up within a yard, or little more of them, and quietly took my stand. I was in black, and scarce seen.

The lady next me was a tall lean figure of a woman, of about thirty-six; the other of the same size and make, of about forty. There was no mark of wife or widow in any one part of either of them: they seem'd to be two upright vestal sisters, unsapp'd by caresses, unbroke in upon by tender salutations. I could have wish'd to have made them happy'— their happiness was destin'd, that night, to come from another quarter.

A low voice, with a good turn of expression, and sweet cadence at the end of it, begg'd for a twelve-sous piece betwixt them, for the love of Heaven. I thought it singular that a beggar should fix the quota of an alms, and that the sum should be twelve times as much as what is usually given in the dark. They both seem'd astonish'd at it as much as myself. Twelve sous! said one. A twelve-sous piece! said the other, and made no reply.

The poor man said, he knew not how to ask less of ladies of their rank; and bow'd down his head to the ground.

Poo! said they; we have no money.

The beggar remained silent for a moment or two, and renew'd his supplication.

Do not, my fair young ladies, said he, stop your good ears against me. Upon my word, honest man! said the younger, we have no change. Then God bless you, said the poor man, and multiply those joys which you can give to others without change! I observed the elder sister put her hand into her pocket. I'll see, said she, if I have a sous. A sous! give twelve, said the supplicant; Nature has been bountiful to you, be bountiful to a poor man.

I would, friend, with all my heart, said the younger, if I had it.

My fair charitable! said he, addressing himself to the elder; what is it but your goodness and humanity which makes your bright eyes so sweet, that they outshine the morning even in this dark passage? and what was it which made the Marquis de Santerre and his brother say so much of you both as they just pass'd by?

The two ladies seemed much affected; and impulsively at the same time they both put their hands into their pocket, and each took out a twelve-sous piece.

The contest betwixt them and the poor supplicant was no more: it was continued betwixt themselves, which of the two should give the twelve-sous piece in charity, and to end the dispute, they both gave it together, and the man went away.

LAURENCE STERNE (1713–1768)

Trunnion gives up the Ghost

About four o'clock in the morning our hero arrived at the garrison, where he found his generous uncle in extremity, supported in bed by Julia on one side, and Lieutenant Hatchway on the other, while Mr Jolter administered spiritual consolation to his soul; and between whiles comforted Mrs Trunnion, who, with her maid, sat by the fire, weeping with great decorum; the physician having just taken his last fee, and retired, after pronouncing the fatal prognostic, in which he anxiously wished he might be mistaken.

Though the commodore's speech was interrupted by a violent hic-cup, he still retained the use of his senses; and, when Peregrine approached, stretched out his hand with manifest signs of satisfaction. The young gentleman, whose heart overflowed with gratitude and affection, could not behold such a spectacle unmoved. He endeavoured to conceal his tenderness, which, in the wildness of his youth, and the pride of his disposition, he considered as a derogation from his man-hood; but, in spite of all his endeavours, the tears gushed from his eyes, while he kissed the old man's hand; and he was so utterly disconcerted by his grief, that, when he attempted to speak, his tongue denied its office;—so that the commodore, perceiving his disorder, made a last effort of strength, and consoled him in these words—

'Swab the spray from your bowsprit, my good lad, and coil up your spirits. You must not let the toplifts of your heart give way, because you see me ready to go down at these years. Many a better man has foundered before he has made half my way; thof I trust, by the mercy of God, I shall be sure in port in a very few glasses, and fast moored in a most blessed riding; for my good friend Jolter hath overhauled the journal of my sins, and, by the observation he hath taken of the state of my soul, I hope I shall happily conclude my voyage, and be brought up in the latitude of heaven. Here has been a doctor that wanted to stow me chock full of physic; but, when a man's hour is come, what signifies his taking his departure with a 'pothecary's shop in his hold? Those fellows come alongside of dying men, like the messengers of the Admiralty with sailing orders; but I told him as how I could slip my cable without his direction or assistance, and so he hauled off in dudgeon. This cursed hiccup makes such a rippling in the current of my speech, that mayhap you don't understand what I say. Now, while the sucker of my wind-pump will go, I would willingly mention a few things, which I hope you will set down in the log-book of your remembrance, when I am stiff, d'ye see. There's your aunt sitting whimpering by the fire; I desire you will keep her tight, warm, and easy in her old age; she's an honest heart in her own way, and, thof she goes a little crank and humoursome, by being often overstowed with Nantz and religion, she has been a faithful shipmate to me, and I daresay she never turned in with another man since we first embarked in the same bottom. Jack Hatchway, you know the trim of her as well as e'er a man in England, and I believe she has a kindness for you; whereby, if you two will grapple in the way of matrimony, when I am gone, I do suppose that my godson, for love of me, will allow you to live in the garrison all the days of your life.'

Peregrine assured him, he would with pleasure comply with any request he should make in behalf of two persons whom he esteemed so much. The lieutenant, with a waggish sneer, which even the gravity of the situation could not prevent, thanked them both for their good-will, telling the commodore, he was obliged to him for his friendship, in seeking to promote him to the command of a vessel which he himself had wore out in the service; but that, notwithstanding, he should be content to take charge of her, though he could not help being shy of coming after such an able navigator.

Trunnion, exhausted as he was, smiled at this sally, and, after some pause, resumed his admonitions in this manner:—'I need not talk of Pipes, because I know you'll do for him without any recommendation; the fellow has sailed with me in many a hard gale, and I'll warrant him as stout a seaman as ever set face to the weather. But I hope you'll take care of the rest of my crew and not disrate them after I am dead, in favour of new followers. As for that young woman, Ned Gauntlet's daughter, I'm informed as how she's an excellent wench, and has a respect for you; whereby, if you run her on board in an unlawful way, I leave my curse upon you, and trust you will never prosper in the voyage of life. But I believe you are more of an honest man, than to behave so much like a pirate. I beg of all love you wool take care of your constitution, and beware of running foul of harlots, who are no better than so many mermaids, that sit upon rocks in the sea, and hang out a fair face for the destruction of passengers; thof I must say, for my own part, I never met with any of those sweet singers, and yet I have gone to sea for the space of thirty years. But howsomever, steer your course clear of all such brimstone b—es. Shun going to law, as you would shun the devil; and look upon all attorneys as devouring sharks, or ravenous fish of prey. As soon as the breath is out of my body, let minute guns be fired, till I am safe under ground. I would also be buried in the red jacket I had on when I boarded and took the *Renummy*. Let my pistols, cutlass, and pocket-compass be laid in the coffin along with me. Let me be carried to the grave by my own men, rigged in the black caps and white shirts which my barge's crew were wont to wear; and they must keep a good lookout, that none of your pilfering rascallions may come and heave me up again, for the lucre of what they can get, until the carcass is belayed by a tombstone. As for the motto, or what you call it, I leave that to you and Mr Jolter, who are scholars; but I do desire, that it may not be engraved in the Greek or Latin lingos, and much less in the French, which I abominate, but in plain English, that, when the angel comes to pipe all hands, at the great day, he may know that I am a British man, and speak to me in my mother tongue. And now I have no more to say, but God in heaven have mercy upon my soul, and send you all fair weather, wheresoever you are bound.'

So saying, he regarded every individual around him with a look of complacency, and closing his eye, composed himself to rest, while the whole audience, Pipes himself not excepted, were melted with sorrow; and Mrs Trunnion consented to quit the room, that she might not be exposed to the unspeakable anguish of seeing him expire.

His last moments, however, were not so near as they imagined. He began to doze, and enjoyed small intervals of ease, till next day in the afternoon; during which remissions, he was heard to pour forth many pious ejaculations, expressing his hope, that, for all the heavy cargo of his sins, he should be able to surmount the puttock-shrouds of despair, and get aloft to the cross-trees of God's good favour. At last his voice sunk so low as not to be distinguished; and, having lain about an hour, almost without any perceptible signs of life, he gave up the ghost with a groan which announced his decease.

TOBIAS SMOLLETT (1721–1771)

Jeanie pleads with the Duke

'Did you wish to speak with me, my bonny lass?' said the Duke, using the encouraging epithet which at once acknowledged the connection betwixt them as country-folk; 'or did you wish to see the Duchess?'

'My business is with your honour, my Lord—I mean your Lordship's Grace.'

'And what is it, my good girl?' said the Duke, in the same mild and encouraging tone of voice. Jeanie looked at the attendant. 'Leave us, Archibald,' said the Duke, 'and wait in the anteroom.' The domestic retired. 'And now sit down, my good lass,' said the Duke; 'take your breath—take your time, and tell me what you have got to say. I guess by your dress, you are just come up from poor old Scotland— Did you come through the streets in your tartan plaid?'

'No, sir,' said Jeanie; 'a friend brought me in ane o' their street coaches—a very decent woman,' she added, her courage increasing as she became familiar with the sound of her own voice in such a presence; 'your Lordship's Grace kens her—it's Mrs Glass, at the sign o' the Thistle.'

'Oh, my worthy snuff-merchant—I have always a chat with Mrs Glass when I purchase my Scotch high-dried.—Well, but your business, my bonny woman—time and tide, you know, wait for no one.'

'Your honour—I beg your Lordship's pardon—I mean your Grace,'—for it must be noticed, that this matter of addressing the Duke by his appropriate title had been anxiously inculcated upon Jeanie by her friend Mrs Glass, in whose eyes it was a matter of such importance, that her last words, as Jeanie left the coach, were, 'Mind to say your Grace;' and Jeanie, who had scarce ever in her life spoke to a person of higher quality than the Laird of Dumbiedikes, found great difficulty in arranging her language according to the rules of ceremony.

The Duke, who saw her embarrassment, said, with his usual affability, 'Never mind my grace, lassie; just speak out a plain tale, and show you have a Scotch tongue in your head.'

'Sir, I am muckle obliged—Sir, I am the sister of that poor unfortunate criminal, Effie Deans, who is ordered for execution at Edinburgh.'

'Ah!' said the Duke, 'I have heard of that unhappy story, I think—a case of child-murder, under a special act of parliament—Duncan Forbes mentioned it at dinner the other day.'

'And I was come up frae the north, sir, to see what could be done for her in the way of getting a reprieve or pardon, sir, or the like of that.'

'Alas! my poor girl,' said the Duke, 'you have made a long and a sad journey to very little purpose—Your sister is ordered for execution.'

'But I am given to understand that there is law for reprieving her, if it is in the king's pleasure,' said Jeanie.

'Certainly there is,' said the Duke; 'but that is purely in the king's breast. The crime has been but too common—the Scotch crown-lawyers think it is right there should be an example. Then the late disorders in Edinburgh have excited a prejudice in government against the nation at large, which they think can only be managed by measures of intimidation and severity. What argument have you, my poor girl, except the warmth of your sisterly affection, to offer against all this?—What is your interest?—What friends have you at court?'

'None, excepting God and your Grace,' said Jeanie, still keeping her ground resolutely, however.

'Alas!' said the Duke, 'I could almost say with old Ormond, that there could not be any, whose influence was smaller with kings and ministers. It is a cruel part of our situation, young woman—I mean of the situation of men in my circumstances, that the public ascribe to them influence which they do not possess; and that individuals are led to expect from them assistance which we have no means of rendering. But candour and plain dealing is in the power of every one, and I must not let you imagine you have resources in my influence, which do not exist, to make your distress the heavier—I have no means of averting your sister's fate—She must die.'

'We must a' die, sir,' said Jeanie; 'it is our common doom for our father's transgression; but we shouldna hasten ilk other out o' the world, that's what your honour kens better than me.'

'My good young woman,' said the Duke mildly, 'we are all apt to blame the law under which we immediately suffer; but you seem to have been well educated in your line of life, and you must know that it is alike the law of God and man, that the murderer shall surely die.'

'But, sir, Effie—that is, my poor sister, sir—canna be proved to be a murderer; and if she be not, and the law take her life notwithstanding, wha is it that is the murderer then?'

'I am no lawyer,' said the Duke; 'and I own I think the statute a very severe one.'

'You are a law-maker, sir, with your leave; and, therefore, ye have power over the law,' answered Jeanie.

'Not in my individual capacity,' said the Duke; 'though, as one of a large body, I have a voice in the legislation. But that cannot serve you —nor have I at present, I care not who knows it, so much personal influence with the sovereign, as would entitle me to ask from him the most insignificant favour. What could tempt you, young woman, to address yourself to me?'

'It was yoursell, sir.'

'Myself?' he replied—'I am sure you have never seen me before.'

'No, sir; but a' the world kens that the Duke of Argyle is his country's friend; and that ye fight for the right, and speak for the right, and that there's nane like yours in our present Israel, and so they that think themselves wranged draw to refuge under your shadow; and if ye wunna stir to save the blood of an innocent countrywoman of your ain, what should we expect frae southrons and strangers? And maybe I had another reason for troubling your honour.'

'And what is that?' asked the Duke.

'I hae understood from my father, that your honour's house, and especially your gudesire and his father, laid down their lives on the scaffold in the persecuting time. And my father was honoured to gie his testimony baith in the cage and in the pillory, as is specially mentioned in the books of Peter Walker, the packman that your honour, I dare say, kens, for he uses maist partly the westland of Scotland. And, sir, there's ane that takes concern in me, that wished me to gang to your Grace's presence, for his gudesire had done your gracious gudesire some good turn, as ye will see frae these papers.'

With these words, she delivered to the Duke the little parcel which she had received from Butler. He opened it, and, in the envelope, read with some surprise, 'Muster-roll of the men serving in the troop of that godly gentleman, Captain Salathiel Bangtext.—Obadiah Muggleton, Sin-Despise Double-knock, Stand-fast-in-faith Gipps, Turn-to-the-right Thwack-away—What the deuce is this? A list of Praise-God Barebone's Parliament, I think, or of old Noll's evangelical army—that last fellow should understand his wheelings to judge by his name.— But what does all this mean, my girl?'

'It was the other paper, sir,' said Jeanie, somewhat abashed at the mistake.

'Oh, this is my unfortunate grandfather's hand sure enough—

To all who may have friendship for the house of Argyle, these are to certify, that Benjamin Butler, of Monk's regiment of dragoons, having been, under God, the means of saving my life from four English troopers who were about to slay me, I, having no other present means of recompense in my power, do give him this acknowledgment, hoping that it may be useful to him or his during these troublesome times; and do conjure my friends, tenants, kinsmen, and whoever will do aught for me, either in the Highlands or Lowlands, to protect and assist the said Benjamin Butler, and his friends or family, on their lawful occasions, giving them such countenance, maintenance, and supply, as may correspond with the benefit he hath bestowed on me; witness my hand—LORNE.

'This is a strong injunction—This Benjamin Butler was your grandfather, I suppose?—You seem too young to have been his daughter.'

'He was nae akin to me, sir—he was grandfather to ane—to a neighbour's son—to a sincere weel-wisher of mine, sir,' dropping her little courtesy as she spoke.

'Oh, I understand,' said the Duke—'a true-love affair. He was the grandsire of one you are engaged to?'

'One I *was* engaged to, sir,' said Jeanie, sighing; 'but this unhappy business of my poor sister——'

'What!' said the Duke hastily,—'he has not deserted you on that account, has he?'

'No, sir; he wad be the last to leave a friend in difficulties,' said Jeanie; 'but I maun think for him, as weel as for mysell. He is a clergyman, sir, and it would not beseem him to marry the like of me, wi' this disgrace on my kindred.'

'You are a singular young woman,' said the Duke. 'You seem to me to think of every one before yourself. And have you really come up from Edinburgh on foot, to attempt this hopeless solicitation for your sister's life?'

SIR WALTER SCOTT (1771–1832)

An Expectation Confounded

Elinor now found the difference between the expectation of an unpleasant event, however certain the mind may be told to consider it, and certainty itself. She now found, that in spite of herself, she had always admitted a hope, while Edward remained single, that something would occur to prevent his marrying Lucy; that some resolution of his own, some mediation of friends, or some more eligible opportunity of establishment for the lady, would arise to assist the happiness of all, But he was now married, and she condemned her heart for the lurking flattery, which so much heightened the pain of the intelligence.

That he should be married so soon, before (as she imagined) he could be in orders, and consequently before he could be in possession of the living, surprised her a little at first. But she soon saw how likely it was that Lucy, in her self-provident care, in her haste to secure him, should overlook every thing but the risk of delay. They were married, married in town, and now hastening down to her uncle's. What had Edward felt on being within four miles of Barton, on seeing her mother's servant, on hearing Lucy's message!

They would soon, she supposed, be settled at Delaford.—Delaford, —that place in which so much conspired to give her an interest; which she wished to be acquainted with, and yet desired to avoid. She saw them in an instant in their parsonage-house; saw in Lucy, the active, contriving manager, uniting at once a desire of smart appearance, with the utmost frugality, and ashamed to be suspected of half her economical practices;—pursuing her own interest in every thought, courting the favour of Colonel Brandon, of Mrs Jennings, and of every wealthy friend. In Edward,—she knew not what she saw, nor what she wished to see;—happy or unhappy,—nothing pleased her;—she turned away her head from every sketch of him.

Elinor flattered herself that some one of their connections in London would write to them to announce the event, and give farther particulars,—but day after day passed off, and brought no letter, no tidings. Though uncertain that any one were to blame, she found fault with every absent friend. They were all thoughtless or indolent.

'When do you write to Colonel Brandon, ma'am?' was an inquiry which sprung from the impatience of her mind to have something going on.

'I wrote to him, my love, last week, and rather expect to see, than to hear from him again. I earnestly pressed his coming to us, and should not be surprised to see him walk in to-day or to-morrow, or any day.'

This was gaining something, something to look forward to. Colonel Brandon *must* have some information to give.

Scarcely had she so determined it, when the figure of a man on horseback drew her eyes to the window. He stopt at their gate. It was a gentleman, it was Colonel Brandon himself. Now she should hear more; and she trembled in expectation of it. But—it was *not* Colonel Brandon—neither his air—nor his height. Were it possible, she should say it must be Edward. She looked again. He had just dismounted;—she could not be mistaken;—it *was* Edward. She moved away and sat down. 'He comes from Mr Pratt's purposely to see us. I *will* be calm; I *will* be mistress of myself.'

In a moment, she perceived that the others were likewise aware of the mistake. She saw her mother and Marianne change colour; saw them look at herself, and whisper a few sentences to each other. She would have given the world to be able to speak—and to make them understand that she hoped no coolness, no slight, would appear in their behaviour to him;—but she had no utterance, and was obliged to leave all to their own discretion.

Not a syllable passed aloud. They all waited in silence for the appearance of their visitor. His footsteps were heard along the gravel path; in a moment he was in the passage; and in another, he was before them.

His countenance, as he entered the room, was not too happy, even for Elinor. His complexion was white with agitation, and he looked as if fearful of his reception, and conscious that he merited no kind one. Mrs Dashwood, however, conforming, as she trusted, to the wishes of that daughter, by whom she then meant in the warmth of her heart to be guided in everything, met him with a look of forced complacency, gave him her hand, and wished him joy.

He coloured, and stammered out an unintelligible reply. Elinor's lips had moved with her mother's, and when the moment of action was over, she wished that she had shaken hands with him too. But it was then too late, and with a countenance meaning to be open, she sat down again and talked of the weather.

Marianne had retreated as much as possible out of sight, to conceal her distress; and Margaret, understanding some part, but not the whole, of the case, thought it incumbent on her to be dignified, and therefore took a seat as far from him as she could, and maintained a strict silence.

When Elinor had ceased to rejoice in the dryness of the season, a very awful pause took place. It was put an end to by Mrs Dashwood, who felt obliged to hope that he had left Mrs Ferrars very well. In a hurried manner, he replied in the affirmative.

Another pause.

Elinor, resolving to exert herself, though fearing the sound of her own voice, now said,

'Is Mrs Ferrars at Longstaple?'

'At Longstaple!' he replied, with an air of surprise—'No, my mother is in town.'

'I meant,' said Elinor, taking up some work from the table, 'to inquire after Mrs *Edward* Ferrars.'

She dared not look up;—but her mother and Marianne both turned their eyes on him. He coloured, seemed perplexed, looked doubtingly, and after some hesitation, said—

'Perhaps you mean—my brother—you mean Mrs—Mrs *Robert* Ferrars.'

'Mrs Robert Ferrars!'—was repeated by Marianne and her mother in an accent of the utmost amazement;—and though Elinor could not speak, even *her* eyes were fixed on him with the same impatient wonder. He rose from his seat and walked to the window, apparently from not knowing what to do; took up a pair of scissars that lay there, and while spoiling both them and their sheath by cutting the latter to pieces as he spoke, said, in an hurried voice,

'Perhaps you do not know—you may not have heard that my brother is lately married to—to the youngest—to Miss Lucy Steele.'

His words were echoed with unspeakable astonishment by all but Elinor, who sat with her head leaning over her work, in a state of such agitation as made her hardly know where she was.

'Yes,' said he, 'they were married last week and are now at Dawlish.'

Elinor could sit it no longer. She almost ran out of the room, and as soon as the door was closed, burst into tears of joy, which at first she thought would never cease.

JANE AUSTEN (1775–1817)

Mrs Gamp awaits a Visitor

Mrs Gamp's apartment in Kingsgate Street, High Holborn, wore, metaphorically speaking, a robe of state. It was swept and garnished for the reception of a visitor. That visitor was Betsey Prig: Mrs Prig, of Bartlemy's: or as some said Barklemy's, or as some said Bardlemy's; for by all these endearing and familiar appellations, had the hospital of Saint Bartholomew become a household word among the sisterhood which Betsey Prig adorned.

Mrs Gamp's apartment was not a spacious one, but, to a contented mind, a closet is a palace; and the first-floor front at Mr Sweedlepipe's may have been, in the imagination of Mrs Gamp, a stately pile. If it were not exactly that, to restless intellects, it at least comprised as much accommodation as any person, not sanguine to insanity, could have looked for in a room of its dimensions. For only keep the bedstead always in your mind; and you were safe. That was the grand secret. Remembering the bedstead, you might even stoop to look under the little round table for anything you had dropped, without hurting yourself much against the chest of drawers, or qualifying as a patient of Saint Bartholomew, by falling into the fire.

Visitors were much assisted in their cautious efforts to preserve an unflagging recollection of this piece of furniture, by its size: which was great. It was not a turn-up bedstead, nor yet a French bedstead, nor yet a four-post bedstead, but what is poetically called a tent: the sacking whereof was low and bulgy, insomuch that Mrs Gamp's box would not go under it, but stopped half-way, in a manner which, while it did violence to the reason, likewise endangered the legs of a stranger. The frame too, which would have supported the canopy and hangings if there had been any, was ornamented with divers pippins carved in timber, which on the slightest provocation, and frequently on none at all, came tumbling down; harassing the peaceful guest with inexplicable terrors.

The bed itself was decorated with a patchwork quilt of great antiquity; and at the upper end, upon the side nearest to the door, hung a scanty curtain of blue check, which prevented the Zephyrs that were abroad in Kingsgate Street, from visiting Mrs Gamp's head too roughly. Some rusty gowns and other articles of that lady's wardrobe depended from the posts; and these had so adapted themselves by long usage to her figure, that more than one impatient husband coming in precipitately, at about the time of twilight, had been for an instant stricken dumb by the supposed discovery that Mrs Gamp had hanged herself. One gentleman, coming on the usual hasty errand, had said indeed, that they looked like guardian angels 'watching of her in her sleep.' But that, as Mrs Gamp said, 'was his first;' and he never repeated the sentiment, though he often repeated his visit.

The chairs in Mrs Gamp's apartment were extremely large and broad-backed, which was more than a sufficient reason for there being but two in number. They were both elbow-chairs, of ancient mahogany; and were chiefly valuable for the slippery nature of their seats, which had been originally horsehair, but were now covered with a shiny substance of a bluish tint, from which the visitor began to slide away with a dismayed countenance, immediately after sitting down. What Mrs Gamp wanted in chairs she made up in bandboxes; of which she had a great collection, devoted to the reception of various miscellaneous valuables, which were not, however, as well protected as the good woman, by a pleasant fiction, seemed to think: for, though every band-box had a carefully closed lid, not one among them had a bottom: owing to which cause the property within was merely, as it were, extinguished. The chest of drawers having been originally made to stand upon the top of another chest, had a dwarfish, elfin look, alone; but in regard of its security it had a great advantage over the band-boxes, for as all the handles had been long ago pulled off, it was very difficult to get at its contents. This indeed was only to be done by one of two devices; either by tilting the whole structure forward until all the drawers fell out together, or by opening them singly with knives, like oysters.

Mrs Gamp stored all her household matters in a little cupboard by the fire-place; beginning below the surface (as in nature) with the coals, and mounting gradually upwards to the spirits, which, from motives of delicacy, she kept in a teapot. The chimney-piece was ornamented with a small almanack, marked here and there in Mrs Gamp's own hand with a memorandum of the date at which some lady was expected to fall due. It was also embellished with three profiles: one, in colours, of Mrs Gamp herself in early life; one, in bronze, of a lady in feathers, supposed to be Mrs Harris, as she appeared when dressed for a ball; and one, in black, of Mr Gamp, deceased. The last was a full length, in order that the likeness might be rendered more obvious and forcible by the introduction of the wooden leg.

A pair of bellows, a pair of pattens, a toasting-fork, a kettle, a pap-boat, a spoon for the administration of medicine to the refractory, and lastly, Mrs Gamp's umbrella, which as something of great price and rarity, was displayed with particular ostentation, completed the decorations of the chimney-piece and adjacent wall. Towards these objects Mrs Gamp raised her eyes in satisfaction when she had arranged the tea-board, and had concluded her arrangements for the reception of Betsey Prig, even unto the setting forth of two pounds of Newcastle salmon, intensely pickled.

'There! Now drat you, Betsey, don't be long!' said Mrs Gamp, apostrophising her absent friend. 'For I can't abear to wait, I do assure you. To wotever place I goes, I sticks to this one mortar, "I'm easy pleased; it is but little as I wants; but I must have that little of the best, and to the minute when the clock strikes, else we do not part as I could wish, but bearin' malice in our arts."'

Her own preparations were of the best, for they comprehended a delicate new loaf, a plate of fresh butter, a basin of fine white sugar, and other arrangements on the same scale. Even the snuff with which she now refreshed herself, was so choice in quality that she took a second pinch. . .

At this juncture the little bell rang, and the deep voice of Mrs Prig struck into the conversation.

'Oh! You're a-talkin' about it, are you!' observed that lady. 'Well, I hope you've got it over, for I ain't interested in it myself.'

'My precious Betsey,' said Mrs Gamp, 'how late you are!'

The worthy Mrs Prig replied, with some asperity, 'that if perwerse people went off dead, when they was least expected, it warn't no fault of her'n.' And further, 'that it was quite aggravation enough to be made late when one was dropping for one's tea, without hearing on it again.'

Mrs Gamp, deriving from this exhibition of repartee some clue to the state of Mrs Prig's feelings, instantly conducted her up-stairs: deeming that the sight of pickled salmon might work a softening change.

But Betsey Prig expected pickled salmon. It was obvious that she did; for her first words, after glancing at the table, were:

'I know'd she wouldn't have a cowcumber!'

Mrs Gamp changed colour, and sat down upon the bedstead.

'Lord bless you, Betsey Prig, your words is true. I quite forgot it!'

Mrs Prig, looking steadfastly at her friend, put her hand in her pocket, and with an air of surly triumph drew forth either the oldest of lettuces or youngest of cabbages, but at any rate, a green vegetable of an expansive nature, and of such magnificent proportions that she was obliged to shut it up like an umbrella before she could pull it out. She also produced a handful of mustard and cress, a trifle of the herb called dandelion, three bunches of radishes, an onion rather larger than an average turnip, three substantial slices of beetroot, and a short prong or antler of celery; the whole of this garden-stuff having been publicly exhibited, but a short time before, as a twopenny salad, and purchased by Mrs Prig on condition that the vendor could get it all into her pocket. Which had been happily accomplished, in High Holborn, to the breathless interest of a hackney-coach stand. And she laid so little stress on this surprising forethought, that she did not even smile, but returning her pocket into its accustomed sphere, merely recommended that these productions of nature should be sliced up, for immediate consumption, in plenty of vinegar.

'And don't go a-droppin' none of your snuff in it,' said Mrs Prig.

'In gruel, barley-water, apple-tea, mutton-broth, and that, it don't signify. It stimilates a patient. But I don't relish it myself.'

'Why, Betsey Prig!' cried Mrs Gamp, 'how *can* you talk so!'

'Why, ain't your patients, wotever their diseases is, always a-sneezin' their wery heads off, along of your snuff?' said Mrs Prig.

'And wot if they are!' said Mrs Gamp.

'Nothing if they are,' said Mrs Prig. 'But don't deny it, Sairah.'

'Who deniges of it?' Mrs Gamp inquired.

Mrs Prig returned no answer.

'WHO deniges of it, Betsey?' Mrs Gamp inquired again. Then Mrs Gamp, by reversing the question, imparted a deeper and more awful character of solemnity to the same. 'Betsey, who deniges of it?'

It was the nearest possible approach to a very decided difference of opinion between these ladies; but Mrs Prig's impatience for the meal being greater at the moment than her impatience of contradiction, she replied for the present, 'Nobody, if you don't, Sairah,' and prepared herself for tea. For a quarrel can be taken up at any time, but a limited quantity of salmon cannot.

Her toilet was simple. She had merely to 'chuck' her bonnet and shawl upon the bed; give her hair two pulls, one upon the right side and one upon the left, as if she were ringing a couple of bells; and all was done. The tea was already made, Mrs Gamp was not long over the salad, and they were soon at the height of their repast.

The temper of both parties was improved, for the time being, by the enjoyments of the table. When the meal came to a termination (which it was pretty long in doing), and Mrs Gamp having cleared away, produced the teapot from the top-shelf, simultaneously with a couple of wine-glasses, they were quite amiable.

'Betsey,' said Mrs Gamp, filling her own glass, and passing the teapot, 'I will now propoge a toast. My frequent pardner, Betsey Prig!'

'Which, altering the name to Sairah Gamp; I drink,' said Mrs Prig, 'with love and tenderness.'

From this moment symptoms of inflammation began to lurk in the nose of each lady; and perhaps, notwithstanding all appearances to the contrary, in the temper also.

'Now, Sairah,' said Mrs Prig, 'joining business with pleasure, wot is this case in which you wants me?'

Mrs Gamp betraying in her face some intention of returning an evasive answer, Betsey added:

'*Is* it Mrs Harris?'

'No, Betsey Prig, it ain't,' was Mrs Gamp's reply.

'Well!' said Mrs Prig, with a short laugh. 'I'm glad of that, at any rate.'

'Why should you be glad of that, Betsey?' Mrs Gamp retorted, warmly. 'She is unbeknown to you except by hearsay, why should you be glad? It you have anythink to say contrairy to the character of Mrs Harris, which well I knows behind her back, afore her face, or anywheres, is not to be impeaged, out with it, Betsey. I have know'd that sweetest and best of women,' said Mrs Gamp, shaking her head, and shedding tears, 'ever since afore her First, which Mr Harris who was dreadful timid went and stopped his ears in a empty dog-kennel, and never took his hands away or come out once till he was showed the baby, wen bein' took with fits, the doctor collared him and laid him on his back upon the airy stones, and she was told to ease her mind, his owls was organs. And I have know'd her, Betsey Prig, when he has hurt her feelin' art by sayin' of his Ninth that it was one too many, if not two, while that dear innocent was cooin' in his face, which thrive it did though bandy, but I have never know'd as you had occagion to be glad, Betsey, on accounts of Mrs Harris not requiring you. Require she never will, depend upon it, for her constant words in sickness is, and will be, "Send for Sairey!"'

During this touching address, Mrs Prig adroitly feigning to be the victim of that absence of mind which has its origin in excessive attention to one topic, helped herself from the teapot without appearing to observe it. Mrs Gamp observed it, however, and came to a premature close in consequence.

'Well, it ain't her, it seems,' said Mrs Prig, coldly: 'who is it then?'

CHARLES DICKENS (1812–1870)

The Last of the Neros

'Oh! my lord, I am so sorry for this accident,' said the signora, putting out her hand so as to force the bishop to take it. 'My brother is so thoughtless. Pray sit down, and let me have the pleasure of making your acquaintance. Though I am so poor a creature as to want a sofa, I am not so selfish as to require it all.' Madeline could always dispose herself so as to make room for a gentleman, though, as she declared, the crinoline of her lady friends was much too bulky to be so accommodated.

'It was solely for the pleasure of meeting you that I have had myself dragged here,' she continued. 'Of course, with your occupation, one cannot even hope that you should have time to come to us, that is, in the way of calling. And at your English dinner-parties all is so dull and so stately. Do you know, my lord, that in coming to England my only consolation has been the thought that I should know you;' and she looked at him with the look of a she-devil.

The bishop, however, thought that she looked very like an angel, and accepting the proffered seat, sat down beside her. He uttered some platitude as to his deep obligation for the trouble she had taken, and wondered more and more who she was.

'Of course you know my sad story?' she continued.

The bishop didn't know a word of it. He knew, however, or thought he knew, that she couldn't walk into a room like other people, and so made the most of that. He put on a look of ineffable distress, and said that he was aware how God had afflicted her.

The signora just touched the corner of her eyes with the most lovely of pocket-handkerchiefs. Yes, she said—she had been sorely tried— tried, she thought, beyond the common endurance of humanity; but while her child was left to her, everything was left. 'Oh! my lord,' she exclaimed, 'you must see that infant—the last bud of a wondrous tree: you must let a mother hope that you will lay your holy hands on her innocent head, and consecrate her for female virtues. May I hope it?' said she, looking into the bishop's eye, and touching the bishop's arm with her hand.

The bishop was but a man, and said she might. After all, what was it but a request that he would confirm her daughter?—a request, indeed, very unnecessary to make, as he should do so as a matter of course, if the young lady came forward in the usual way.

'The blood of Tiberius,' said the signora, in all but a whisper; 'the blood of Tiberius flows in her veins. She is the last of the Neros!'

The bishop had heard of the last of the Visigoths, and had floating in his brain some indistinct idea of the last of the Mohicans, but to have the last of the Neros thus brought before him for a blessing was very staggering. Still he liked the lady: she had a proper way of thinking, and talked with more propriety than her brother. But who were they? It was now quite clear that that blue madman with the silky beard was not a Prince Vicinironi. The lady was married, and was of course one of the Vicinironi's by the right of her husband. So the bishop went on learning.

'When will you see her?' said the signora with a start.

'See whom?' said the bishop.

'My child,' said the mother.

'What is the young lady's age?' asked the bishop.

'She is just seven,' said the signora.

'Oh,' said the bishop, shaking his head; 'she is much too young—very much too young.'

'But in sunny Italy, you know, we do not count by years,' and the signora gave the bishop one of her sweetest smiles.

'But indeed, she is a great deal too young,' persisted the bishop; 'we never confirm before——'

'But you might speak to her; you might let her hear from your consecrated lips, that she is not a castaway because she is a Roman; that she may be a Nero and yet a Christian; that she may owe her black locks and dark cheeks to the blood of the pagan Cæsars, and yet herself be a child of grace; you will tell her this, won't you, my friend?'

The friend said he would, and asked if the child could say her catechism.

'No,' said the signora, 'I would not allow her to learn lessons such as those in a land ridden over by priests, and polluted by the idolatry of Rome. It is here, in Barchester, that she must first be taught to lisp those holy words. Oh, that you could be her instructor!'

Now, Dr Proudie certainly liked the lady, but, seeing that he was a bishop, it was not probable that he was going to instruct a little girl in the first rudiments of her catechism; so he said he'd send a teacher.

'But you'll see her, yourself, my lord?'

The bishop said he would, but where should he call?

'At papa's house,' said the signora, with an air of some little surprise at the question.

The bishop actually wanted the courage to ask her who was her papa; so he was forced at last to leave her without fathoming the mystery. Mrs Proudie, in her second best, had now returned to the rooms, and her husband thought it as well that he should not remain in too close conversation with the lady whom his wife appeared to hold in such slight esteem. Presently he came across his youngest daughter.

'Netta,' said he, 'do you know who is the father of that Signora Vicinironi?'

'It isn't Vicinironi, papa,' said Netta; 'but Vesey Neroni, and she's Doctor Stanhope's daughter. But I must go and do the civil to Griselda Grantly; I declare nobody has spoken a word to the poor girl this evening.'

Dr Stanhope! Dr Vesey Stanhope! Dr Vesey Stanhope's daughter, of whose marriage with a dissolute Italian scamp he now remembered to have heard something! And that impertinent blue cub who had examined him as to his episcopal bearings was old Stanhope's son, and the lady who had entreated him to come and teach her child the catechism was old Stanhope's daughter! the daughter of one of his own prebendaries! As these things flashed across his mind, he was nearly as angry as his wife had been. Nevertheless, he could not but own that the mother of the last of the Neros was an agreeable woman.

ANTHONY TROLLOPE (1815–1882)

Retribution

Before three minutes had passed, however, as if by some sorcery, the brilliant smiling young woman above the mantelpiece seemed to be appearing at the doorway withered and frosted by many winters, and with lips and eyes from which the smile had departed. Jermyn advanced, and they shook hands, but neither of them said anything by way of greeting. Mrs Transome seated herself, and pointed to a chair opposite and near her.

'Harold has gone to Loamford,' she said, in a subdued tone. 'You had something particular to say to me?'

'Yes,' said Jermyn, with his soft and deferential air. 'The last time I was here I could not take the opportunity of speaking to you. But I am anxious to know whether you are aware of what has passed between me and Harold?'

'Yes, he has told me everything.'

'About his proceedings against me? and the reason he stopped them?'

'Yes: have you had notice that he has begun them again?'

'No,' said Jermyn, with a very unpleasant sensation.

'Of course he will now,' said Mrs Transome. 'There is no reason in his mind why he should not.'

'Has he resolved to risk the estate then?'

'He feels in no danger on that score. And if there were, the danger doesn't depend on you. The most likely thing is, that he will marry this girl.'

'He knows everything then?' said Jermyn, the expression of his face getting clouded.

'Everything. It's of no use for you to think of mastering him: you can't do it. I used to wish Harold to be fortunate—and he is fortunate,' said Mrs Transome, with intense bitterness. 'It's not my star that he inherits.'

'Do you know how he came by the information about this girl?'

'No; but she knew it all before we spoke to her. It's no secret.'

Jermyn was confounded by this hopeless frustration to which he had no key. Though he thought of Christian, the thought shed no light; but the more fatal point was clear: he held no secret that could help him.

'You are aware that these Chancery proceedings may ruin me?'

'He told me they would. But if you are imagining that I can do anything, dismiss the notion. I have told him as plainly as I dare that I wish him to drop all public quarrel with you, and that you could make an arrangement without scandal. I can do no more. He will not listen to me; he doesn't mind about my feelings. He cares more for Mr Transome than he does for me. He will not listen to me any more than if I were an old ballad-singer.'

'It's very hard on *me*, I know,' said Jermyn, in the tone with which a man flings out a reproach.

'I besought you three months ago to bear anything rather than quarrel with him.'

'I have not quarrelled with him. It is he who has been always seeking a quarrel with me. I have borne a good deal—more than any one else would. He set his teeth against me from the first.'

'He saw things that annoyed him; and men are not like women,' said Mrs Transome. There was a bitter innuendo in that truism.

'It's very hard on me—I know that,' said Jermyn, with an intensification of his previous tone, rising and walking a step or two, then turning and laying his hand on the back of the chair. 'Of course the law in this case can't in the least represent the justice of the matter. I made a good many sacrifices in times past. I gave up a great deal of fine business for the sake of attending to the family affairs, and in that lawsuit they would have gone to rack and ruin, if it hadn't been for me.'

He moved away again, laid down his hat, which he had been previously holding, and thrust his hands into his pockets as he returned. Mrs Transome sat motionless as marble, and almost as pale. Her hands lay crossed on her knees. This man, young, slim, and graceful, with a selfishness which then took the form of homage to her, had at one time kneeled to her and kissed those hands fervently; and she had thought there was a poetry in such passion beyond any to be found in everyday domesticity.

'I stretched my conscience a good deal in that affair of Bycliffe, as you know perfectly well. I told you everything at the time. I told you I was very uneasy about those witnesses, and about getting him thrown into prison. I know it's the blackest thing anybody could charge me with, if they knew my life from beginning to end; and I should never have done it, if I had not been under an infatuation such as makes a man do anything. What did it signify to me about the loss of the lawsuit? I was a young bachelor—I had the world before me.'

'Yes,' said Mrs Transome, in a low tone. 'It was a pity you didn't make another choice.'

'What would have become of you?' said Jermyn, carried along a climax, like other self-justifiers. 'I had to think of you. You would not have liked me to make another choice then.'

'Clearly,' said Mrs Transome, with concentrated bitterness, but still quietly; 'the greater mistake was mine.'

Egoism is usually stupid in a dialogue; but Jermyn's did not make him so stupid that he did not feel the edge of Mrs Transome's words. They increased his irritation.

'I hardly see that,' he replied, with a slight laugh of scorn. 'You had an estate and a position to save, to go no further. I remember very well what you said to me—"A clever laywer can do anything if he has the will; if it's impossible, he will make it possible. And the property is sure to be Harold's some day." He was a baby then.'

'I remember most things a little too well: you had better say at once what is your object in recalling them.'

'An object that is nothing more than justice. With the relation I stood in, it was not likely I should think myself bound by all the forms that are made to bind strangers. I had often immense trouble to raise the money necessary to pay off debts and carry on the affairs; and, as I said before, I had given up other lines of advancement which would have been open to me if I had not stayed in this neighbourhood at a critical time when I was fresh to the world. Anybody who knew the whole circumstances would say that my being hunted and run down on the score of my past transactions with regard to the family affairs, is an abominably unjust and unnatural thing.'

Jermyn paused a moment, and then added, 'At my time of life . . . and with a family about me—and after what has passed . . . I should have thought there was nothing you would care more to prevent.'

'I do care. It makes me miserable. That is the extent of my power—to feel miserable.'

'No, it is not the extent of your power. You could save me if you would. It is not to be supposed that Harold would go on against me . . . if he knew the whole truth.'

Jermyn had sat down before he uttered the last words. He had lowered his voice slightly. He had the air of one who thought that he had prepared the way for an understanding. That a man with so much sharpness, with so much suavity at command—a man who piqued himself on his persuasiveness towards women,—should behave just as Jermyn did on this occasion, would be surprising, but for the constant experience that temper and selfish insensibility will defeat excellent gifts—will make a sensible person shout when shouting is out of place, and will make a polished man rude when his polish might be of eminent use to him.

As Jermyn, sitting down and leaning forward with an elbow on his knee, uttered his last words—'if he knew the whole truth'—a slight shock seemed to pass through Mrs Transome's hitherto motionless body, followed by a sudden light in her eyes, as in an animal's about to spring.

'And you expect me to tell him?' she said, not loudly, but yet with a clear metallic ring in her voice.

'Would it not be right for him to know?' said Jermyn, in a more bland and persuasive tone than he had yet used.

Perhaps some of the most terrible irony of the human lot is this of a deep truth coming to be uttered by lips that have no right to it.

'I will never tell him!' said Mrs Transome, starting up, her whole frame thrilled with a passion that seemed almost to make her young again.

GEORGE ELIOT (1819–1880)

Themistocles in Exile

Themistocles started inland with one of the coast Persians, and sent a letter to King Artaxerxes, Xerxes's son, who had just come to the throne. Its contents were as follows: 'I, Themistocles, am come to you, who did your house more harm than any of the Hellenes, when I was compelled to defend myself against your father's invasion—harm, however, far surpassed by the good that I did him during his retreat, which brought no danger for me but much for him. For the past, you are a good turn in my debt'—here he mentioned the warning sent to Xerxes from Salamis to retreat, as well as his finding the bridges unbroken, which, as he falsely pretended, was due to him—'for the present, able to do you great service, I am here, pursued by the Hellenes for my friendship for you. However, I desire a year's grace, when I shall be able to declare in person the objects of my coming.'

It is said that the king approved his intention, and told him to do as he said. He employed the interval in making what progress he could in the study of the Persian tongue, and of the customs of the country. Arrived at court at the end of the year, he attained to very high consideration there, such as no Hellene has ever possessed before or since; partly from his splendid antecedents, partly from the hopes which he held out of effecting for him the subjugation of Hellas, but principally by the proof which experience daily gave of his capacity. For Themistocles was a man who exhibited the most indubitable signs of genius; indeed, in this particular he has a claim on our admiration quite extraordinary and unparalleled. By his own native capacity, alike unformed and unsupplemented by study, he was at once the best judge in those sudden crises which admit of little or of no deliberation, and the best prophet of the future, even to its most distant possibilities. An able theoretical expositor of all that came within the sphere of his practice, he was not without the power of passing an adequate judgment in matters in which he had no experience. He could also excellently divine the good and evil which lay hid in the unseen future. In fine, whether we consider the extent of his natural powers, or the slightness of his application, this extraordinary man must be allowed to have surpassed all others in the faculty of intuitively meeting an emergency. Disease was the real cause of his death; though there is a story of his having ended his life by poison, on finding himself unable to fulfil his promises to the king. However this may be, there is a monument to him in the market-place of Asiatic Magnesia. He was governor of the district, the king having given him Magnesia, which brought in fifty talents a year, for bread, Lampsacus, which was considered to be the richest wine country, for wine, and Myos for other provisions. His bones, it is said, were conveyed home by his relatives in accordance with his wishes, and interred in Attic ground. This was done without the knowledge of the Athenians; as it is against the law to bury in Attica an outlaw for treason.

THUCYDIDES (c. 460–401 B.C.)

The Chancellor yields up the Great Seal

But Sir Thomas More, in process of time, seeing the King fully determined to proceed forth in the marriage of Queen Anne, and when he, with the bishops and nobles of the Higher House of the Parliament, were, for the furtherance of that marriage, commanded by the King to go down to the Common House to shew unto them both what the Universities, as well as of other parts beyond the seas as of Oxford and Cambridge, had done in that behalf, and their seals also testifying the same—all which matters, at the King's request, not shewing of what mind himself was therein, he opened to the Lower House of the Parliament—nevertheless, doubting lest further attempts after should follow, which, contrary to his conscience, by reason of his office, he was likely to be put unto, he made suit unto the Duke of Norfolk, his singular dear friend, to be a means to the King that he might, with His Grace's favour, be discharged of that chargeable room of the Chancellorship, wherein, for certain infirmities of his body, he pretended himself unable any longer to serve.

This Duke, coming on a time to Chelsea to dine with him, fortuned to find him at the Church, singing in the Choir, with a surplice on his back; to whom, after service, as they went homeward together, arm in arm, the Duke said, 'God body! God body! My Lord Chancellor, a parish Clerk, a parish Clerk! You dishonour the King and his office.' 'Nay,' quoth Sir Thomas More, smiling upon the Duke, 'Your Grace may not think that the King, your master and mine, will with me, for serving of God, his master, be offended, or thereby count his office dishonoured.'

When the Duke, being thereunto often solicited, by importunate suit had at length of the King obtained for Sir Thomas More a clear discharge of his office, then, at a time convenient, by his Highness's appointment, repaired he to His Grace, to yield up unto him the Great Seal. Which, as His Grace, with thanks and praise for his worthy service in that office, courteously at his hands received, so pleased it His Highness further to say unto him, that for the service that he before had done him, in any suit which he should after have unto him, that either should concern his honour (for that word it liked His Highness to use unto him) or that should appertain unto his profit, he should find His Highness good and gracious Lord unto him.

After he had thus given over the Chancellorship, and placed all his gentlemen and yeomen with bishops and noblemen, and his eight watermen with the Lord Audley, that in the same office succeeded him, to whom also he gave his great barge, then, calling us all that were his children unto him, and asking our advice how we might now, in this decay of his ability (by the surrender of his office so impaired that he could not, as he was wont, and gladly would, bear out the whole charges of them all himself) from thenceforth be able to live and continue together, as he wished we should, when he saw us silent, and in that case not ready to shew our opinions to him, 'Then will I,' said he, 'shew my poor mind unto you. I have been brought up,' quoth he, 'at Oxford, at an Inn of Chancery, at Lincoln's Inn and also in the King's Court, and so forth from the lowest degree to the highest, and yet have I in yearly revenues at this present left me little above an hundred pounds by the year, so that now must we hereafter, if we like to live together, be contented to become contributories together. But, by my counsel, it shall not be best for us to fall to the lowest fare first. We will not therefore descend to Oxford fare, nor to the fare of New Inn, but we will begin with Lincoln's Inn diet, where many right worshipful and of good years do live full well; which, if we find not ourselves the first year able to maintain, then will we the next year go one step down to New Inn fare, wherewith many an honest man is well contented. If that exceed our ability too, then will we the next year after descend to Oxford fare, where many grave, learned and ancient fathers be continually conversant, which if our power stretch not to maintain neither, then may we yet with bags and wallets, go a begging together, and hoping that for pity some good folk will give us their charity, at every man's door to sing *Salve Regina*, and so still keep company and be merry together.'

And whereas you have heard before, he was by the King from a very worshipful living taken into His Grace's service, with whom, in all the great and weighty causes that concerned His Highness or the Realm, he consumed and spent with painful cares, travels and troubles, as well beyond the seas as within the Realm, in effect the whole substance of his life, yet with all the gain he got thereby, being never wasteful spender thereof, was he not able, after the resignation of his office of Lord Chancellor, for the maintenance of himself and such as necessarily belonged unto him, sufficiently to find meat, drink, fuel, apparel and such other necessary charges. All the land that ever he purchased, which also he purchased before he was Lord Chancellor, was not, I am well assured, above the value of twenty marks by the year. And after his debts paid, he had not, I know, his chain excepted, in gold and silver left him the worth of one hundred pounds.

And whereas upon the holy-days during his High Chancellorship, one of his gentlemen, when service at the Church was done, ordinarily used to come to my lady his wife's pew, and say unto her, 'Madame, my Lord is gone,' the next holy-day after the surrender of his office and departure of his gentleman, he came unto his lady his wife's pew himself, and making a low curtsy, said unto her, 'Madame, my lord is gone.'

WILLIAM ROPER (1496–1578)

Louis XIV and James 'III'

On the following day he went again to Saint Germains, and, attended by a splendid retinue, entered James's bedchamber. The dying man scarcely opened his heavy eyes, and then closed them again. 'I have something,' said Lewis, 'of great moment to communicate to Your Majesty.' The courtiers who filled the room took this as a signal to retire, and were crowding towards the door, when they were stopped by that commanding voice: 'Let nobody withdraw. I come to tell Your Majesty that, whenever it shall please God to take you from us, I will be to your son what I have been to you, and will acknowledge him as King of England, Scotland and Ireland.' The English exiles who were standing round the couch fell on their knees. Some burst into tears. Some poured forth praises and blessings with clamour such as was scarcely becoming in such a place and at such a time. Some indistinct murmurs which James uttered, and which were drowned by the noisy gratitude of his attendants, were interpreted to mean thanks. But from the most trustworthy accounts it appears that he was insensible to all that was passing around him.

As soon as Lewis was again at Marli, he repeated to the Court assembled there the announcement which he had made at Saint Germains. The whole circle broke forth into exclamations of delight and admiration. What piety! What humanity! What magnanimity! Nor was this enthusiasm altogether feigned. For, in the estimation of the greater part of that brilliant crowd, nations were nothing and princes every thing. What could be more generous, more amiable, than to protect an innocent boy, who was kept out of his rightful inheritance by an ambitious kinsman? The fine gentlemen and fine ladies who talked thus forgot that, besides the innocent boy and that ambitious kinsman, five millions and a half of Englishmen were concerned, who were little disposed to consider themselves as the absolute property of any master, and who were still less disposed to accept a master chosen for them by the French King.

James lingered three days longer. He was occasionally sensible during a few minutes, and, during one of these lucid intervals, faintly expressed his gratitude to Lewis. On the sixteenth he died. His Queen retired that evening to the nunnery of Chaillot, where she could weep and pray undisturbed. She left Saint Germains in joyous agitation. A herald made his appearance before the palace gate, and, with sound of trumpet, proclaimed, in Latin, French and English, King James the Third of England and Eighth of Scotland. The streets, in consequence doubtless of orders from the government, were illuminated; and the townsmen with loud shouts wished a long reign to their illustrious neighbour. The poor lad received from his ministers, and delivered back to them, the seals of their offices, and held out his hand to be kissed. One of the first acts of his mock reign was to bestow some mock peerages in conformity with directions which he found in his father's will. Middleton, who had as yet no English title, was created Earl of Monmouth. Perth, who had stood high in the favour of his late master, both as an apostate from the Protestant religion, and as the author of the last improvements on the thumb screw, took the title of Duke.

Meanwhile the remains of James were escorted, in the dusk of the evening by a slender retinue to the Chapel of the English Benedictines at Paris, and deposited there in the vain hope that, at some future time, they would be laid with kingly pomp at Westminster among the graves of the Plantagenets and Tudors.

Three days after these humble obsequies Lewis visited Saint Germains in form. On the morrow the visit was returned. The French Court was now at Versailles; and the Pretender was received there, in all points, as his father would have been, sate in his father's arm chair, took, as his father had always done, the right hand of the great monarch, and wore the long violet coloured mantle which was by ancient usage the mourning garb of the Kings of France. There was on that day a great concourse of ambassadors and envoys; but one well known figure was wanting. Manchester had sent off to Loo intelligence of the affront which had been offered to his country and his master, had solicited instructions, and had determined that, till these instructions should arrive, he would live in strict seclusion. He did not think that he should be justified in quitting his post without express orders; but his earnest hope was that he should be directed to turn his back in contemptuous defiance on the Court which had dared to treat England as a subject province.

THOMAS BABINGTON MACAULAY (1800–59)

The Queen of the Adriatic

I stood in Venice, on the Bridge of Sighs;
A palace and a prison on each hand:
I saw from out the wave her structures rise
As from the stroke of the enchanter's wand:
A thousand years their cloudy wings expand
Around me, and a dying Glory smiles
O'er the far times, when many a subject land
Look'd to the winged Lion's marble piles,
Where Venice sate in state, throned on her hundred isles!

She looks a sea Cybele, fresh from ocean,
Rising with her tiara of proud towers
At airy distance, with majestic motion,
A ruler of the waters and their powers:
And such she was;—her daughters had their dowers
From spoils of nations, and the exhaustless East
Pour'd in her lap all gems in sparkling showers.
In purple was she robed, and of her feast
Monarchs partook, and deem'd their dignity increased.

In Venice Tasso's echoes are no more,
And silent rows the songless gondolier;
Her palaces are crumbling to the shore,
And music meets not always now the ear;
Those days are gone—but Beauty still is here.
States fall, arts fade—but Nature doth not die,
Nor yet forget how Venice once was dear,
The pleasant place of all festivity,
The revel of the earth, the masque of Italy!

But unto us she hath a spell beyond
Her name in story, and her long array
Of mighty shadows, whose dim forms despond
Above the dogeless city's vanish'd sway;
Ours is a trophy which will not decay
With the Rialto; Shylock and the Moor,
And Pierre, can not be swept or worn away—
The keystones of the arch! though all were o'er,
For us repeopled were the solitary shore.

LORD BYRON (1788–1824)

The Inimitable Livers

Antony was so captivated by her that, while Fulvia his wife maintained his quarrels in Rome against Cæsar by actual force of arms, and the Parthian troops, commanded by Labienus (the king's generals having made him commander-in-chief), were assembled in Mesopotamia, and ready to enter Syria, he could yet suffer himself to be carried away by her to Alexandria, there to keep holiday, like a boy, in play and diversion, squandering and fooling away in enjoyments that most costly, as Anliphon says, of all valuables, time. They had a sort of company, to which they gave a particular name, calling it that of the Inimitable Livers. The members entertained one another daily in turn, with an extravagance of expenditure beyond measure or belief. Philotas, a physician of Amphissa, who was at that time a student of medicine in Alexandria, used to tell my grandfather Lamprias that, having some acquaintance with one of the royal cooks, he was invited by him, being a young man, to come and see the sumptuous preparations for supper. So he was taken into the kitchen, where he admired the prodigious variety of all things; but particularly, seeing eight wild boars roasting whole, says he, 'Surely you have a great number of guests.' The cook laughed at his simplicity, and told him there were not above twelve to sup, but that every dish was to be served up just roasted to a turn, and if anything was but one minute ill-timed, it was spoiled. 'And,' said he, 'maybe Antony will sup just now, maybe not this hour, maybe he will call for wine, or begin to talk, and will put it off. So that,' he continued, 'it is not one, but many suppers must be had in readiness, as it is impossible to guess at his hour.' This was Philotas's story; who related besides, that he afterwards came to be one of the medical attendants of Antony's eldest son by Fulvia, and used to be invited pretty often, among other companions, to his table, when he was not supping with his father. One day another physician had talked loudly, and given great disturbance to the company, whose mouth Philotas stopped with this sophistical syllogism: 'In some states of fever the patient should take cold water; every one who has a fever is in some state of fever; therefore in a fever cold water should always be taken.' The man was quite struck dumb, and Antony's son, very much pleased, laughed aloud, and said, 'Philotas, I make you a present of all you see there,' pointing to a sideboard covered with plate. Philotas thanked him much, but was far enough from ever imagining that a boy of his age could dispose of things of that value. Soon after, however, the plate was all brought to him, and he was desired to set his mark upon it; and when he put it away from him, and was afraid to accept the present, 'What ails the man?' said he that brought it; 'do you know that he who gives you this is Antony's son, who is free to give it, if it were all gold? but if you will be advised by me, I would counsel you to accept of the value in money from us; for there may be amongst the rest some antique or famous piece of workmanship, which Antony would be sorry to part with.' These anecdotes, my grandfather told us, Philotas used frequently to relate.

PLUTARCH (c. 46–120)

A Six-Pint Fellow

At my first admission into this printing-house I took to working at press, imagining I felt a want of the bodily exercise I had been used to in America, where presswork is mixed with composing. I drank only water; the other workmen, near fifty in number, were great guzzlers of beer. On occasion, I carried up and down stairs a large form of types in each hand, when others carried but one in both hands. They wondered to see, from this and several instances, that the *Water-American*, as they called me, was *stronger* than themselves, who drank *strong* beer! We had an alehouse boy who attended always in the house to supply the workmen. My companion at the press drank every day a pint before breakfast, a pint at breakfast with his bread and cheese, a pint between breakfast and dinner, a pint at dinner, a pint in the afternoon about six o'clock, and another when he had done his day's work. I thought it a detestable custom; but it was necessary, he supposed, to drink *strong* beer, that he might be *strong* to labor. I endeavored to convince him that the bodily strength afforded by beer could only be in proportion to the grain or flour of the barley dissolved in the water of which it was made; that there was more flour in a pennyworth of bread; and therefore, if he would eat that with a pint of water, it would give him more strength than a quart of beer. He drank on, however, and had four or five shillings to pay out of his wages every Saturday night for that muddling liquor; an expense I was free from. And thus these poor devils keep themselves always under.

Watts, after some weeks, desiring to have me in the composing-room, I left the pressmen; a new bien venu or sum for drink, being five shillings, was demanded of me by the compositors. I thought it an imposition, as I had paid below; the master thought so too, and forbad my paying it. I stood out two or three weeks, was accordingly considered as an excommunicate, and had so many little pieces of private mischief done me, by mixing my sorts, transposing my pages, breaking my matter, etc., etc., if I were ever so little out of the room, and all ascribed to the chappel ghost, which they said ever haunted those not regularly admitted, that, notwithstanding the master's protection, I found myself obliged to comply and pay the money, convinced of the folly of being on ill terms with those one is to live with continually.

I was now on a fair footing with them, and soon acquired considerable influence. I proposed some reasonable alterations in their chappel laws, and carried them against all opposition. From my example, a great part of them left their muddling breakfast of beer, and bread, and cheese, finding they could with me be supplied from a neighboring house with a large porringer of hot water-gruel, sprinkled with pepper, crumbed with bread, and a bit of butter in it, for the price of a pint of beer, viz., three half-pence. This was a more comfortable as well as cheaper breakfast, and kept their heads clearer. Those who continued sotting with beer all day, were often, by not paying, out of credit at the alehouse, and used to make interest with me to get beer; their *light*, as they phrased it, *being out*. I watched the pay-table on Saturday night, and collected what I stood engaged for them, having to pay sometimes near thirty shillings a week on their accounts. This, and my being esteemed a pretty good *riggite*, that is, a jocular verbal satirist, supported my consequence in the society. My constant attendance (I never making a St Monday) recommended me to the master; and my uncommon quickness at composing occasioned my being put upon all work of dispatch, which was generally better paid. So I went on now very agreeably.

My lodging in Little Britain being too remote, I found another in Duke-street, opposite to the Romish Chapel. It was two pair of stairs backwards, at an Italian warehouse. A widow lady kept the house; she had a daughter, and a maid servant, and a journeyman who attended the warehouse, but lodged abroad. After sending to inquire my character at the house where I last lodged she agreed to take me in at the same rate, 3s. 6d. per week; cheaper, as she said, from the protection she expected in having a man lodge in the house. She was a widow, an elderly woman; had been bred a Protestant, being a clergyman's daughter, but was converted to the Catholic religion by her husband, whose memory she much revered; had lived much among people of distinction, and knew a thousand anecdotes of them as far back as the times of Charles the Second. She was lame in her knees with the gout, and, therefore, seldom stirred out of her room, so sometimes wanted company; and hers was so highly amusing to me, that I was sure to spend an evening with her whenever she desired it. Our supper was only half an anchovy each, on a very little strip of bread and butter, and half a pint of ale between us; but the entertainment was in her conversation. My always keeping good hours, and giving little trouble in the family, made her unwilling to part with me; so that, when I talked of a lodging I had heard of, nearer my business, for two shillings a week, which, intent as I now was on saving money, made some difference, she bid me not think of it, for she would abate me two shillings a week for the future; so I remained with her at one shilling and sixpence as long as I staid in London.

BENJAMIN FRANKLIN (1706–1790)

Mr Jorrocks's Dinner Party

The dining-room was the breadth of the passage narrower than the front drawing-room, and, as Mr Jorrocks truly said, was rayther small—but the table being excessively broad, made the room appear less than it was. It was lighted up with spermaceti candles in silver holders, one at each corner of the table, and there was a lamp in the wall between the red-curtained windows, immediately below a brass nail, on which Mr Jorrocks's great hunting-whip and a bunch of boot garters were hung. Two more candles in the hands of bronze Dianas on the marble mantelpiece, lighted up a coloured copy of Barraud's picture of John Warde on Blue Ruin; while Mr Ralph Lambton, on his horse Undertaker, with his hounds and men, occupied a frame on the opposite wall. The old-fashioned cellaret sideboard, against the wall at the end, supported a large bright-burning brass lamp, with raised foxes round the rim, whose effulgent rays shed a brilliant halo over eight black hats and two white ones, whereof the four middle ones were decorated with evergreens and foxes' brushes. The dinner table was crowded, not covered. There was scarcely a square inch of cloth to be seen on any part. In the centre stood a magnificent finely spun barley-sugar windmill, two feet and a half high, with a spacious sugar foundation, with a cart and horses and two or three millers at the door, and a she-miller working a ball-dress flounce at a lower window.

The whole dinner, first, second, third, fourth course—everything, in fact, except dessert—was on the table, as we sometimes see it at ordinaries and public dinners. Before both Mr and Mrs Jorrocks were two great tureens of mock-turtle soup, each capable of holding a gallon, and both full up to the brim. Then there were two sorts of fish; turbot and lobster sauce, and a great salmon. A round of boiled beef and an immense piece of roast occupied the rear of these, ready to march on the disappearance of the fish and soup—and behind the walls, formed by the beef of old England, came two dishes of grouse, each dish holding three brace. The side dishes consisted of a calf's head hashed, a leg of mutton, chickens, ducks, and mountains of vegetables; and round the windmill were plum-puddings, tarts, jellies, pies, and puffs.

Behind Mrs Jorrocks's chair stood 'Batsay' with a fine brass-headed comb in her hair, and stiff ringlets down her ruddy cheeks. She was dressed in a green silk gown, with a coral necklace, and one of Mr Jorrocks's lavender and white coloured silk pocket-handkerchiefs made into an apron. 'Binjimin' stood with the door in his hand, as the saying is, with a towel twisted round his thumb, as though he had cut it.

'Now, gentlemen,' said Mr Jorrocks, casting his eye up the table, as soon as they had all got squeezed and wedged round it, and the dishes were uncovered, 'you see your dinner, eat whatever you like except the windmill—hope you'll be able to satisfy nature with what's on—would have had more but Mrs J—— is so werry fine, she won't stand two joints of the same sort on the table.'

Mrs J. Lauk, John, how can you be so wulgar! Who ever saw two rounds of beef, as you wanted to have? Besides, I'm sure the gentlemen will excuse any little de*fish*ency, considering the short notice we have had, and that this is not an elaborate dinner.

Mr Spiers. I'm sure, ma'm, there's no de*fish*ency at all. Indeed, I think there's as much fish as would serve double the number—and I'm sure you look as if you had your soup 'on sale or return,' as we say in the magazine line.

Mr J. Haw! haw! haw! werry good, Mr Spiers. I owe you one. Not bad soup though—had it from Birch's. Let me send you some; and pray lay into it, or I shall think you don't like it. Mr Happerley, let me send you some—and, gentlemen, let me observe, once for all, that there's every species of malt liquor under the side table. Prime stout, from the Marquess Cornwallis, hard by. Also ale, table, and what my friend Crane there calls lamen*table*—he says, because it's so werry small—but, in truth, because I don't buy it of him. There's all sorts of drench, in fact, except water—a thing I never touch—rots one's shoes, don't know what it would do with one's stomach if it was to get there. Mr Crane, you're eating nothing. I'm quite shocked to see you;

you don't surely live upon hair? Do help yourself, or you'll faint from werry famine. Belinda, my love, does the Yorkshireman take care of you? Who's for some salmon?—bought at Luckey's, and there's both Tallyho and Tantivy sarce to eat with it. Somehow or other I always fancies I rides harder after eating these sarces with fish. Mr Happerley Nimrod, you are the greatest man at table, consequently I axes you to drink wine first, according to the book of etiquette—help yourself, sir. Some of Crane's particklar, hot and strong, real stuff, none of your wan de bones (vin de beaume) or rot-gut French stuff—hope you like it—if you don't, pray speak your mind freely, now that we have Crane among us. Binjimin, get me some of that duck before Mr Spiers, a leg and a wing, if you please, sir, and a bit of the breast.

Mr Spiers. Certainly, sir, certainly. Do you prefer a right or left wing, sir?

Mr Jorrocks. Oh, either. I suppose it's all the same.

Mr Spiers. Why no, sir, it's not exactly all the same; for it happens there is only one remaining, therefore it must be the *left* one.

Mr J. (chuckling). Haw! haw! haw! Mr S——, werry good that— werry good indeed. I owes you two.

'I'll trouble you for a little, Mr Spiers, if you please,' says Crane, handing his plate round the windmill.

'I'm sorry, sir, it is all gone,' replies Mr Spiers, who had just filled Mr Jorrocks's plate; 'there's nothing left but the neck,' holding it up on the fork.

'Well, send it,' rejoins Mr Crane; 'neck or nothing, you know, Mr Jorrocks, as we say with the Surrey.'

'Haw! haw! haw!' grunts Mr Jorrocks, who is busy sucking a bone; 'haw! haw! haw! werry good, Crane, werry good—owes you one. Now, gentlemen,' added he, casting his eye up the table as he spoke, 'let me adwise ye, before you attack the grouse, to take the hedge (edge) **off** your appetites, or else there won't be enough, and, you know, it does not do to eat the farmer after the gentlemen. Let's see, now— three and three are six, six brace among eight—oh dear, that's nothing like enough. I wish, Mrs J——, you had followed my adwice, and roasted them all. And now, Binjimin, you're going to break the wind- mill with your clumsiness, you little dirty rascal! Why von't you let Batsay arrange the table? Thank you, Mr Crane, for your assistance— your politeness, sir, exceeds your beauty.' [A barrel organ strikes up before the window, and Jorrocks throws down his knife and fork in an agony.] 'Oh dear, oh dear, there's that cursed horgan again. It's a regular annihilator. Binjimin, run and kick the fellow's werry soul out

of him. There's no man suffers so much from music as I do. I wish I
had a pocketful of sudden deaths, that I might throw one at every
thief of a musicianer that comes up the street. I declare the scoundrel
has set all my teeth on edge. Mr Nimrod, pray take another glass of
wine after your roast beef.—Well, with Mrs J—— if you choose, but
I'll join you—always says that you are the werry cleverest man of the
day—read all your writings—anny-tommy (anatomy) of gaming, and
all. Am a hauthor myself, you know—once set to, to write a werry long
and elaborate harticle on scent, but after cudgelling my brains, and
turning the thing over and over again in my mind, all that I could brew
on the subject was, that scent was a werry rum thing: nothing rummer
than scent, except a woman.'. .

A single, but very resolute knock at the street door, sounding quite
through the house, stopped all further ebullition, and Benjamin, slip-
ping out, held a short conversation with someone in the street, and
returned.

'What's happened now, Binjimin?' inquired Mr Jorrocks, with
anxiety on his countenance, as the boy re-entered the room; 'the
'osses arn't amiss, I 'ope?'

'Please, sir, Mr Farrell's young man has come for the windmill—he
says you've had it two hours,' replied Benjamin.

'The deuce be with Mr Farrell's young man! he does not suppose
we can part with the mill before the cloth's drawn—tell him to mizzle,
or I'll mill him. "Now's the day and now's the hour"; who's for some
grouse? Gentlemen, make your game, in fact. But first of all let's have
a round robin. Pass the wine, gentlemen. What wine do you take,
Stubbs.'

'Why, champagne is good enough for me.'

Mr Jorrocks. I dare say; but if you wait till you get any here, you
will have a long time to stop. Shampain, indeed! had enough of that
nonsense abroad—declare you young chaps drink shampain like hale.
There's red and wite port, and sherry, in fact, and them as carn't drink,
they must go without.

> X. was expensive and soon became poor,
> Y. was the wise man and kept want from the door.

'Now for the grouse!' added he, as the two beefs disappeared, and
they took their stations at the top and bottom of the table. 'Fine birds,
to be sure! Hope you havn't burked your appetites, gentlemen, so as
not to be able to do justice to them—smell high—werry good—gamey,

in fact. Binjimin, take an 'ot plate to Mr Nimrod—sarve us all round
with them.'

The grouse being excellent, and cooked to a turn, little execution was
done upon the pastry, and the jellies had all melted long before it came
to their turn to be eat. At length everyone, Mr Jorrocks and all,
appeared satisfied, and the noise of knives and forks was succeeded by
the din of tongues and the ringing of glasses, as the eaters refreshed
themselves with wine or malt liquors. Cheese and biscuit being handed
about on plates, according to the *Spirit of Etiquette*. Binjimin and
Batsay at length cleared the table, lifted off the windmill, and removed
the cloth.

ROBERT S. SURTEES (1803–1864)

Not Made with a Hen Lobster

Her father, of course, was the lion of the party, but seeing that we were
all meek and quite willing to be eaten, he roared to us rather than at us.
It was a fine sight to see him tucking his napkin under his rosy old
gills, and letting it fall over his capacious waistcoat while the high light
from the chandelier danced about the bump of benevolence on his bald
old head like a star of Bethlehem.

The soup was real turtle; the old gentleman was evidently well
pleased and he was beginning to come out. Gelstrap stood behind his
master's chair. I sat next Mrs Theobald on her left hand, and was
thus just opposite her father-in-law, whom I had every opportunity of
observing.

During the first ten minutes or so, which were taken up with the
soup and the bringing in of the fish, I should probably have thought,
if I had not long since made up my mind about him, what a fine old
man he was and how proud his children should be of him; but suddenly as he was helping himself to lobster sauce, he flushed crimson, a
look of extreme vexation suffused his face, and he darted two furtive
but fiery glances to the two ends of the table, one for Theobald and one
for Christina. They, poor simple souls, of course saw that something
was exceedingly wrong, and so did I, but I couldn't guess what it was
till I heard the old man hiss in Christina's ear: 'It was not made with a
hen lobster. What's the use,' he continued, 'of my calling the boy
Ernest, and getting him christened in water from the Jordan, if his
own father does not know a cock from a hen lobster?'

This cut me too, for I felt that till that moment I had not so much as known that there were cocks and hens among lobsters, but had vaguely thought that in the matter of matrimony they were even as the angels in heaven, and grew up almost spontaneously from rocks and seaweed.

SAMUEL BUTLER (1835-1902)

The Admiral calls for Bubbly

At dinner Mrs Schwellenberg presided, attired magnificently. Miss Goldsworthy, Mrs Stainforth, Messrs de Luc and Stanhope dined with us; and, while we were still eating fruit, the Duke of Clarence entered.

He had just risen from the King's table, and waiting for his equipage to go home and prepare for the ball. To give you an idea of the energy of his Royal Highness's language, I ought to set apart a general objection to writing, or rather intimating, certain forcible words, and beg leave to show you, in genuine colours, a Royal sailor.

We all rose, of course, upon his entrance, and the two gentlemen placed themselves behind their chairs, while the footmen left the room; but he ordered us all to sit down, and called the men back to hand about some wine. He was in exceeding high spirits and in the utmost good humour. He placed himself at the head of the table, next to Mrs Schwellenberg, and looked remarkably well, gay, and full of sport and mischief, yet clever withal as well as comical.

'Well, this is the first day I have ever dined with the King at St James's on his birthday. Pray, have you all drunk his Majesty's health?'

'No, your Roy'l Highness: your Roy'l Highness might make dem do dat,' said Mrs Schwellenberg.

'Oh, by —— will I! Here, you (to the footman); bring champagne! I'll drink the King's health again, if I die for it! Yet, I have done pretty well already: so has the King, I promise you! I believe his Majesty was never taken such good care of before. We have kept his spirits up, I promise you; we have enabled him to go through his fatigues; and I should have done more still, but for the ball and Mary —I have promised to dance with Mary!'

Princess Mary made her first appearance at Court to-day: she looked most interesting and unaffectedly lovely: she is a sweet creature, and perhaps, in point of beauty, the first of this truly beautiful race, of which Princess Mary may be called *pendant* to the Prince of Wales.

Champagne being now brought for the Duke, he ordered it all round.

When it came to me I whispered to Westerhaults to carry it on: the Duke slapped his hand violently on the table and called out: 'Oh, by ——, you shall drink it!'

There was no resisting this. We all stood up, and the Duke sonorously gave the Royal toast.

'And now,' cried he, making us all sit down again, 'where are my rascals of servants? I sha'n't be in time for the ball; besides, I've got a deuced tailor waiting to fix on my epaulette! Here, you, go and see for my servants! d'ye hear? Scamper off!'

Off ran William.

'Come, let's have the King's health again. De Luc, drink it. Here, champagne to de Luc!'

I wish you could have seen Mr de Luc's mixed simper—half pleased, half alarmed. However, the wine came and he drank it, the Duke taking a bumper for himself at the same time.

'Poor Stanhope!' cried he: 'Stanhope shall have a glass, too! Here, champagne! what are you all about? Why don't you give champagne to poor Stanhope?'

Mr Stanhope, with great pleasure, complied, and the Duke again accompanied him.

'Come hither, do you hear?' cried the Duke to the servants, and on the approach, slow and submissive, of Mrs Stainforth's man, he hit him a violent slap on the back, calling out: 'Hang you! Why don't you see for my rascals?'

Away flew the man, and then he called out to Westerhaults: 'Hark'ee! Bring another glass of champagne to Mr de Luc!'

Mr de Luc knows these Royal youths too well to venture at so vain an experiment as disputing with them; so he only shrugged his shoulders and drank the wine. The Duke did the same.

'And now, poor Stanhope,' cried the Duke; 'give another glass to poor Stanhope, d'ye hear?'

'Is not your Royal Highness afraid,' cried Mr Stanhope, displaying the full circle of his borrowed teeth, 'I shall be apt to be rather up in the world, as the folks say, if I tope on at this rate?'

'Not at all! You can't get drunk in a better cause. I'd get drunk myself if it was not for the ball. Here, champagne! Another glass for the philosopher! I keep sober for Mary.'

'Oh, your Royal Highness!' cried Mr de Luc, gaining courage as he drank, 'you will make me quite droll of it if you make me go on— quite droll!'

'So much the better! so much the better! it will do you a monstrous deal of good. Here, another glass of champagne for the Queen's philosopher!'

Mr de Luc obeyed, and the Duke then addressed Mrs Schwellenberg's George. 'Here, you! you! why, where is my carriage? Run and see, do you hear?'

Off hurried George, grinning irrepressibly.'

FANNY BURNEY (1752–1840)

Poet to Patron

My dear Maecenas, thou shalt drink with me
   In modest goblets my *vin ordinaire*,
Which I laid down the year they gave to thee
   The acclamation in the theatre, where
Out of the Tiber's banks thy praises ran,
   The river by whose waters thou wast reared,
And sportive echoes of the Vatican
   Repeated them. By vineyards thou art cheered
Of Caecubum, or wine that from the stills
   Of Cales comes; but in my cups shall be
Nought from the vines upon Falernian hills
   Nor those that flourish under Formiae.

HORACE (65–8 B.C.)

Afternoon Tea

One of the shining moments of my day is that when, having returned a little weary from an afternoon walk, I exchange boots for slippers, out-of-doors coat for easy, familiar, shabby jacket, and, in my deep, soft-elbowed chair, await the tea-tray. Perhaps it is while drinking tea that I most of all enjoy the sense of leisure. In days gone by, I could but gulp down the refreshment, hurried, often harassed, by the thought of the work I had before me; often I was quite insensible of the aroma, the flavour, of what I drank. Now, how delicious is the soft yet penetrating odour which floats into my study with the appearance of the teapot! What solace in the first cup, what deliberate sipping of that which follows! What a glow does it bring after a walk in chilly rain! The while, I look around at my books and pictures, tasting the happiness of their tranquil possession. I cast an eye towards my pipe; perhaps I prepare it, with seeming thoughtfulness, for the reception of tobacco. And never, surely, is tobacco more soothing, more suggestive of humane thoughts, than when it comes just after tea—itself a bland inspirer.

In nothing is the English genius for domesticity more notably declared than in the institution of this festival—almost one may call it so—of afternoon tea. Beneath simple roofs, the hour of tea has something in it of sacred; for it marks the end of domestic work and worry, the beginning of restful, sociable evening. The mere chink of cups and saucers tunes the mind to happy repose. I care nothing for your five o'clock tea of modish drawing-rooms, idle and wearisome like all else in which that world has part; I speak of tea where one is *at home* in quite another than the worldly sense. To admit mere strangers to your tea-table is profanation; on the other hand, English hospitality has here its kindliest aspect; never is friend more welcome than when he drops in for a cup of tea. Where tea is really a meal, with nothing between it and nine o'clock supper, it is—again in the true sense—the *homeliest* meal of the day. Is it believable that the Chinese, in who knows how many centuries, have derived from tea a millionth part of the pleasure or the good which it has brought to England in the past one hundred years?

I like to look at my housekeeper when she carries in the tray. Her mien is festal, yet in her smile there is a certain gravity, as though she performed an office which honoured her. She has dressed for the evening; that is to say, her clean and seemly attire of working hours is exchanged for garments suitable to fireside leisure; her cheeks are warm, for she has been making fragrant toast. Quickly her eye glances about my room, but only to have the pleasure of noting that all is in order; inconceivable that anything serious should need doing at this hour of the day. She brings the little table within the glow of the hearth, so that I can help myself without changing my easy position. If she speaks, it will only be a pleasant word or two; should she have anything important to say, the moment will be *after* tea.

GEORGE GISSING (1857–1903)

A Negative Relief

My next more immediate companions were and are persons of such intrinsic and felt worth, that though accidentally their acquaintance has proved pernicious to me, I do not know that if the thing were to do over again, I should have the courage to eschew the mischief at the price of forfeiting the benefit. I came to them reeking from the steams of my late over-heated notions of companionship; and the slightest fuel which they unconsciously afforded, was sufficient to feed my old fires into a propensity.

They were no drinkers, but, one from professional habits, and another from a custom derived from his father, smoked tobacco. The devil could not have devised a more subtle trap to re-take a backsliding penitent. The transition, from gulping down draughts of liquid fire to puffing out innocuous blasts of dry smoke, was so like cheating him. But he is too hard for us when we hope to commute. He beats us at barter; and when we think to set off a new failing against an old infirmity, 'tis odds but he puts the trick upon us of two for one. That (comparatively) white devil of tobacco brought with him in the end seven worse than himself.

It were impertinent to carry the reader through all the processes by which, from smoking at first with malt liquor, I took my degrees through thin wines, through stronger wine and water, through small punch, to those juggling compositions, which, under the name of mixed liquors, slur a great deal of brandy or other poison under less and less water continually, until they come next to none, and so to none at all. But it is hateful to disclose the secrets of my Tartarus.

I should repel my readers, from a mere incapacity of believing me, were I to tell them what tobacco has been to me, the drudging service which I have paid, the slavery which I have vowed to it. How, when I have resolved to quit it, a feeling as of ingratitude has started up; how it has put on personal claims and made the demands of a friend upon me. How the reading of it casually in a book, as where Adams takes his whiff in the chimney-corner of some inn in Joseph Andrews, or Piscator in the Complete Angler breaks his fast upon a morning pipe in that delicate room *Piscatoribus Sacrum*, has in a moment broken down the resistance of weeks. How a pipe was ever in my midnight path before me, till the vision forced me to realise it,—how then its ascending vapours curled, its fragrance lulled, and the thousand delicious ministerings conversant about it, employing every faculty, extracted the sense of pain. How from illuminating it came to darken, from a quick solace it turned to a negative relief, thence to a restlessness and dissatisfaction, thence to a positive misery. How, even now, when the whole secret stands confessed in all its dreadful truth before me, I feel myself linked to it beyond the power of revocation. Bone of my bone——

CHARLES LAMB (1775–1834)

The Hospital for the Mind

At home I betake me somwhat the oftner to my library, whence all at once I command and survay all my houshold; It is seated in the chiefe entrie of my house, thence I behold under me my garden, my base court, my yard, and looke even into most roomes of my house. There without order, without method, and by peece-meales I turne over and ransacke, now one booke and now another. Sometimes I muse and rave; and walking up and downe I endight and enregister these my humours, these my conceits. It is placed on the third storie of a tower. The lowermost is my Chapell; the second a chamber with other lodgings, where I often lie, because I would be alone. Above it is a great ward-robe. It was in times past the most unprofitable place of all my house. There I [passe] the greatest part of my lives dayes, and weare out most houres of the day. I am never there a nights: Next unto it is a handsome neat cabinet, able and large enough to receive fire in winter, and very pleasantly windowed. And if I feared not care, more then cost; (care which drives and diverts me from all businesse) I might easily joyne a convenient gallerie of a hundred paces long, and twelve broad, on each side of it, and upon one floore; having already, for some other purpose, found all the walles raised unto a convenient height. Each retired place requireth a walke. My thoughts are prone to sleepe, if I sit long. My minde goes not alone as if [legges] did moove it. Those that studie without bookes, are all in the same case.

The forme of it is round, and hath no flat side, but what serveth for my table and chaire: In which bending or circling manner, at one looke it offreth me the full sight of all my books, set round about upon shelves or desks, five rankes one upon another. It hath three bay-windowes, of a farre-extending, rich and unresisted prospect, and is in diameter sixteene paces void. In winter I am lesse continually there: for my house (as the name of it importeth) is pearched upon an over-pearing hillocke; and hath no part more subject to all wethers then this: which pleaseth me the more, both because the accesse unto it is somwhat troublesome and remote, and for the benefit of the exercise which is to be respected; and that I may the better seclude my selfe from companie, and keepe incrochers from me: There is my seat, that is my throne. I endevour to make my rule therein absolute, and to sequester that only corner from the communitie of wife, of children and of acquaintance. Elsewhere I have but a verball authoritie, of confused essence. Miserable, in my minde is he, who in his owne home, hath no where to be to himselfe; where hee may particularly court, and at his pleasure hide or with-draw himself. . . *Bookes have and containe divers pleasing qualities to those that can duly choose them.* But *no good without paines ; no Roses without prickles.* It is a pleasure not absolutely pure and neate, no more then all others; it hath his inconveniences attending on it and somtimes waighty ones: The minde is therein exercised, but the body (the care whereof I have not yet forgotten) remaineth there-whilst without action, and is wasted, and ensorrowed. I know no excesse more hurtfull for me, nor more to be avoided by me, in this declining age. Loe here my three most favoured and particular employments. I speake not of those I owe of dutie to the world.

MICHEL EYQUEM DE MONTAIGNE (1533–1592)

NOTES

Throughout the notes, volume and page references are to editions in Everyman's Library. Places and dates contained within square brackets are those of the first edition, not of the Everyman title cited. When the date alone appears, first publication was in London.

9 LEIGH HUNT, *The Literary Examiner* [1823] in *Selected Essays*, pp. 346–8. A short-lived section of *The Examiner* (which in 1812 libelled the Prince Regent, 'This Adonis of loveliness', &c., for which Hunt was imprisoned for two years).

11 ADDISON, *The Spectator* [12 April 1711], II, 110–12. The first 'feature' journalism, read and re-read in book form by the emerging middle class throughout the eighteenth century.

13 BEDE, *Ecclesiastical History of the English Nation* [Strassburg *c.* 1475], pp. 4–5. Finished 731. Bede, 'the only native Englishman to join the small band of indispensable authors to be found in every great collection of manuscripts in north-western Europe'.

14 GREEN, *A Short History of the British People* [1874], II, 431–2. The Stepney parson who wrote a superb best-seller, after leaving Oxford without distinction.

16 PEPYS, *Diary* [1825, in part], III, 138–9. The private diary, written in cypher, covers the period 1659–69 almost day by day.

17 GRAY to Dr Wharton, 22 April 1760, in *Letters and Essays*, pp. 227–30. Even if esteemed more as a poet, Gray, with Horace Walpole and Byron, is one of the supremely great English letter-writers.

19 HEINE, 'London', in *English Fragments* [1828] in *Prose and Poetry*, pp. 220–2. Contributed to *Allgemeinen politischen Annalen*; collected and published in London 1831. A. E. Housman has acknowledged indebtedness to Heine's poems—but, says Heine, 'Send no poet to London.'

22 BLAKE, in *Songs of Experience* [1794] in *Poems and Prophecies*, p. 31.

22 PRIESTLEY, *Angel Pavement* [1931], pp. 11–13.

24 COBBETT, *Rural Rides* [1830], II, 217–18. Journalist and sometime Army sergeant, 'Peter Porcupine' is one of the English masters of the 'plain style'.

26 DEFOE, *A Tour through the whole Island of Great Britain* [1724–6], II, 301–2. The first great reporter. For a time imprisoned in Newgate.

27 WASHINGTON IRVING, *The Sketch Book of Geoffrey Crayon Gent* [1820], pp. 302–7. Praised on publication by Lockhart, Byron, Jeffrey, Scott.

29 DE QUINCEY, in *Recollections of the Lakes and the Lake Poets* [1862], in *Reminiscences of the English Lake Poets*, pp. 166–7. Eye-witness reporting; published in the *Edinburgh Magazine* in and after 1834.

30 MITFORD, *Our Village* [1824–32], pp. 63–4. 'Miniature writing' of the greatest charm.

31 HOBBES, *Leviathan* [1651], pp. 64–6. A politico-philosophical writer, mostly unacceptable to his contemporaries, in whose wit Charles II delighted.

32 BURKE, in Speech at Bristol 3 November 1774 to the Electors, in *British Orations from Ethelbert to Churchill*, pp. 71–3. The Irishman who injected principle into English politics, but whose oratory could empty the House.

35 TOM PAINE, *The Rights of Man* [1791], pp. 274–6. The answer to Burke's attack on the French Revolution. For this Paine was indicted, but evaded trial.

36 BURKE, Speech, on 'American Taxation', 19 April 1774, in *Speeches and Letters on American Affairs*, pp. 48–9.

37 DANTE, 'Paradise', XVII, 46–69, *Divine Comedy* [Foligno 1472], pp. 369–70. No great poem is so untranslatable. Of the verse attempts in English, Cary's [1805–14] has worn best.

38 HAMILTON, in *The Federalist* [New York 1802], pp. 41–3. Written in 1788. A 'keen study in the economic interpretation of politics' by one of the Founding Fathers of the U.S.A. Constitution. Died after a duel. The other contributors were Jay and Madison.

40 HUME, *A Treatise of Human Nature* [1739], II, 265–7. The masterpiece that 'fell still-born from the press'.

41 MAINE, *Ancient Law* [1861], pp. 56–9.

44 BEACONSFIELD, *Coningsby* [1844], pp. 83–5. The novelist who once when Prime Minister, in a letter to Queen Victoria, linked his sovereign and himself as 'we authors'.

46 STOW, *The Survey of London* [1598], pp. 70–2. Elizabethan London through the eyes of a dedicated antiquary and historian.

48 CICERO, *The Offices* [Mainz 1465]; *On Friendship, &c.*, pp. 140–1. The prose stylist whom the neo-Latin writers of the Renaissance took as their model.

49 MILL, *Utilitarianism* [1863], pp. 55–7. Logician and political economist.

51 VOLTAIRE, *The Age of Louis XIV* [Berlin 1751], pp. 376–80. The first great Frenchman to understand the English ethos.

54 WALTON, *The Compleat Angler* [1653], pp. 110–11. His *Lives* was eulogized by Wordsworth, see p. 128.

55 WHITE, *A Natural History of Selborne* [1789], pp. 227–9.

57 DARWIN, *The Voyage of the 'Beagle'* [1839], pp. 379–80. The voyage 1831–6 was both Darwin's education and his opportunity. Sketched in 1841, his theory of evolution when published as *The Origin of Species* [1859] sold out on the day of publication.

58 PEARSON, *The Grammar of Science* [1892], pp. 31–2. First delivered as lectures on Gresham's foundation, by the dedicated biometrist who applied statistical method to the verification of Darwinism.

60 THOREAU, *Walden* [Boston, Mass. 1854], pp. 136–9. A report of 'an experiment in living and thinking' in New England—essays that became a textbook for the British Labour Party.

62 KEATS, 'To a Cat' in *Poems*, p. 228. Written January 1818; published 1848. The cat belonged to his friend Reynolds.

62 ADAM SMITH, *The Wealth of Nations* [1766], I, 118–21. The Glasgow professor who founded modern economic science.

65 MALTHUS, *An Essay on the Principle of Population* [1798], II, 201–3. 'Parson Malthus, the plagiarist and shameless sycophant of the ruling classes', said Marx of the man who 'put up a warning sign for future generations: Human Population: Beware of Explosions'.

67 HOWARD, *The State of the Prisons* [1777], pp. 186–7. Translated into German (Leipzig 1780)

68 BACON, *Essays* [1597; 1612; 1625], pp. 125–6. Lawyer, encyclopaedist, scientist.

69 RICARDO, *The Principles of Political Economy and Taxation* [1817], pp. 244–5. A critical running commentary on *The Wealth of Nations* by a very successful businessman.

71 BURNS, *Poems and Songs*, p. 483. Written 1786.

71 MARX, *Capital* [1867], II, 162–5. The modern materialist's bible, whose data were gleaned from British Government Blue Books consulted in the British Museum.

73 SAMUEL BUTLER, *Erewhon* [1872, revised 1901], pp. 138–40. 'Philosophical writer', as Butler himself chose to be described; Butler also painted.

74 WILDE, 'The Soul of Man Under Socialism' [1891], in *Plays, Prose Writings and Poems*, pp. 269–70. Scholar, dramatist, novelist, wit, Irishman.

75 ARISTOTLE, *Ethics* [Venice 1498], pp. 209–10. Contains the classic analysis of the virtues and vices.

77 GRACIÁN, *The Oracle* [Huesca 1647], pp. 131, 167, 247. A Jesuit's uncommitted comments on the conduct of life in camp and court.

78 CHESTERFIELD, *Letters to his Son : and Others* [1774], pp. 85–6. Letters to a bastard son, which Dr Johnson thought might make a 'pretty book'.

79 BLAKE, 'Proverbs of Hell' in *The Marriage of Heaven and Hell* [*c.* 1793] in *Poem and Prophecies*, p. 45.

80 POPE, 'Epilogue to the Satires', Dialogue I, ll. 137–70 [1738] in *Poems*, pp. 328–9. 'England's genius must be rescued from the Whig forces of fraud and corruption.'

81 MILTON, *Paradise Lost* [1667], IX, 886–916, in *Milton's Poems*, pp. 324–5.

82 DEFOE, *The Fortunes and Misfortunes of Moll Flanders* [1722], pp. 63–5.

83 STEELE, No. 108, *The Tatler* [1709–11], p. 211. Like Cobbett, Steele was an enlisted Army man.

84 CONRAD, *Nostromo* [1904], pp. 127–30.

86 FIELDING, *The Life and Adventures of Jonathan Wild* [1743], pp. 104–7. According to Horace Walpole, Fielding received in all seven hundred pounds for his *Tom Jones*.

89 AUGUSTINE, *Confessions* [Strassburg 1470], pp. 50–1. Pusey's translation. Not till Montaigne does an author tell us as much about himself.

90 RICHARDSON, *Clarissa* [1747–8], II, 334–6. The first English novelist.

91 ARNOLD BENNETT, *The Old Wives' Tale* [1908], pp. 290–4. Contains, *inter alia*, so it has been claimed, the finest depiction of a public execution, by a writer who never witnessed one.

93 BYRON, *Letters*, pp. 317–18. Pisa, 17 November 1821. 'I was perfectly sincere when I wrote it, and am still.'

94 DONNE 'To His Mistress Going to Bed', Elegies, XIX [1633] in *John Donne's Poems*, pp. 87–8. Written *c.* 1590–1601. Donne took Orders in 1615; Dean of St Paul's 1621.

95 PLATO, *Republic* [Venice 1513], pp. 318–25. To teach philosophy is difficult. To teach the history of philosophy is easy—it is just adding footnotes to Plato.

97 PASCAL, *Pensées* [Paris 1670], pp. 112–13. Scintillating *obiter dicta* for a work of formal Christian apologetics that was never written.

98 PLATO, *The Laws* [Venice 1513], pp. 277–8. The work of his old age, and considerably later than *The Republic*.

99 ANTONINUS, 'To Himself', *The Meditations of Marcus Aurelius* [Zürich 1558–9], p. 63. Only when printed did *The Meditations* secure a public, whose size might have amazed its author.

100 TOLSTOY, *War and Peace* [Moscow 1868], I, 398–9. Having seen active service in the Crimean War, 1856–9, Tolstoy knew what war meant.

101 'BHAGAVAD-GITA' [Calcutta 1809], in R. H. Zaehner, *Hindu Scriptures*, 'Gita', I, §§ 27–47. A minute part of the enormous Sanscrit epic, the *Mahabharata* [Calcutta 1834–9], the 'Gita' is 'the bedrock of Hindu theism'. The first English translation [1785] has a preliminary note by Warren Hastings, impeached in 1788.

103 CARLYLE, *Heroes and Hero Worship* [1841], pp. 290–1. The preacher turned lecturer takes a text from Islam.

104 KORAN [Hamburg 1694], p. 420. Rodwell's translation (1861). Translations into European languages began in the sixteenth century: Latin (Basle 1543), Italian (Venice 1547), German (Nuremberg 1623), Dutch (Hamburg 1641), French (Paris 1649), English (1649).

104 EMERSON, *The Conduct of Life* [1860] *and Other Essays*, pp. 251–2. Essayist, poet, lecturer; a friend of the Carlyles.

106 FITZGERALD, *Omar Khayyám* [1859] in *Persian Poems*, pp. 18–19. The text printed is that of the 4th edition, 1879.

107 ECKERMANN, *Conversations with Goethe* [Leipzig and Magdeburg 1836–8], pp. 423–4. These cover Goethe's last years, 1823–32.

108 BERKELEY, *A New Theory of Vision* [1709] *and Other Writings*, pp. 93–4.

109 LOCKE, *An Essay Concerning Human Understanding* [1690], pp. 91–6.

111 *Chinese Philosophy in Classical Times* (ed. E. R. Hughes), pp. 122–3. Kung-sun Lung was a scion of the ruling house of Chao State.

111 KANT, *Critique of Pure Reason* [Riga 1781], pp. 1–3. The counterblast to Hume's epistemology and psychology. Kant could not read English. For an account of Kant's last years, see De Quincey, *The English Mail Coach, &c.*

113 ARISTOTLE, *Metaphysics* [Venice 1498], pp. 345–6. The earliest argued statement of the cosmological 'proof' of the existence of God.

115 MONTAIGNE, 'Of the Institution and Education of Children', *Essays* [Bordeaux 1580, 1588], I, 154–5; 184–5. The father of French prose; inventor of the 'essay'; 'the sturdy womanizer who prized friendship far more than love'; 'The persuasive champion of liberty and toleration.' One-quarter Jewish. The *Essays* were placed on the Index in 1671.

117 RABELAIS, *The Heroic Deeds of Gargantua and Pantagruel* [1532–5], I, 163–4. Rabelais the cleric physician was the first Renaissance medical man to lecture from the Greek of Hippocrates.

119 HAZLITT, 'On Classical Education', *The Round Table* [1817], pp. 4–5. First contributed to *The Examiner*.

120 ROUSSEAU, *Confessions* [1782], pp. 8–9. After the publication of his romance *Emile; or, Education*, and *The Social Contract* [both 1762], Rousseau was forced to flee from France. The *Confessions* were published posthumously in 1782.

122 THACKERAY, *Pendennis* [1848–50], I, 175–8. Like Pendennis, Thackeray dissipated a competence, variously estimated at between £500 and £20,000 per annum.

124 MARY WOLLSTONECRAFT, *A Vindication of the Rights of Woman* [1792], pp. 178–83. After conceiving a daughter, Mary, who was to become Shelley's second wife, Mary Wollstonecraft married William Godwin, who had disliked her at their first meeting, in Paris when she had out-talked Tom Paine.

126 ARNOLD, 'Shakespeare' [1849], in *Matthew Arnold's Poems*, pp. 2–3.

126 ARNOLD, *The Study of Poetry* [1880] in *Essays in Criticism* [Second Series 1888], pp. 247–9. Originally the 'General Introduction' to T. H. Ward, ed., *The English Poets* [1880–1].

128 WORDSWORTH, 'The Book of Walton's Lives', *Ecclesiastical Sonnets* [1822], III, v, in *Poems*, p. 159, composed in 1821. See p. 128.

128 DRYDEN, *Sylvae: or the Second Part of Poetical Miscellanies* [1685] in *Of Dramatic Poesy and other critical Essays*, II, 24–8.

129 BOSWELL, *Life of Johnson* [1791], I, 283–6.

132 JOHNSON, *Lives of the Poets* [1781], I, 225–6.

133 JOHNSON, *op. cit.*, II, 213–15.

135 WALPOLE, to the Rev. William Mason, 18 February 1776, in *Selected Letters*, pp. 210–12. Virtuoso, man of quality, printer, novelist, wit. His letters, which Byron called 'incomparable', were published posthumously.

136 HAZLITT, 'Henry IV' in *Characters of Shakespeare's Plays* [1817] in *The Round Table, &c.,* pp. 278-9.

138 VASARI, *Lives of the Painters* [Florence 1550], II, 247-8. The classic of graphic art criticism—by a Florentine architect and painter, and collector of drawings, who often wrote from considerable personal knowledge.

139 EVELYN, *Diary* [1819], II, 56-60. A self-portrait of a cultivated Royalist, with an account of the Grand Tour.

141 ECKERMANN, *Conversations with Goethe* [1836-8], pp. 134-6. The French *Faust* [Paris 1828] is now a collector's piece. The comparison of Eckermann with Boswell is forced.

142 CELLINI, *Memoirs* [1728; defective], pp. 244-6. Begun in 1558, the manuscript was jealously guarded for over a century. Translated into English in 1771; 1806, II; and subsequently.

144 PEACOCK, *Headlong Hall* [1816], pp. 70-2. Published anonymously.

145 BEACONSFIELD, *Coningsby* [1844], pp. 208-11.

148 KINGLAKE, *Eothen* [1844], pp. 181-2. From an early travel book by one who later became famous as a war correspondent.

149 MUNGO PARK, *Travels* [1799], pp. 309-10. One of the earliest of African explorers, Park discovered the source of the Niger, in whose waters he was later drowned.

151 PRESCOTT, *Conquest of Mexico* [1843], pp. 335-6. The American writer who made 'the matter of Spain' his province.

152 DARWIN, *The Voyage of the 'Beagle'* [1839], pp. 484-7.

155 DE CRÈVECŒUR, *Letters from an American Farmer* [1782], pp. 21-5. Written in English. Emigrating to French Canada, De Crèvecœur served under Montcalm but later returned to France.

158 WAKEFIELD, *A Letter from Sydney* [1829] *and Other Writing on Colonization,* pp. 61-3. The 'first blueprint for the British Commonwealth'; written in Newgate by a man who was yet to emigrate.

160 BORROW, *The Bible in Spain* [1843], pp. 136-9, with *Richard Ford, Gatherings from Spain* [1846], the most incisive nineteenth-century interpreter of the Peninsula.

163 STEVENSON, *New Arabian Nights* [1882], in *Treasure Island, &c.,* pp. 220-3.

166 POE, 'The Pit and the Pendulum' in *Tales of Mystery and Imagination* [1845], pp. 227-9.

171 MELVILLE, *Moby Dick: or The White Whale* [1851], pp. 140-1. The cosmic allegory whose theme is the enormity of evil.

173 'Culhwch and Olwen' in *The Mabinogion,* pp. 135-6. Early thirteenth-century Welsh romance. Much of the subject-matter of this story and of the others 'is very old indeed, coeval maybe with the dawn of the Celtic world'.

174 MALORY, *Le Morte d'Arthur* [Westminster 1485], II, 397-8. The final medieval recension; printed by William Caxton. Malory underwent several spells of imprisonment for felonies.

175 HERODOTUS, *The Histories* [Venice 1502], II, 207-8.

176 CAESAR, *Gallic War* [Rome 1469], pp. 154-7. Political propaganda—and the hated school book—now presented in today's English.

179 STURLUSON, in *Heimskringla* [Copenhagen 1777-83] in *Sagas of the Norse Kings*, I, 229-30. In October 1066, after defeating the Norwegian army near York, Harold marched two hundred and forty miles in ten days to be defeated in his turn and die at Hastings.

180 GIBBON, *The Decline and Fall of the Roman Empire* [1776-88], I, 151-2. Of the trio of English eighteenth-century historians Hume, Robertson, Gibbon, Gibbon alone lives—'a punctilious historian, an interesting writer in spite of a bad style'.

181 RALEIGH, 'A Report of the truth of the fight about the Iles of Azores, this last Sommer' [1591] in Hakluyt, *Principal Navigations* [1598], V, 6-8. Raleigh was prevented from commanding the expedition, and his cousin Grenville took his place.

184 TOLSTOY, *War and Peace* [Moscow 1868], pp. 295-7.

185 LUCY HUTCHINSON, *Memoirs of Colonel Hutchinson* [1806], pp. 18-20.

187 FANNY BURNEY, *Diary* [1842-6], pp. 356-8. Lady in Waiting to Queen Charlotte, wife of George III, and subsequently Madame D'Arblay.

188 SOUTHEY, *Life of Horatio, Lord Nelson* [1813], pp. 26-7, 224-5.

190 MACHIAVELLI, *The Prince* [Rome 1532], pp. 139-43. Renaissance statecraft through the eyes of a great Florentine. The first edition is excessively rare.

192 MARRYAT, *Mr Midshipman Easy* [1836], pp. 245-9.

195 JEROME K. JEROME, *Three Men in a Boat* [1889], pp. 19-21.

198 HANS ANDERSEN, *Fairy Tales and Stories* [1835-72], pp. 354-6. Published 1835-72. Many English translations from 1846 onwards.

199 LEWIS CARROLL, *Alice in Wonderland* [1865], pp. 57-9. Additionally immortalized by Sir John Tenniel's illustrations. The author-artist relationship was not exactly harmonious.

201 THE BROTHERS GROSSMITH, *The Diary of a Nobody* [1894], pp. 203-7. Originally serialized in *Punch*.

203 STERNE, *A Sentimental Journey* [1767], pp. 114-16. Best known for *Tristram Shandy*, which, says Walpole, Warburton recommended to the bench of bishops, calling Sterne the English Rabelais.

205 SMOLLETT, *Peregrine Pickle* [1751], I, 358-61. Smollett was once a ship's surgeon.

208 SCOTT, *The Heart of Mid-lothian* [Edinburgh 1818], pp. 374-7. Eclipsed overnight by Byron, the lawyer poet creates the historical novel.

211 JANE AUSTEN, *Sense and Sensibility* [1811], pp. 301-4.

214 DICKENS, *Martin Chuzzlewit* [1843-4], pp. 714-21. Published in parts.

219 TROLLOPE, *Barchester Towers* [1857], pp. 84-6. The second of the five 'Barchester' novels.

222 GEORGE ELIOT, *Middlemarch* [1872], pp. 367-70. The Welsh woman whose powers Dickens conceded to be greater than his own.

225 THUCYDIDES, *History of the Peloponnesian War* [Venice 1502], pp. 68–9. Military history—plus—by a military man. Soldier historians of the first rank are few: Thucydides, Caesar, Sir Winston Churchill.

226 ROPER, *Life of More* [Paris 1626], pp. 25–8. By More's son-in-law.

229 MACAULAY, *The History of England* [1848, 55], IV, 530–2. Covers the years 1685–1702. The work brought Macaulay £20,000 on one cheque.

231 BYRON, *Childe Harold* [1818], Canto IV, i–iii, in *Byron's Poems*, II, 99. Until the Venetian Republic was conquered in 1797 by Napoleon, the Venetian ambassador was the permanent doyen of the corps diplomatique everywhere.

232 PLUTARCH, *Lives of the Noble Greeks and Romans* [Florence 1517], III, 286–7. Dryden's translation. Only very occasionally, as here, is Plutarch a primary authority.

233 FRANKLIN, *Autobiography* [Paris 1791, in part], pp. 41–4. The printer-publisher from Philadelphia, diplomat, and one of the founding fathers of the U.S.A. Constitution. First published in a French translation. Not until 1868 was the complete English text published.

235 SURTEES, *Jorrocks's Jaunts and Jollities* [1838], pp. 224–6. Contributed to the *New Sporting Magazine*, 1831–4, which he edited till 1836.

239 SAMUEL BUTLER, *The Way of All Flesh* [1901], pp. 67–8. The semi-autobiographical novel written 1872 and published posthumously.

240 FANNY BURNEY, *Diary* [1842–6], pp. 285–7. The Duke of Clarence succeeded to the throne in 1830 as William IV.

242 HORACE, 'To Maecenas', Odes I, 20 [Venice 1471] in *The Collected Works of Horace*, p. 20. The Odes, Books I–III, appeared in 19 B.C. Translated by Lord Dunsany.

242 GISSING, *The Private Papers of Henry Ryecroft* [1903], pp. 295–6.

243 LAMB, 'Confessions of a Drunkard' in *Last Essays of Elia* [1833] in *Essays of Elia, &c.*, pp. 295–6. Not included in the first edition. Written *c.* 1813. The Essays first appeared in 1822 in the *London Magazine*.

245 MONTAIGNE, 'Of Three Commerces or Societies', *Essays* [Bordeaux 1580, 88], III, 49–50.

INDEX

Addison, Joseph, 11
Andersen, Hans, 198
Antoninus, Marcus Aurelius, 99
Aristotle, 75, 113
Arnold, Matthew, 126
Augustine, Saint, 89
Austen, Jane, 211

Bacon, Francis, 68
Beaconsfield, Lord, 44, 145
Bede, 13
Bennett, Arnold, 91
Berkeley, George, 108
Bhagavad-Gita, 101
Blake, William, 22, 79
Borrow, George, 160
Boswell, James, 129
Burke, Edmund, 32, 36
Burney, Fanny, 187, 240
Burns, Robert, 71
Butler, Samuel, 73, 239
Byron, Lord, 93, 231

Caesar, Gaius Julius, 176
Carlyle, Thomas, 103
Carroll, Lewis, 199
Cellini, Benvenuto, 142
Chesterfield, Lord, 78
Cicero, Marcus Tullius, 48
Cobbett, William, 24
Conrad, Joseph, 84
Crèvecœur, Saint John de, 155

Dante Alighieri, 37
Darwin, Charles, 57, 152
Defoe, Daniel, 26, 82
De Quincey, Thomas, 29
Dickens, Charles, 214
Donne, John, 94
Dryden, John, 128

Eckermann, Johann, 107, 141
Eliot, George, 222
Emerson, Ralph Waldo, 104
Evelyn, John, 139

Fielding, Henry, 86
FitzGerald, Edward, 106
Franklin, Benjamin, 233

Gibbon, Edward, 180
Gissing, George, 242
Gracián, Baltasar, 77
Gray, Thomas, 17
Green, John Richard, 14
Grossmith, George and Weedon, 201

Hakluyt, Richard, 181
Hamilton, Alexander, 38
Hazlitt, William, 119, 136
Heine, Heinrich, 19
Herodotus, 175
Hobbes, Thomas, 31
Horace, 242
Howard, John, 67
Hume, David, 40
Hunt, Leigh, 9
Hutchinson, Lucy, 185

Irving, Washington, 27

Jerome, Jerome K., 195
Johnson, Samuel, 132, 133

Kant, Immanuel, 111
Keats, John, 62
Kinglake, Alexander William, 148
Koran, The Holy, 104
Kung-sun Lung, 111

255

INDEX

Lamb, Charles, 243
Locke, John, 109

Mabinogion, 173
Macaulay, Thomas Babington, 229
Machiavelli, Niccolo, 190
Maine, Sir Henry, 41
Malory, Sir Thomas, 174
Malthus, Thomas Robert, 65
Marryat, Frederick, 192
Marx, Karl, 71
Melville, Herman, 171
Mill, John Stuart, 49
Milton, John, 81
Mitford, Mary Russell, 30
Montaigne, Michel de, 115, 245

Paine, Tom, 35
Park, Mungo, 149
Pascal, Blaise, 97
Peacock, Thomas Love, 144
Pearson, Karl, 58
Pepys, Samuel, 16
Plato, 95, 98
Plutarch, 232
Poe, Edgar Allan, 166
Pope, Alexander, 80
Prescott, W. H., 151
Priestley, J. B., 5, 22

Rabelais, François, 117
Raleigh, Sir Walter, 181

Ricardo, David, 69
Richardson, Samuel, 90
Roper, William, 226
Rousseau, Jean-Jacques, 120

Scott, Sir Walter, 208
Smith, Adam, 62
Smollett, Tobias, 205
Southey, Robert, 188
Steele, Sir Richard, 83
Sterne, Laurence, 203
Stevenson, Robert Louis, 163
Stow, John, 46
Sturluson, Snorri, 179
Surtees, Robert Smith, 235

Thackeray, William Makepeace, 122
Thoreau, Henry David, 60
Thucydides, 225
Tolstoy, Count Leo, 100, 184
Trollope, Anthony, 219

Vasari, Giorgio, 138
Voltaire, 51

Wakefield, Edward Gibbon, 158
Walpole, Horace, 135
Walton, Isaak, 54
White, Gilbert, 55
Wilde, Oscar, 74
Wollstonecraft, Mary, 124
Wordsworth, William, 128